W9-AHL-380

**THIRD EDITION**

**2a**

# GRAMMAR IN CONTEXT

## SANDRA N. ELBAUM

Southwest Division of Adult and Continuing Education
Adult Resource Center
450 Moss Street
Chula Vista, CA 91911-1899
(691) 619-5624
(691) 619-5791

**THOMSON**
✴ TM

**HEINLE**

Australia Canada Mexico Singapore Spain United Kingdom United States

**Grammar In Context 2a**
**Third Edition**
*Sandra N. Elbaum*

**Vice President, Editorial Director ESL/EFL:** *Nancy Leonhardt*
**Acquisitions Editor:** *Eric Bredenberg*
**Developmental Editor:** *Thomas Healy*
**Production Editor:** *Michael Burggren*
**Marketing Manager:** *Charlotte Sturdy*
**Manufacturing Coordinator:** *Mary Beth Hennebury*
**Project Management:** *Michael Granger; Modern Graphics, Inc.*
**Composition:** *Modern Graphics, Inc.*
**Photo Research:** *Susan Van Etten*
**Illustration:** *Outlook/Anco*
**Cover/Text Designer:** *Linda Dana Willis*
**Cover Photography:** *Richard Glover/CORBIS*
**Printer:** *Von Hoffman Graphics*

Copyright © 2003 by Sandra N. Elbaum

Printed in the United States of America
1 2 3 4 5 6 7 8   07 06 05 04 03

For more information contact Heinle, 25 Thomson Place, Boston, MA 02210 USA,
or you can visit our Internet site at http://www.heinle.com

All rights reserved. No part of this work covered by the copyright hereon may be reproduced or used in any form or by any means—graphic, electronic, or mechanical, including photocopying, recording, taping, Web distribution or information storage and retrieval systems—without the written permission of the publisher.

**Photo & Illustration Credits:**

**p. 1** © Susan Van Etten, **p. 2** © Lowell Georgia/Corbis, **p. 17** © susan Van Etten, **p. 37** © Susan Van Etten, **p. 38** © Joseph Sohn: Chromo Sohn Inc./Corbis, **p. 38** © Susan Van Etten, **p. 53** © tony Arruza/Corbis, **p. 53** © Jay Syverson/Corbis, **p. 75** © Flip Sghulke/Corbis, **p. 76** © Joseph Schwartz Collection/Corbis, **p. 89** © Bettmann/Corbis, **p. 89** © Lynn Goldsmith/Corbis, **p. 90** © Bettmann/Corbis, **p. 101** © Susan Van Etten, **p. 149** © Sandra Elbaum, **p. 160** © Kevin R. Morris/Corbis, **p. 163** Neal Preston/Corbis, **p. 164** © Robert Holmes/Corbis, **p. 172** © Jennie Woodcock/Corbis, **p. 185** © Bettmann/Corbis, **p. 192** © Bettmann/Corbis, **p. 209** © Susan Van Etten

For permission to use material from this text or product contact us:
Tel      1-800-730-2214
Fax      1-800-730-2215
Web      www.thomsonrights.com

ISBN: 0-75939-661-2

# Contents

## Lesson 1

## Lesson 2

# *Lesson* 3

# *Lesson* 4

# Lesson 5

# Lesson 6

# *Lesson* 7

# *Lesson* 8

**To the Teacher:** This portion of the contents is included for your convenience. This book ends with Lesson 8.

# Lesson 9

# Lesson 10

# Lesson 11

# Lesson 12

# Lesson 13

# Lesson 14

# Lesson 15

# Appendices

# A word from the author

It seems to me that I was born to be an ESL teacher. My parents immigrated to the U.S. from Poland as adults and were confused not only by the English language but by American culture as well. Born in the U.S., I often had the task as a child to explain the intricacies of the language and allay my parents' fears about the culture. It is no wonder to me that I became an ESL teacher, and later, an ESL writer who focuses on explanations of American culture in order to illustrate grammar. My life growing up in an immigrant neighborhood was very similar to the lives of my students, so I have a feel for what confuses them and what they need to know about American life.

ESL teachers often find themselves explaining confusing customs and providing practical information about life in the U.S. Often, teachers are a student's only source of information about American life. With **Grammar in Context, Third Edition,** I enjoy sharing my experiences with you.

**Grammar in Context, Third Edition** connects grammar with American cultural context, providing learners of English with a useful and meaningful skill and knowledge base. Students learn the grammar necessary to communicate verbally and in writing, and learn how American culture plays a role in language, beliefs, and everyday situations.

Enjoy the new edition of **Grammar in Context!**

Each level of Grammar in Context has now been split into two books (1a/1b, 2a/2b, etc.) in the hope that these briefer editions will better meet the needs of programs with shorter terms.

*Sandra N. Elbaum*

# Grammar in Context Unites Learners and Language

**Students learn language in context, increasing their understanding and ability to use new structures.**

Learning a language through meaningful themes and practicing in a contextualized setting promotes both linguistic and cognitive development. In **Grammar in Context,** grammar is presented in interesting and informative readings, and the language is subsequently practiced throughout the chapter. Students learn more, remember more and can use language more effectively when they learn grammar in context.

**Students expand their knowledge of American topics and culture.**

American themes add a historical and cultural dimension to students' learning. The readings in **Grammar in Context** help students gain insight into American culture and the way many Americans think and feel about various topics. Students gain ample exposure to and practice in dealing with situations such as finding an apartment, holiday traditions, and shopping, as well as practicing the language that goes with these situations. Their new knowledge helps them enjoy their stay or life in the U.S.

**Students are prepared for academic assignments and everyday language tasks.**

Discussions, readings, compositions and exercises involving higher level critical thinking skills develop overall language and communication skills. In addition to the numerous exercises in the student text and workbook, teachers will find a wealth of ideas in **Grammar in Context.** Students will have interesting, fulfilling, and successful experiences that they will take with them as they complete their ESL classes.

**Students learn to use their new skills to communicate.**

The exercises and Expansion Activities in **Grammar in Context** help students learn English while practicing their writing and speaking skills. Students work together in pairs and groups to find more information about topics, to make presentations, to play games, and to role-play. Their confidence to use English increases, as does their ability to communicate effectively.

**Students enjoy learning.**

If learning is meaningful, it is motivational and fun. Places, famous people, trends, customs, and everyday American activities all have an impact on our students' lives, and having a better understanding of these things helps them function successfully in the U.S. By combining rich, cultural content with clear grammar presentation and practice, **Grammar in Context** engages the student's attention and provides guidance in grammar usage and writing. And whatever is enjoyable will be more readily learned and retained.

# Welcome to
# **Grammar in Context, Third Edition**
## Spanning language and culture

Students learn more, remember more and can use grammar more effectively when they learn language in context. **Grammar in Context, Third Edition** connects grammar with rich, American cultural context, providing learners of English with a useful and meaningful skill and knowledge base.

**Grammar charts** use simple and clear language taken from the readings to explain structures in context.

**Language Notes** refine students' understanding of the target structure.

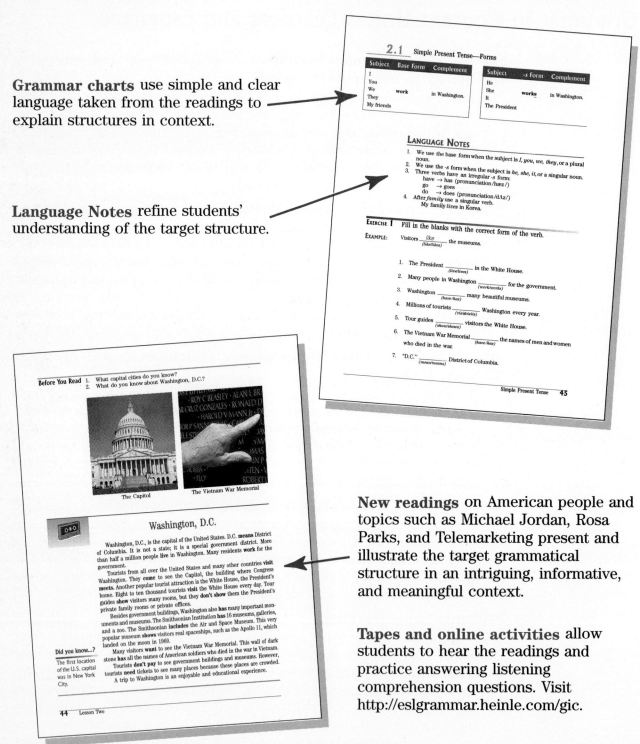

**2.1** Simple Present Tense—Forms

| Subject | Base Form | Complement |
|---|---|---|
| I | | |
| You | | |
| We | **work** | in Washington. |
| They | | |
| My friends | | |

| Subject | -s Form | Complement |
|---|---|---|
| He | | |
| She | | |
| It | **works** | in Washington. |
| The President | | |

**LANGUAGE NOTES**
1. We use the base form when the subject is *I, you, we, they*, or a plural noun.
2. We use the *-s* form when the subject is *he, she, it*, or a singular noun.
3. Three verbs have an irregular *-s* form:
   have → has (pronunciation /hæz /)
   go → goes
   do → does (pronunciation /dʌz/)
4. After *family* use a singular verb.
   My family *lives* in Korea.

**EXERCISE 1** Fill in the blanks with the correct form of the verb.

EXAMPLE: Visitors _____like_____ the museums.
(like/likes)

1. The President _____ in the White House.
(live/lives)
2. Many people in Washington _____ for the government.
(work/works)
3. Washington _____ many beautiful museums.
(have/has)
4. Millions of tourists _____ Washington every year.
(visit/visits)
5. Tour guides _____ visitors the White House.
(show/shows)
6. The Vietnam War Memorial _____ the names of men and women who died in the war.
(have/has)
7. "D.C." _____ District of Columbia.
(mean/means)

Simple Present Tense **45**

The Capitol          The Vietnam War Memorial

### Washington, D.C.

Washington, D.C., is the capital of the United States. D.C. **means** District of Columbia. It is not a state; it is a special government district. More than half a million people **live** in Washington. Many residents **work** for the government.

Tourists from all over the United States and many other countries **visit** Washington. They **come** to see the Capitol, the building where Congress **meets**. Another popular tourist attraction is the White House, the President's home. Eight to ten thousand tourists **visit** the White House every day. Tour guides **show** visitors many rooms, but they **don't show** them the President's private family rooms or private offices.

Besides government buildings, Washington also **has** many important monuments and museums. The Smithsonian Institution **has** 16 museums, galleries, and a zoo. The Smithsonian **includes** the Air and Space Museum. This very popular museum **shows** visitors real spaceships, such as the Apollo 11, which landed on the moon in 1969.

Many visitors **want** to see the Vietnam War Memorial. This wall of dark stone **has** all the names of American soldiers who died in the war in Vietnam. Tourists **don't pay** to see government buildings and museums. However, tourists **need** tickets to see many places because these places are crowded.

A trip to Washington is an enjoyable and educational experience.

**Did you know...?**
The first location of the U.S. capital was in New York City.

**44** Lesson Two

**New readings** on American people and topics such as Michael Jordan, Rosa Parks, and Telemarketing present and illustrate the target grammatical structure in an intriguing, informative, and meaningful context.

**Tapes and online activities** allow students to hear the readings and practice answering listening comprehension questions. Visit http://eslgrammar.heinle.com/gic.

**A wide array of exercises** keeps the classroom lively and targets a variety of learning styles.

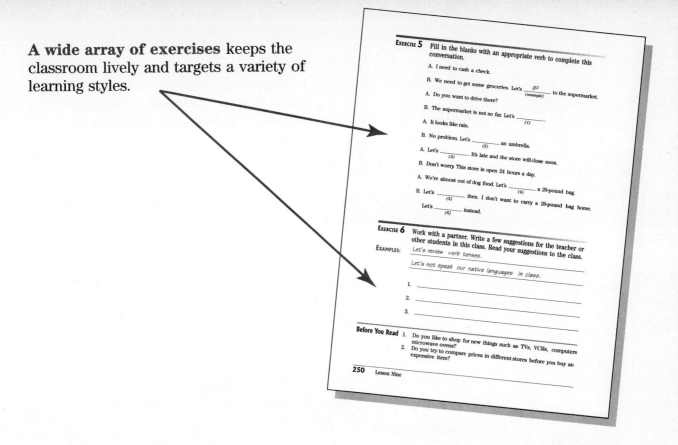

**EXERCISE 5** Fill in the blanks with an appropriate verb to complete this conversation.

A. I need to cash a check.

B. We need to get some groceries. Let's __go__ to the supermarket.
*(example)*

A. Do you want to drive there?

B. The supermarket is not so far. Let's _____.
*(1)*

A. It looks like rain.

B. No problem. Let's _____ an umbrella.
*(2)*

A. Let's _____. It's late and the store will close soon.
*(3)*

B. Don't worry. This store is open 24 hours a day.

A. We're almost out of dog food. Let's _____ a 20-pound bag.
*(4)*

B. Let's _____ then. I don't want to carry a 20-pound bag home.
*(5)*

Let's _____ instead.
*(6)*

**EXERCISE 6** Work with a partner. Write a few suggestions for the teacher or other students in this class. Read your suggestions to the class.

EXAMPLES: *Let's review verb tenses.*

*Let's not speak our native languages in class.*

1. _____

2. _____

3. _____

**Before You Read** 1. Do you like to shop for new things such as TVs, VCRs, computers microwave ovens?
2. Do you try to compare prices in different stores before you buy an expensive item?

250    Lesson Nine

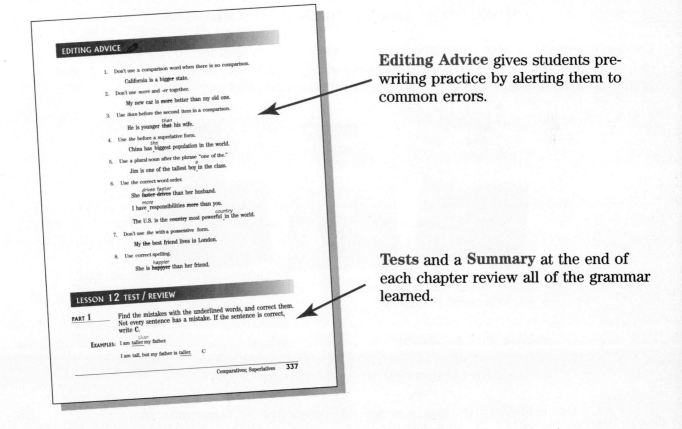

**EDITING ADVICE**

1. Don't use a comparison word when there is no comparison.
   California is a ~~bigger~~ state.

2. Don't use *more* and *-er* together.
   My new car is ~~more~~ better than my old one.

3. Use *than* before the second item in a comparison.
   He is younger ~~that~~ *than* his wife.

4. Use *the* before a superlative form.
   *the*
   China has ∧ biggest population in the world.

5. Use a plural noun after the phrase "one of the."
   *s*
   Jim is one of the tallest boy∧ in the class.

6. Use the correct word order.
   *drives faster*
   She ~~faster drives~~ than her husband.
   *more*
   I have ∧ responsibilities ~~more~~ than you.
   *country*
   The U.S. is the ~~country~~ most powerful ∧ in the world.

7. Don't use *the* with a possessive form.
   My ~~the~~ best friend lives in London.

8. Use correct spelling.
   *happier*
   She is ~~happyer~~ than her friend.

**Editing Advice** gives students prewriting practice by alerting them to common errors.

**LESSON 12 TEST / REVIEW**

PART 1    Find the mistakes with the underlined words, and correct them. Not every sentence has a mistake. If the sentence is correct, write C.

EXAMPLES: I am ~~taller~~ *than* my father.

I am tall, but my father is taller.    C

**Tests** and a **Summary** at the end of each chapter review all of the grammar learned.

Comparatives; Superlatives    **337**

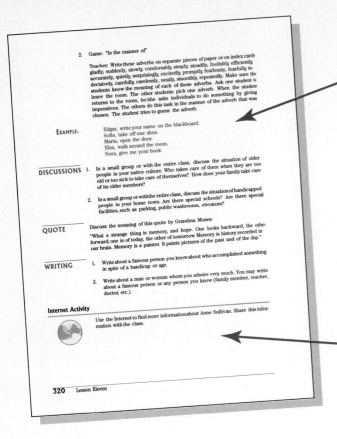

**Expansion Activities** provide many fun opportunities for students to interact with one another and further develop their skills in speaking and writing.

New **Internet** activities encourage students to use technology to explore a wealth of online resources. Also available at http://eslgrammar.heinle.com/gic.

# More Grammar Practice Workbooks

Used in conjunction with **Grammar in Context** or as a companion to any reading, writing, or listening skills text, **More Grammar Practice** helps students learn and review the essential grammar skills to make language learning comprehensive and ongoing.

- Clear grammar charts

- Extensive exercises

- Great for in-class practice or homework

- Follows the same scope and sequence as **Grammar in Context, Third Edition**

# *Lesson One*

## GRAMMAR
The Simple Present Tense
Frequency Words

## CONTEXT
Pets
Letter About American Customs

## LESSON FOCUS
We use the simple present tense to talk about facts.
The U.S. *has* about 275 million people.
The U.S. *is* in North America.

We use the simple present tense to talk about regular activities, habits, or customs. We use frequency words to show how often an action happens.
Americans *often* wear shorts in the summer.
Americans *sometimes* say, "Have a nice day."

**Before You Read**
1. Do you like animals?
2. Do you have a pet?

Read the following article. Pay special attention to the verb *be* and other verbs in the simple present tense.

# Pets

Americans **love** pets. About 60 percent of Americans **live** with one or more animals. About four in ten households **have** at least one dog. Three in ten households **own** at least one cat.

Americans **think** of their pets as part of the family: 79 percent of pet owners **give** their pets holiday or birthday presents,[1] and 33 percent of pet owners **talk** to their pets on the phone or through the answering machine. Many pet owners **sleep** with their dogs or cats. Many people **travel** with their pets. (It **costs** about $50 to fly with a pet.) Some hotels **allow** guests to bring their pets.

Americans **pay** a lot of money to keep pets. They **spend** $12 billion a year in vet[2] bills and pet supplies. There **are** schools, toys, hotels, restaurants, clothes, and cemeteries for pets. There **are** magazines for pet owners. There **are** hundreds of Web sites for pet owners.

Pets **are** a lot of fun. They **are** affectionate, too. People who **are** lonely **get** a lot of love from their animals. Medical research **shows** that contact with a dog or a cat can lower a person's blood pressure.

Pets **need** a lot of attention. Before you buy a pet, it's important to ask yourself these questions:

- **Are** you patient?
- **Are** you home a lot?
- If you **have** children, **are** they responsible?
- **Are** pets allowed where you live?

**Did you know...?**

The most common registered breed of dog in the U.S. is the labrador retriever.

Unfortunately, some people **don't realize** that pets need a lot of care. Some people **see** a cute puppy or kitten, **buy** it, and later **abandon** it because they **don't want** to take care of it. It **is** important to understand that a pet **is** a long-term responsibility.

Labrador Retrievers

[1] These statistics are from the American Animal Hospital Association, 1995.
[2] *Vet* is short for *veterinarian*. This is an animal doctor.

| Examples | Explanation |
|---|---|
| I **am** patient.<br>Dogs **are** friendly.<br>My grandmother **is** lonely.<br>It **is** important to choose the right pet.<br>There **are** toys for dogs. | I → am<br>you, we, they → are<br>he, she, it, → is<br>there → is or are |
| She **is not** home much.<br>Some children **are not** responsible. | Negatives:<br>am not, are not, is not |

## LANGUAGE NOTES

1.  We can make a contraction with the subject pronoun and *am, is,* or *are.*

    | | |
    |---|---|
    | I am → I'm | he is → he's |
    | you are → you're | she is → she's |
    | we are → we're | it is → it's |
    | they are → they're | |

2.  We can make a contraction with most nouns and *is.*
    My grandmother**'s** lonely.
    Your dog**'s** beautiful.

3.  We don't make a contraction with *is* if the noun ends in these letters: *s, se, ce, ze, sh, ch,* or *x.*
    A mouse *is* a small animal.
    A fo<u>x</u> <u>*is*</u> a relative of a dog.

    fox

4.  In writing, we don't make a contraction with a noun and *are.*
    My *children are* responsible.

5.  In writing, we don't make a contraction with *there are.*
    *There are* many kinds of dogs.

6.  The negative contractions are: *isn't* and *aren't.*
    She *isn't* home much.
    You *aren't* patient.
    There is no contraction for *am not.*

**EXERCISE 1**   Fill in the blanks with the correct form of *be*. Make a contraction wherever possible.

**EXAMPLE:**   My dog__'s__ very small.

1. You take care of your dog. You _____ responsible.

2. Pet ownership _____ a big responsibility.

3. My cat _____ soft.

4. Dogs _____ great pets because they _____ affectionate.

    They _____ also good protection for a house.

5. My dog _____ a member of my family.

6. Some cats _____ very affectionate. Other cats _____ very independent.

7. It _____ a big responsibility to own a pet.

8. Kittens and puppies _____ cute.

9. We _____ ready to get a pet.

10. Some people _____ lonely.

**EXERCISE 2**   Fill in the blank with the correct form of *be*. Then fill in the second blank with a negative form. Use contractions wherever possible.

**EXAMPLE:**   Today__'s__ my daughter's birthday. It __isn't__ a holiday.

1. My daughter and I _____ at the pet shop. We _____ at home.

2. My husband _____ at work now. He _____ with me.

3. I _____ patient. My husband _____ patient.

4. This puppy _____ for my daughter. It _____ for my son.

5. My daughter _____ responsible. My son _____ responsible.

6. Dogs _____ good for protection. Cats _____ good for protection.

7. My daughter _____ excited. She _____ bored.

8. This _____ a lab.[3] It _____ a small dog.

---

[3] *Lab* is short for *labrador retriever*.

**4**   Lesson One

| Examples | Uses |
|---|---|
| I **am** patient.<br>The pet shop **is** located on the corner.<br>The children **are** excited about the new puppy. | With a description (adjective)<br>NOTE: Some words that end in *-ed* are adjectives: *tired, married, worried, interested, bored, excited, crowded, located* |
| This **is** a labrador.<br>A labrador **is** a big dog. | With a classification or definition of the subject |
| My dog **is** in the yard. | With a location |
| My husband **is** from Guatemala. | With a place of origin |
| My dog **is** three (years old). | With age |
| The cat **is** hungry.<br>The window is open. I **am** cold. | With physical states |
| There **are** toys for dogs.<br>There **is** a dog restaurant near my house. | With *there* |
| It **is** ten o'clock now.<br>It **is** warm today. | With time and weather. |

## LANGUAGE NOTES

*Be cold* means to feel a low temperature. *Have a cold* shows an illness.
Please bring me my sweater. *I'm cold.*
I'm sick. *I have a cold.*

**EXERCISE 3**   Fill in the blanks with the missing words.

**EXAMPLE:**   My dog __'s__ hungry. He wants to eat.

1. Your son _____ responsible because he _____ only four
         *(not)*

   years _____ .

2. My aunt _____ married. Her dog _____ her only companion.
     *(not)*

3. In the U.S., there _____ cemeteries for pets.

4. Some cats _____ very affectionate.

5. My dog _____ thirsty. Put water in his dish.

6. This _____ a kitten. It _____ only two weeks _____.

7. Don't leave your dog in the car. _____ hot today.

8. My dog _____ cold in the winter. She needs a sweater.

9. _____ is a picture of my dog.

10. My cat is near the _____.

11. I _____ worried about my dog because she _____ sick.

12. My vet's office _____ located about two miles from my house.

## 1.3   Questions with *Be*

| Statement | Yes/No Question and Short Answer |
|---|---|
| **Dogs are** fun. | **Are dogs** affectionate? Yes, they are. |
| **My dog is** big. | **Is your dog** big? No, he isn't. |
| **I am** responsible. | **Am I** patient? Yes, you are. |

| Statement | Wh- Question |
|---|---|
| **You are** at home. | When **are you** at home? |
| **My son isn't** responsible. | Why **isn't your son** responsible? |
| **You aren't** patient. | Why **aren't you** patient? |

## LANGUAGE NOTES

1.  In a statement, we put the subject before the verb *be*. In a question, we put *be* before the subject.
    *The dog is* big.
    *Is the dog* friendly?

2.  If a short answer is negative, we can make a contraction with *be*. If a short answer is affirmative, we can't make a contraction.
    Is your dog small? No, he *isn't*. OR No, *he's not*.
    Is your dog friendly? Yes, he *is*. (NO CONTRACTION)

3.  Most question words can contract with *is*. (EXCEPTION: *which is*)
    *Where's* your cat?
    *What's* your cat's name?
    *Which is* bigger, a Collie or a Lab? (NO CONTRACTION)

4.  Some common questions with *be* are:
    What's your name? My name is Linda.
    What time is it? It's 4:32.
    What color is the flag? It's red, white, and blue.
    What kind of dog is this? It's a Lab.
    What's this? It's a leash.
    What's a Collie? It's a dog.
    How are you? I'm fine.
    How's the weather? It's sunny and warm.
    How old is your daughter? She's 10 (years old).[4]
    How tall are you? I'm five feet, three inches tall (or 5′3″).[5]
    Where are you from? I'm from Mexico.

leash

---

**EXERCISE 4**  Read each question. Answer with a short answer. Do not make a contraction for a short answer after *yes*.

**EXAMPLES:**  Is the teacher a native speaker of English?
Yes, she is.
Is the teacher near the door?
No, she isn't.

1.  Are you from Africa?

2.  Are you tired?

3.  Is the teacher from your native country?

4.  Are the students bored?

5.  Are the windows of the classroom open?

6.  Is the door open?

7.  Are you an immigrant?

8.  Is it warm in the classroom?

9.  Is there a map in the classroom?

10. Is the school located near your house?

---

[4] It is not polite to ask an adult American about his or her age.
[5] For conversion to the metric system, see Appendix D.

Ask and answer. (You may work with a partner.)

EXAMPLE: Where are you from?
I'm from El Salvador.

1. What city are you from?
2. What color is the flag of your native country?
3. What time is it now in your hometown?
4. What sports are popular in your native country?
5. What pets are popular in your native country?
6. What kind of cars are popular in your native country?
7. What's the capital of your native country?
8. Who's the president (or leader) of your native country?
9. When's Labor Day in your native country?
10. What's a popular holiday in your native country?

EXERCISE 6 Fill in the blanks in this phone conversation between Betty (B) and Alice (A).

B. Hello?

A. Hi. This ___is___ Alice.
        (example)

B. Hi, Alice. How _____?
                        (1)

A. I'm fine. This _____ a long distance call. I _____ at home
                    (2)                               (3 not)
now.

B. Where _____?
              (4)

A. I'm at Disneyland.

B. What's Disneyland? _____ a city?
                          (5)

A. No, it _____ . _____ a park in California.
              (6)          (7)

B. What kind of park _____?
                        (8)

A. It's a place for children to have fun. There _____ a lot of things
                                                    (9)
to do here.

B. _____ with you?
      (10)

A. My daughter _____ with me. We _____ here for her birthday.
                  (11)                  (12)

B. How _____ she?
   (13)

A. She _____ 10 _____. She _____ very excited about
   (14)      (15)        (16)
the trip.

B. Why _____ with you?
       (17)

A. My husband isn't here because he _____ too busy. Anyway, he
                                    (18)

_____ interested in Disneyland.
(19 not)

B. _____ the weather in California?
   (20)

A. _____ sunny and warm. _____ warm in New York?
   (21)                     (22)

B. No. The weather here _____ terrible. _____ only 50° and
                        (23)              (24)

rainy. You _____ lucky to be in California.
           (25)

A. Yes, I _____. My daughter and I _____ tired now. And
          (26)                       (27)

we _____ hungry. I'll talk to you when I get home.
   (28)

B. Thanks for calling. Bye.

## 1.4   The Simple Present Tense—Forms

| Base Form | -S Form |
|-----------|---------|
| I **love** animals. | My mother **loves** children. |
| We **love** animals. | My father **loves** children. |
| You **love** animals. | My family **loves** children. |
| My children **love** animals. | My dog **loves** children. |
| They **love** animals. | Everyone **loves** children. |

## LANGUAGE NOTES

1.  The simple present tense has two forms: the base form and the -s
    form.
        love—loves
        want—wants

2.  We use the -s form after *he, she, it,* singular nouns, *everyone, every-
    body, everything, no one, nobody, nothing,* and *family.*
3.  We use the base form after *I, you, we, they,* and plural nouns.
4.  Three verbs have an irregular -s form:
        have → has (pronunciation /hæz/)
        go → goes
        do → does (pronunciation: /dəz/)

5. For a review of the spelling and pronunciation of the *-s* form, see Appendix A.

---

**EXERCISE 7** Fill in the blanks with the base form or the *-s* form.

**EXAMPLE:** Americans ___love___ pets.
(love)

My son ___loves___ his new kitten.
(love)

1. My girlfriend _____ her dog a present on his birthday.
(give)

2. People _____ affection from animals.
(get)

3. Everyone _____ affection.
(need)

4. It _____ a lot of money to have a pet.
(cost)

5. Some pet owners _____ to their pets on the phone.
(talk)

6. My daughter _____ a puppy for her birthday.
(want)

7. My neighbor's dog _____ all the time.
(bark)

8. Some people _____ with their dogs.
(travel)

9. Forty percent of Americans _____ at least one dog.
(have)

10. My brother _____ three dogs.
(have)

11. Dogs _____ their owners.
(protect)

12. My family _____ animals.
(love)

13. Nobody _____ the dog's age.
(know)

14. Everybody _____ that puppies and kittens are cute.
(think)

## 1.5 Negative Statements with the Simple Present Tense

| Examples | Explanation |
|---|---|
| My neighbors **have** two dogs. They **don't have** a cat. | We use *don't* + the base form with *I, you, we, they,* or a plural noun. |
| My daughter **wants** a puppy. She **doesn't want** a kitten. | We use *doesn't* + the base form with *he, she, it,* or a singular noun. |

# LANGUAGE NOTES

1. *Don't* is the contraction for *do not*. *Doesn't* is the contraction for *does not*.
2. Always use the base form after *don't* and *doesn't*.

---

**EXERCISE 8** Write the negative form of the underlined verb.

**EXAMPLE:** We <u>have</u> two cats. We ___*don't have*___ a dog.

1. My cats <u>eat</u> special food. They _____ food from our table.

2. My cats <u>like</u> tuna. They _____ chicken.

3. One cat <u>sleeps</u> in my bed. She _____ alone.

4. I <u>buy</u> cat food. I _____ dog food.

5. My landlord <u>allows</u> cats. He _____ dogs.

6. My cats <u>need</u> attention. They _____ a lot of my time.

7. Some cats <u>go</u> outside. My cats _____ outside.

8. You <u>like</u> dogs. You _____ cats.

9. We <u>have</u> cats. We _____ children.

10. I <u>like</u> cats. My sister _____ cats.

---

**EXERCISE 9** Check (√) the items that describe you. Make an affirmative or negative statement about yourself. Then ask a question. Another student will answer.

**EXAMPLE:** ___√___ I speak Spanish.
A. I speak Spanish. Do you speak Spanish?
B. No, I don't. I speak Romanian.

**EXAMPLE:** _____ I live in a suburb.
A. I don't live in a suburb. Do you live in a suburb?
B. Yes, I do.

1. _____ I speak Spanish.

2. _____ I like American movies.

3. _____ I have a cell phone.

4. _____ I take the bus to school.

5. _____ I have a pet.

6. _____ I like cats.

7. _____ I like to wake up early.

8. _____ I have a CD player.

9. _____ I like to use computers.

10. _____ I know a lot about American history.

## 1.6 Questions with the Simple Present Tense

| Wh- Word | Do/Does Don't/Doesn't | Subject | Verb | Complement | Short Answer |
|---|---|---|---|---|---|
| | | My friend | **has** | a dog. | |
| | | She | **doesn't have** | a cat. | |
| | **Does** | she | **have** | a Labrador? | No, she **doesn't.** |
| What kind of dog | **does** | she | | **have**? | |
| Why | **doesn't** | she | **have** | a cat? | |

## LANGUAGE NOTES

We use the base form in questions.[6]

---

**EXERCISE 10** Fill in the blanks to complete this conversation.

A. Do you _____ like _____ animals?
       (example)

B. Yes, I _____. In fact, I love animals very much. I especially
          (1)
like dogs.

A. _____ you have a dog?
     (2)

B. No, I _____.
        (3)

A. If you love dogs, why _____ a dog?
                                (4)

B. Because my landlord _____ dogs.
                          (5 not/permit)

A. _____ he permit cats?
     (6)

B. Yes, he _____.
           (7)

[6] You will see an exception to this rule in Lesson Four, "Questions About the Subject."

A. _____ a cat?
(8 have)

B. Yes, I do, but I _____ to find a new home for my cat.
(9 need)

_____ you know anyone who wants a cat?
(10)

A. Why _____ your cat?
(11)

B. I'm getting married in three months and my girlfriend _____

_____ to live with cats.
(12 not/want)

A. Why _____ to live with cats? Doesn't she
(13)

_____ them?
(14)

B. She _____ them, but she's allergic to them. When she
(15 like)

_____ over, she _____ and _____ .
(16 come)            (17 sneeze)              (18 cough)

She _____ to come over any more.
(19 not/want)

A. That's a big problem.

B. Yes, it is. I _____ to find a good home for my cat.
(20 need)

_____ you want my cat?
(21)

A. Sorry. My landlord _____ dogs or cats. Maybe you need
(22 not/allow)

a new girlfriend.

B. I _____ so. I _____ her and she _____
(23 not/think)        (24 love)                    (25 love)
me.

A. Well, I _____ you find a good home for your cat soon.
(26 hope)

## 1.7 Wh- Questions with a Preposition

| Preposition | Wh- Word | Do/Does | Subject | Verb | Preposition |
|---|---|---|---|---|---|
| With | whom | do | you | live? | |
| | Who | do | you | live | with? |
| On | what floor | does | he | live? | |
| | What floor | does | he | live | on? |
| | Where | do | you | come | from? |

# LANGUAGE NOTES

1. Putting the preposition before a question word is very formal. In conversation, most people put the preposition at the end.
   FORMAL: *With* whom do you live?
   INFORMAL: Who do you live *with*?

2. We omit *at* in a question about time.
   What time does the class begin?
   It begins *at* 3 o'clock.

3. For country of origin, you can use *be from* or *come from*.
   Where are you from?
   Where do you come from?

**EXERCISE 11** Ask a question using the words given. Then use the words in parentheses ( ) to ask a *wh-* question whenever possible. Another student will answer.

**EXAMPLE:** you/eat in the cafeteria (with whom) OR (who . . . with)
A. Do you eat in the cafeteria?
B. Yes, I do.
A. Who do you eat with? OR With whom do you eat?
B. I eat with my friends.

1. you/live alone (with whom) OR (who . . . with)

2. you/go to bed early (what time)

3. the teacher/come to class on time (what time)

4. the teacher/come from this city (where . . . from)

5. you/practice English outside of class (with whom) OR (who . . . with)

6. you/think about your future (what else)

7. you/complain about English grammar (what else)

8. you/listen to the radio (what station)

9. the teacher/talk about spelling (what else)

10. you/interested in animals (what animals)

11. you/come from Mexico (where)

12. you/go to sleep at midnight (what time)

## 1.8 Questions About Meaning, Spelling, and Cost

| *Wh-* Word | *Do/Does* | Subject | Verb Phrase | Answer |
|---|---|---|---|---|
| What | **does** | vet | **mean**? | It means veterinarian or animal doctor. |
| How | **do** | you | **spell** vet? | V - E - T |
| How | **do** | you | **say** "dog" in Spanish? | "Perro" |
| How much | **does** | dog food | **cost**? | It costs about $10 a bag. |

## LANGUAGE NOTES

*Mean*, *spell*, *say*, and *cost* are verbs and should be in the verb position of a question.

**EXERCISE 12** Fill in the blanks with the missing words.

**EXAMPLE:** What _____*does*_____ "vet" mean?

1. How _____ does the textbook cost?

2. How much _____ bananas cost this week?

3. How much _____ a phone call to your country _____ per minute?

4. I need to buy the textbook. How much _____?

5. I want to buy this computer. How _____?

6. What does "kitten" _____? It means baby cat.

7. I don't know the word "puppy." What does _____?

8. I don't know the word "cemetery." What _____?

9. In Spanish, we say "maestro" for teacher. How do _____ teacher in your language?

10. In Spanish, we say "estudiante" for student. How _____ student in your language?

11. In Spanish, we say "escuela" for school. How _____ in your native language?

12. I want to write your last name. How do you _____ your last name?

13. How _____ spell your first name?

14. How _____ the name of this college?

**EXERCISE 13** Fill in the blanks to complete the questions.

A. How _____is_____ your cousin Bill? I never see him.
   (example)

B. He's fine. But he doesn't live here anymore.

A. Where _____? 
   (1)

B. He lives in L.A. now.

A. What _____? 
   (2)

B. L.A. means Los Angeles. We say L.A. for short.

A. Where _____? 
   (3)

B. L.A. is on the west coast. It's in California. I plan to visit him next month.

A. How much _____? 
   (4)

B. An airplane ticket to Los Angeles costs about $200.

A. Why _____ in L.A.? 
   (5)

B. He lives in L.A. because he goes to school there now.

A. What college _____? 
   (6)

B. He goes to Los Angeles City College.

A. _____ California? 
   (7)

B. Oh, he likes it very much.

A. _____ his address? I want to write to him. 
   (8)

B. Yes, I have his address. He lives at 734 Sierra Avenue.

A. How _____ "Sierra"? 
   (9)

B. S-I-E-R-R-A.

A. Sierra sounds like a Spanish word. What _____? 
   (10)

B. It means "mountain." Many places in California have Spanish names. In fact, Los Angeles means "the angels."

Read the following letter from Elena in the U.S. to Sofia in Russia. Pay special attention to the frequency words.

# Letter About American Customs

Dear Sofia,

I want to tell you about life in the U.S. Some American customs are so strange for me.

Americans treat their pets like a member of the family. My friend Marianne lives alone but she has a dog, Sparky. She **always** carries a picture of Sparky in her wallet. She **often** buys toys for him, especially on his birthday. **Once a month**, she takes him to a dog groomer. The groomer gives him a bath and cuts his nails. When Marianne travels, she **sometimes** takes her dog with her. She **often** calls her dog on the telephone when she's not home and talks into the answering machine. Sparky even sleeps in bed with her.

Another strange custom is this: **Sometimes** Marianne invites me to go to a restaurant. When the check arrives, she **usually** starts to divide the bill in half. Or she says, "Your part is $10.95 and my part is $12.75." In our country, **whenever** I invite someone to a restaurant, I pay.

There's another strange custom. When Americans don't finish their meal in a restaurant, they **often** ask for a doggie bag. Even people who don't have a dog ask for a doggie bag. They take the food home and eat it later. But in Marianne's case, she **usually** likes to share her food with Sparky. She **often** orders a steak in a restaurant because Sparky likes a good steak.

There is another custom that is strange for me. Americans **often** ask, "How are you?" but they **rarely** wait for an answer. Marianne asks me this question **whenever** she sees me, but she **never** listens to my answer. If I start to say, "I don't feel well," she doesn't hear me and says, "That's nice." **Sometimes** I hear her ask other pet owners, "How's your dog?" or, "How's your cat?" She seems more interested in animals' health than in people's health.

I learn a lot about American customs from Marianne. If I don't understand something, she **always** explains it to me. But life is still strange for me here.

Please write me soon. How are you? I'm not American. I REALLY want to know the answer.

Your good friend,
Elena

## 1.9  Simple Present Tense—Uses

| Examples | Uses of the Simple Present Tense |
|---|---|
| Sixty percent of Americans **have** a pet.<br>Pets **need** attention. | To state a fact |
| Marianne **comes** from the U.S.<br>Elena **comes** from Russia. | To show one's country or city of origin |
| Marianne **always** carries a picture of her dog in her wallet.<br>She **often** buys toys for her dog.<br>When Americans don't finish their meal in a restaurant, they **sometimes** ask for a doggie bag.<br>**Whenever** we go to a restaurant, we divide the check. | To show a regular activity, a habit, or a custom |

## LANGUAGE NOTES

1.  For place of origin, we use the simple present tense, not the past tense.
    I *come* from China. NOT: I *came* from China.

2.  For a place of origin, we can also use *be from*.
    I *am from* China.

**EXERCISE 14** Fill in the blanks with the correct form of the verb in parentheses ( ).

**EXAMPLE:** Marianne always ___explains___ American customs to Elena.
                                   *(explain)*

1. Elena often _____ about American customs.
                      *(think)*

2. Marianne always _____ a picture of her dog in her wallet.
                          *(carry)*

3. They sometimes _____ in a restaurant.
                        *(eat)*

4. Marianne sometimes _____ for a doggie bag.
                         *(ask)*

5. She often _____ her food with her dog.
                      *(share)*

6. When the check _____, the two women usually _____ it.
                   *(arrive)*                                                 *(divide)*

7. Americans often _____, "How are you?"
                          *(ask)*

8. Sometimes they _____ for an answer.
                     *(not/wait)*

## 1.10   Frequency Words

| Frequency Word | | Example |
|---|---|---|
| always | 100% | Elena **always** pays when she invites someone to a restaurant. |
| usually/generally | ↑ | Marianne **usually** (**generally**) divides the bill in half. |
| often/frequently | | Americans **often** (**frequently**) ask, "How are you?" |
| sometimes/occasionally | | Marianne **sometimes** (**occasionally**) invites me to a restaurant. |
| rarely/seldom/hardly ever | | Elena **rarely** (**seldom**) (**hardly ever**) eats in a restaurant. |
| never/not ever | 0% | Marianne **never** waits for an answer to her question. |
| | | She does**n't ever** wait for an answer. |

**EXERCISE 15** Fill in the blanks with an appropriate frequency word.

**EXAMPLE:** Americans ___*often*___ say, "Have a nice day."

1. I _____ say, "How are you?" when I meet a friend.

2. I'm _____ confused about American customs.

3. I _____ smile when I pass someone I know.

4. I _____ shake hands when I get together with a friend.

5. Americans _____ ask me, "What country are you from?"

6. I _____ celebrate my birthday in a restaurant.

7. I _____ buy birthday presents for my good friends.

8. If I invite a friend to a restaurant, I _____ pay for both of us.

9. I _____ ask for a "doggie bag" in a restaurant.

10. I _____ eat in fast-food restaurants.

**EXERCISE 16** Fill in the blanks with an appropriate frequency word. (You may find a partner and compare your answers.)

**EXAMPLE:** People in my native country ___*rarely*___ ask, "How are you?"

1. Women in my native country _____ kiss their friends when they get together.

2. People in my native country _____ visit each other without calling first.

3. Men in my native country _____ do housework.

4. Most people in my native country _____ work hard.

5. Students in my native country _____ stand up when the teacher enters the room.

6. Married women in my native country _____ wear a wedding ring.

7. Married men in my native country _____ wear a wedding ring.

8. Women in my native country _____ wear shorts in the summer.

9. People in my native country _____ complain about the political situation.

10. People in my native country _____ eat in restaurants.

11. People in my native country _____ leave a tip in a restaurant.

12. People in my native country _____ take food home from a restaurant.

## 1.11 Position of Frequency Words

| Subject | Frequency Word | Verb | Complement |
|---------|----------------|------|------------|
| I | **often** | ask | about American customs. |
| We | **rarely** | eat | in a restaurant. |

| Subject | Be | Frequency Word | Complement |
|---------|-----|----------------|------------|
| I | am | **often** | confused about American customs. |
| We | are | **always** | interested in American customs. |

## LANGUAGE NOTES

1. Frequency words come after the verb *be* but before other verbs.

    I*'m often* confused about American customs.

    I *always ask* questions about American customs.

2. The following words can also come at the beginning of a sentence: *usually, generally, often, frequently, sometimes, occasionally.*
    I *usually* eat at home.
    *Usually* I eat at home.
    We *sometimes* talk about American customs in class.
    *Sometimes* we talk about American customs in class.
    Americans *often* ask, "How are you?"
    *Often* Americans ask, "How are you?"

**EXERCISE 17** Add a frequency word to each sentence to make a **true** statement about yourself.

**EXAMPLE:**    I drink coffee at night.
    I never drink coffee at night.

1. I talk to my neighbors.

2. I pay my rent on time.

3. I'm busy on Saturdays.

4. I receive letters from my friends.

5. I call my family in my country.

6. I travel in the summer.

7. I speak English at home with my family.

8. I eat meat for dinner.

9. I go downtown.

10. I study in the library.

11. I eat cereal for breakfast.

12. I bring my dictionary to class.

**EXERCISE 18** Add a verb (phrase) to make a **true** statement.

**EXAMPLE:**    I/usually

*I usually drink coffee in the morning.*

OR _*I'm usually afraid to go out at night.*_____

1. I/rarely/on Sunday

   _____

2. I/usually/on the weekend

   _____

3. I/hardly ever

   _____

4. I/sometimes/at night

   _____

5. people from my native country/often

   _____

6. people from my native country/seldom

   _____

7. Americans/sometimes

   _____

8. Americans/rarely

   _____

9. women from my native country/hardly ever

_____

10. men from my native country/hardly ever

_____

## 1.12    Questions with *Ever*

| Examples | Explanation |
|---|---|
| Do you **ever** eat in a restaurant?<br>   Yes, I **sometimes** do.<br>Does the teacher **ever** give surprise tests?<br>   No, he **never** does. | We use *ever* in a *yes/no* question when we want an answer that has a frequency word. |
| Are you **ever** afraid to go out at night?<br>   Yes, I **sometimes** am.<br>Is the teacher **ever** late to class?<br>   No, he **never** is. | In a short answer, the frequency word comes between the subject and the verb. |

## LANGUAGE NOTES

1.  The verb after *never* is affirmative. We do not put two negatives together.
    Do Americans ever bow? No, they *never* do.

2.  We can give a short answer with *yes* or *no* and the frequency word.
    Do you *ever* shake hands when you meet your friends?
    *Yes, always.*
    Do the students *ever* stand up when the teacher enters the room?
    No, *never.*

**EXERCISE 19**  Fill in the blanks with a frequency word to make a **true** statement about yourself. Then ask a question with *ever*. Another student will answer.

**EXAMPLE:**    I __*rarely*__ eat breakfast in a restaurant.
A. Do you ever eat breakfast in a restaurant?
B. No, I never do.

1. I _____ sleep with the light on.

2. I _____ watch TV in the morning.

3. I _____ take a bubble bath.

4. I _____ spend money on foolish things.

5. I'm _____ afraid to go out at night.

6. I'm _____ tired while I'm in class.

7. I _____ cry at a sad movie.

8. I _____ dream in English.

9. I _____ take off my shoes when I enter my house.

10. I _____ babysit for a member of my family.

11. I _____ eat fast food.

12. I _____ wear a watch.

13. I _____ use cologne or perfume.

14. I _____ fall asleep with the TV on.

15. I _____ fall asleep in class.

**bubble bath**

## 1.13    Frequency Expressions and Questions with *How Often*

| Examples | Explanation |
|---|---|
| I eat in a restaurant **once a month**.<br><br>**How often** do you eat in a restaurant?<br><br>My mother writes to me **every week**.<br><br>**How often** does your mother write to you?<br><br>I walk my dog **three times a day**.<br><br>**How often** do you walk your dog? | Expressions that show frequency are:<br>• every day (week, month, year)<br>• every other day (week, month, year)<br>• from time to time<br>• once in a while<br>We can ask a question with *how often* when we want to know the frequency of an activity. |
| **How often** does the teacher review grammar?<br><br>She reviews grammar **whenever** she has time. | We can show frequency with *whenever*. |

## Language Notes

Frequency expressions can come at the beginning of a sentence or at the end of a sentence.

I talk to my friend *every day.*
*Every day* I talk to my friend.
*From time to time,* I go to the theater.
I go to the theater *from time to time.*

**EXERCISE 20** Ask a question with "How often do you...?" and the words given. Another student will answer.

EXAMPLES: eat in a restaurant
A. How often do you eat in a restaurant?
B. I eat in a restaurant once a week.

go downtown
A. How often do you go downtown?
B. I go downtown whenever I have a doctor's appointment.

1. need to renew your driver's license
2. shop for groceries
3. exercise
4. get a haircut
5. use your dictionary
6. water your plants

7. use public transportation
8. use the Internet
9. go to the post office
10. go to the dentist
11. watch the news on TV
12. go to the teacher's office

## SUMMARY OF LESSON 1

1.  Observe the simple present tense with the verb *be*.

You **are** from California.
You **aren't** from Massachusetts.
**Are** you from Los Angeles? No, **I'm** not.
Where **are** you from?

She**'s** late.
She **isn't** on time.
**Is** she here?
No, she **isn't**.
Where **is** she?
Why **isn't** she here?

2.  Observe the simple present tense with other verbs.

BASE FORM
They **have** a car.
They **don't have** a bike.
**Do** they **have** an American car?
Yes, they **do**. OR No, they **don't**.
What kind of car **do** they **have**?
Why **don't** they **have** a foreign car?

-*S* FORM
She **speaks** Spanish.
She **doesn't speak** Portuguese.
**Does** she **speak** English?
Yes, she **does**. OR No, she **doesn't**.
When **does** she **speak** English?
Why **doesn't** she **speak** Portuguese?

3. Frequency words:

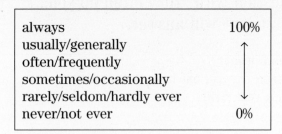

| | |
|---|---|
| always | 100% |
| usually/generally | ↑ |
| often/frequently | |
| sometimes/occasionally | |
| rarely/seldom/hardly ever | ↓ |
| never/not ever | 0% |

4. Questions with frequency words:
Does he **ever** work at night? Yes, he sometimes does.
**How often** does he work on Saturdays? Once a month.

## EDITING ADVICE

1. Do not use a contraction in a short affirmative answer.

Are you happy in the U.S. Yes, ~~I'm~~ *I am*.

2. Do not make a contraction with a word that ends with *s, se, ce, ze, sh, ch,* or *x.*

English~~'s~~ *is* a difficult language.

3. Do not use *have* with age. Do not use *years* without *old.*

My daughter ~~has~~ *is* 10 years *old*.

4. Do not use *have* with *hungry, thirsty, hot, cold, afraid.*

Please open the window. I ~~have~~ *am* hot.

5. Don't forget the subject *it* with time and weather and impersonal expressions.

*It i*~~I~~s cold today.

*It i*~~I~~s important to know English.

6. Don't forget the verb *be.* Remember that some words that end in *-ed* are adjectives, not verbs.

The college *is* located downtown.

*am* I very tired.

7. Don't confuse *your* (possession) and *you're (you are)*.

       *You're*
      ~~Your~~ a very good student.

8. Use correct word order in questions.

          *are you*
      Why ~~you are~~ late?

          *doesn't your sister*
      Why ~~your sister doesn't~~ drive?

9. In a contraction, be careful to put the apostrophe in place of the missing letter. Put the apostrophe above the line.

             *isn't*
      The teacher ~~is'nt~~ here today.

         *doesn't*
      He ~~doesn,t~~ know the answer.

10. There's no contraction for *am not*.

      *I'm not*
      ~~I amn't~~ sick today.

11. Don't repeat the subject with a pronoun.

      My brother ~~he~~ lives in Puerto Rico.

12. Don't use *be* with another present tense verb.

      I~~'m~~ come from Poland.

      We~~'re~~ have a new computer.

13. Use the *-s* form when the subject is *he, she, it, everyone,* or *family*.

             *s*
      My father live in New York.

             *s*
      Everyone know the answer.

             *s*
      My family live in Egypt.

14. Use *doesn't* when the subject is *he, she, it,* or *family*.

         *doesn't*
      He ~~don't~~ have a car.

15. Use the base form after *does*.

      He doesn't speak~~s~~ English.

      Where does he live~~s~~?

16. Don't forget to use *do* or *does* to form the question.

      *does*
Where ⌄your father works?

17. Don't put an object between *don't* or *doesn't* and the main verb.

      *know your friend.*
I don't ~~your friend know.~~

18. Use normal question formation for *spell*, *mean*, and *cost*.

      *does "custom" mean?*
What ~~means "custom"?~~

      *do you*
How ⌄spell "responsible"?

      *does*     *cost*
How much ~~costs~~ the newspaper ⌄?

19. Use the correct word order with frequency words.

      *sometimes goes*
He ~~goes sometimes~~ to the zoo.

      *I never*
~~Never I~~ eat in a restaurant.

      *am never*
I ~~never am~~ late to class.

20. Don't put a frequency phrase between the subject and the verb.

      *all the time*
She ~~all the time~~ talks on the phone ⌄.

21. Don't use *ever* in an affirmative answer.

Does he ever go to church?

      *sometimes*
Yes, ~~ever.~~

# LESSON 1 TEST / REVIEW

**PART 1**    Find the mistakes with the underlined words and correct them. Not every sentence has a mistake. If the sentence is correct, write **C**.

**EXAMPLES:**  Does your mother <u>speaks</u> Polish?

Where <u>do</u> they live?    C

1. How often <u>does</u> they go shopping?

2. I <u>don't need</u> help.

3. Why <u>you don't</u> answer my question?

4. How many languages <u>speaks your brother</u>?

5. My brother <u>don't</u> like American food.

6. Who does your sister <u>lives</u> with?

7. She <u>doesn't understand</u> your question.

8. She <u>doesn't pizza like.</u>

9. <u>How you spell</u> "occasion"?

10. What <u>means</u> "occasion"?

11. How much <u>costs the textbook</u>?

12. I <u>never am</u> bored in class.

13. I <u>never go</u> out at night.

14. <u>Do you ever</u> rent a video? Yes, often.

15. Does she ever wear jeans? No, <u>ever.</u>

16. <u>Sometimes I don't understand</u> Americans.

17. <u>What often</u> do you get a haircut?

18. <u>She every other day</u> writes a letter.

19. Everyone <u>need</u> love.

20. My family <u>live</u> in Colombia.

21. Is your father an engineer? Yes, <u>he's.</u>

22. <u>France's</u> a beautiful country.

23. I want to eat. I <u>am</u> hungry.

24. <u>Is</u> very hot today.

25. The college <u>located</u> on Main and Green.

26. <u>You're</u> my favorite teacher.

27. Why <u>the teacher isn't</u> here today?

28. My little brother <u>has 10 years.</u>

29. I <u>don't interested</u> in sports.

30. She <u>doesn't have</u> a cell phone.

31. I have my sweater, so I <u>amn't</u> cold.

32. <u>I'm have</u> a new TV.

33. <u>She's comes</u> from Mexico.

## PART 2

Fill in the blanks with the affirmative form of the verb in parentheses ( ). Then write the negative form of the verb.

**EXAMPLES:** Elena _____*wants*_____ to write about strange American customs.
(want)

She _____*doesn't want*_____ to write about the weather.

1. Marianne _____ Elena.
   (know)

   She _____ Sofia.

2. Marianne _____ a dog.
   (have)

   Elena _____ a dog.

3. Elena _____ in the U.S.
   (live)

   Sofia _____ in the U.S.

4. Marianne _____ American.
   (be)

   Elena _____ American.

5. You _____ some American customs.
   (understand)

   You _____ all American customs.

6. American customs _____ strange for Elena.
   (be)

   American customs _____ strange for Marianne.

7. I _____ for an answer to "How are you?"
   (wait)

   Americans _____ for an answer.

8. Everyone _____ questions.
   (ask)

   Elena _____ "How are you?" if she's not interested
   in the answer.

Read each statement. Then write a *yes/no* question about the words in parentheses ( ). Write a short answer.

EXAMPLE: Elena lives in the U.S. (Marianne)

*Does Marianne live in the U.S.? Yes, she does.*

1. Marianne has a dog. (Elena) (no)

   _____

2. Elena and Marianne live in the U.S. (Sofia) (no)

   _____

3. Elena has an American friend. (Sofia) (no)

   _____

4. Americans often ask, "How are you?" (ever ask, "How's it going?") (yes/ sometimes)

   _____

5. You live in the U.S. (in New York City) [Give a true answer about yourself.]

   _____

6. American customs are strange for Elena. (for Marianne) (no)

   _____

PART **4**

Read each sentence. Then write a *wh-* question about the word in parentheses ( ). An answer is not necessary.

EXAMPLE: Americans often ask, "How are you?" (why)

*Why do they ask, "How are you?"*

1. You spell "America" A-M-E-R-I-C-A. (How/spell/custom)

   _____

2. Elena lives in the U.S. (where/Sofia)

   _____

3. "Puppy" means baby dog. (kitten)

   _____

The Simple Present Tense; Frequency Words **31**

4. You say "How are you?" in English. You say "¿Cómo está usted?" in Spanish. (how/"how are you"/in Russian)

_____

5. "How are you?" is not a serious question in the U.S. (why)

_____

6. Marianne doesn't wait for an answer. (why)

_____

7. Elena writes to Sofia once a week. (Sofia/write to Elena)

_____

8. They divide the check in a restaurant. (why)

_____

9. Elena doesn't have a dog. (why)

_____

10. You pay for your friends in a restaurant. (why)

_____

# EXPANSION ACTIVITIES

**CLASSROOM ACTIVITIES**

1. Put a check (√) to indicate which of the following are American customs and which are customs in your native culture. Discuss your answers in a small group or with the entire class. (If you don't have information about Americans, ask the teacher.)

| Customs | Americans | People in my native culture |
|---|---|---|
| Students wear jeans to class. | √ | |
| Students call their teachers by their first names. | | |
| Students talk to each other during a test. | | |
| Students write in their textbooks. | | |
| Teachers stand in class. | | |
| People talk a lot about politics. | | |
| People drink a lot of soft drinks. | | |
| Children watch TV a lot. | | |

*(continued)*

| Customs | Americans | People in my native culture |
|---|---|---|
| Friends get together in coffeehouses. | | |
| Most women wear makeup. | | |
| People eat some foods with their hands. | | |
| People are friendly with their neighbors. | | |
| People say, "How are you?" | | |
| Most people use credit cards. | | |
| Men open doors for women. | | |
| Young people give their seats to older people on the bus. | | |
| People eat with chopsticks. | | |
| Most people have a car. | | |
| A lot of people wear gym shoes. | | |
| People travel in the summer. | | |
| Most people take off their shoes when they enter a house. | | |
| Young adults live separately from their parents. | | |
| People usually leave a tip in a restaurant. | | |
| Most people know how to use a computer. | | |
| People pay attention to the weather report. | | |
| Most students study a foreign language. | | |

2.  Fill in the blanks with a frequency word to tell how often you do these activities. Find a partner and discuss your activities with your partner.

EXAMPLE:     I __*often*__ wear jeans to class.

a) I _____ write personal letters to my friends and family.

b) I _____ sit in the sun to get a suntan.

c) I _____ carry a personal stereo.

d) I _____ wear running shoes.

e) I _____ take off my shoes when I enter a house.

f) I _____ discuss politics with my friends.

g) I _____ wear sandals in warm weather.

h) I'm _____ friendly with my neighbors.

3.   Work with a partner or in a small group. Tell if you think this animal is a good pet. Why or why not?

a) A snake

snake

b) A parakeet

parakeet

c) A rabbit

d) A lizard

lizard

e) A turtle

turtle

f) A hamster

hamster

g) A cat

h) A dog

i) Tropical fish (Note: *Fish* can be singular or plural)

**DISCUSSION**

1. Do a lot of people you know have a pet? Do they treat their pet like a member of the family? Do you have a pet now? What kind?

2. Americans tip a waitress or waiter, a taxi driver, and a hair stylist. Discuss tipping customs in other countries.

**PROVERBS**

The following proverbs mention animals. Discuss the meaning of each proverb. Do you have a similar proverb in your native language?

1. You can't teach an old dog new tricks.

2. While the cat's away, the mice will play.

3. Man's best friend is his dog.

4. Curiosity killed the cat.

5. His bark is worse than his bite.

**JOKE**

A woman is outside of her house. A dog is near her. A man walks by and is interested in the dog. He wants to pet the dog. He asks the woman, "Does your dog bite?" The woman answers no. The man pets the dog and the dog bites him. He says, "You told me that your dog doesn't bite." The woman answers, "This is not my dog. My dog is in the house."

**WRITING**

1. Write a letter to a friend or relative in another country. Write about customs that are strange for you. Use the letter on pages 17–18 as your model.

2. Write a letter to an American who plans to visit your community or native country. Explain customs in your culture that the American will find strange.

3. Write about the advantages or disadvantages of owning a dog, a cat, or other pet.

**OUTSIDE ACTIVITY**

Go to the cafeteria. Observe what people are doing. Make note of any behavior that you think is strange. Talk about your observations with the class.

1. Type in "pet" at a search engine. Find a Web site that advertises pet supplies. Make a list of all the unusual things Americans buy for their pets.

2. Find information about a breed of dog that you like. (Try the Web site of the American Kennel Club or AKC.)

# Lesson Two

## GRAMMAR
The Present Continuous Tense
The Future Tense

## CONTEXT
Sunday Afternoon in the Park
The Graying of America

## LESSON FOCUS
We use the present continuous tense[1] to talk about
an action that is in progress now.

> We *are studying* Lesson Two now. The teacher *is explaining* the
> grammar now.

We use the future tense to talk about plans or
predictions about the future.

> We *will have* a test at the end of this lesson.
> We *are going to study* the past tense in Lesson Three.

[1] The present continuous is sometimes called the present progressive.

**Before You Read**
1. Do you like to go to the park? Do you like to sit in the sun?
2. Do you think elderly Americans are physically active?

Read the following article. Pay special attention to present continuous tense verbs.

# Sunday Afternoon in the Park

Dear Fatima,

It's a beautiful Sunday afternoon and I'**m sitting** in the park now under a big, old tree. I'**m taking** a break from my studies to write you this letter. I'**m watching** Americans and their strange behaviors. I want to describe some of these behaviors to you. I want to know what you think of them.

I'**m sitting** in the shade, but most of the people **are sitting** in the sun.

A lot of people **are wearing** short-sleeved shirts and shorts. They**'re trying** to get a suntan. Don't they know that the sun is bad for the skin?

Most of the people **are sitting** alone. Some of them **are reading** magazines. One woman **is talking** on her cell phone. A man **is playing** Frisbee with his dog. He**'s throwing** it to the dog, and the dog **is running** to catch it. Why **isn't** he **playing** with a friend? Why **is** he **playing** with a dog? Another woman **is working** on a computer. Why **isn't** she **relaxing**? Some people **are listening** to a personal stereo. I don't think they**'re having** fun. Some people have a big boom box. They**'re playing** their music loud and **bothering** other people.

Most of the people in the park are young, but I see a few elderly people too. Two elderly men **are playing** tennis. Another elderly man **is jogging**. They seem to be in very good health. But I also see an elderly woman in a wheelchair. A young woman **is pushing** the wheelchair, but I don't think it's her daughter. Don't American children spend time with their parents when they are old and sick?

**I'm learning** a lot about American customs. In fact, **I'm keeping** a diary and **writing** my observations.

Please write to me soon and let me know what **is happening** back home.
Your friend,
Sarah

---

## 2.1 The Present Continuous Tense—Forms

| Examples | Explanation |
|---|---|
| I **am taking** a break now.<br>Some people **are listening** to the radio.<br>A man **is playing** with his dog. | The present continuous tense uses *am, is, are* + verb + *-ing.* |
| Sarah**'s writing** a letter.<br>She**'s sitting** in the park.<br>We**'re learning** about American customs. | We can make a contraction with the subject pronoun and a form of *be.* Most nouns can also contract with *is.*[2] |
| Sarah **isn't** wearing a bathing suit.<br>Most people **aren't** sitting in the shade. | To form the negative, put *not* after *is, am,* or *are.* We can make a contraction for *are not (aren't)* and *is not (isn't).* |
| Sarah **is looking** at Americans and **writing** about her impressions. | When the subject is doing two or more things, don't repeat the *be* verb. |

[2] See Lesson 1, page 3 for exceptions.

# LANGUAGE NOTES

For a review of the spelling of the *-ing* form of verbs, see Appendix A.

**EXERCISE 1** Fill in the blanks with the present continuous form of the verb in parentheses ( ). Use correct spelling.

**EXAMPLE:** Sarah _____*is writing*_____ a letter.
(write)

1. Sarah _____ in the park.
(sit)

2. She _____ in the sun.
(not/sit)

3. She _____ Americans.
(watch)

4. She _____ to her friend.
(write)

5. A lot of people _____ bathing suits.
(wear)

6. Sarah _____ a bathing suit.
(not/wear)

7. One woman _____ on her cell phone.
(talk)

8. Another woman _____ on her computer.
(work)

9. A young woman _____ an elderly woman in a wheelchair.
(push)

10. Some people _____ to their personal stereos.
(listen)

11. Two elderly men _____ tennis.
(play)

12. An elderly man _____ .
(jog)

13. A young man _____ with his dog.
(play)

14. He _____ with a friend.
(not/play)

15. The dog _____ to catch a Frisbee.
(run)

16. We _____ about American customs.
(read)

17. I _____ in the blanks with the correct answers.
(fill)

18. We _____ the past tense now.
(not/study)

## 2.2 Uses of the Present Continuous Tense

| Examples | Uses |
|---|---|
| A man **is playing** with his dog. A woman **is talking** on her cell phone. Sarah **is writing** a letter. | To show that an action is in progress now, at this moment. |
| Sarah **is learning** about American customs. She **is keeping** a diary. | To show a long-term action that is in progress. It may not be happening at this exact moment. |
| A lot of people **are wearing** bathing suits. Sarah **is sitting** in the shade. | To describe a state or condition, using the following verbs: *sit, stand, wear, sleep.* |

**EXERCISE 2** Fill in the blanks with an affirmative or negative verb to make a **true** statement about what is happening now.

**EXAMPLES:** I _____'m wearing_____ jeans now.
(wear)

The teacher _____isn't writing_____ on the blackboard now.
(write)

1. The sun _____ now.
(shine)

2. It _____ now.
(rain)

3. I _____ my answers in my book.
(write)

4. I _____ a pencil to write this exercise.
(use)

5. We _____ this exercise together.
(do)

6. The teacher _____ the students with this exercise.
(help)

7. The teacher _____ a watch.
(wear)

8. I _____ my dictionary now.
(use)

9. We _____ possessive forms now.
(practice)

10. I _____ jeans.
(wear)

11. The teacher _____.
(stand)

12. I _____ near the door.
(sit)

**EXERCISE 3** Write three sentences about being a student. Tell what is happening in your life as a student. (You may share your sentences with the class.)

**EXAMPLES:**   I'm taking five courses this semester.
I'm staying with my sister this semester.
I'm majoring in math.

You may use these verbs: *learn, study, take courses, stay, live, major, plan.*

1. _____

2. _____

3. _____

**EXERCISE 4** Write three sentences to tell which things in your life are changing. Then find a partner and ask your partner if he or she is experiencing the same changes.

**EXAMPLES:**   I'm gaining weight. Are you gaining weight?
I'm planning to buy a house. Are you planning to buy a house?
My English pronunciation is improving. Is your pronunciation improving?

You may use the following verbs: *plan, get (become), learn, grow, gain, lose, improve, think about, change, start.*

1. _____

2. _____

3. _____

## 2.3 Questions with the Present Continuous Tense

Compare statements, questions, and short answers using the present continuous tense.

| Wh- Word | Be (+ N't) | Subject | Be (+ N't) | Verb + -ing | Complement | Short Answer |
|---|---|---|---|---|---|---|
| | | Sarah | **is** | **writing** | a letter. | |
| | | She | **isn't** | **writing** | a composition. | |
| | **Is** | she | | **writing** | to her family? | No, she **isn't**. |
| What | **is** | she | | **writing** | about? | Her observations. |
| Why | **isn't** | she | | **writing** | to her family? | |

# LANGUAGE NOTES

1. Don't use a contraction for a short *yes* answer.
   Is she writing a letter? Yes, *she is*. (NOT: Yes, *she's*.)

2. When the question is "What...doing?" we usually answer with another verb.
   What is Sarah *doing*? She's *writing* a letter.
   What are you *doing*? I'm *studying* verbs.

3. Informally, Americans often put the preposition at the end of a question. COMPARE:
   INFORMAL:  What is Sarah writing *about*?
   FORMAL:    *About* what is she writing?
   INFORMAL:  Who are you talking *to*?
   FORMAL:    *To* whom are you talking?

---

**EXERCISE 5**  Fill in the blanks to make *yes/no* questions about the reading on pages 38–39.

**EXAMPLE:**  _Is Sarah reading a book?_ _____ No. She isn't reading a book.

1. _____ about American customs? Yes, she's learning about American customs.

2. _____ a bathing suit? No, she isn't. She's wearing a dress.

3. _____ in the sun? No, she isn't. She's sitting in the shade.

4. _____ with his friend? No, he isn't. He's playing with his dog.

5. _____ in her diary? Yes, she is. She's writing in her diary about American customs.

6. _____ tennis? Yes, they are. The elderly men are playing tennis.

7. _____ bathing suits? Yes, they are. Most people are wearing bathing suits.

8. _____ to get a suntan? No, she isn't. Sarah isn't trying to get a suntan.

---

Read each statement. Then write a question about the words in parentheses ( ). An answer is not necessary.

**EXAMPLE:**     Sarah's writing something. (what)
*What is she writing?*

1. Sarah is watching Americans. (why)

2. Sarah isn't wearing a bathing suit. (why)

3. A man and a dog are playing with something. (what)

4. Some people aren't relaxing. (why)

5. Sarah is learning about American customs. (how)

6. Most people are sitting alone. (why)

7. A dog is running. (why)

8. Sarah isn't sitting in the sun. (why)

9. Sarah is writing to someone. (who . . . to)

10. Sarah is looking at someone. (who . . . at)

11. Sarah is writing about something. (what . . . about)

12. Two elderly men are playing. (what)

13. Some people are reading. (what)

14. Sarah is doing something. (what)

## 2.4 Contrasting the Simple Present and the Present Continuous

FORMS

| Simple Present | Present Continuous |
|---|---|
| She sometimes **wears** a dress. | She**'s wearing** sunglasses now. |
| She **doesn't wear** shorts. | She **isn't wearing** shoes. |
| **Does** she ever **wear** a bathing suit? | **Is** she **wearing** a T-shirt? |
| No, she **doesn't**. | No, she **isn't**. |
| How often **does** she **wear** a dress? | What **is** she **wearing**? |
| Why **doesn't** she ever **wear** a bathing suit? | Why **isn't** she **wearing** shoes? |

USE

| Examples | Explanation |
|---|---|
| The President **lives** in the White House. <br> I usually **study** in the library. <br> Americans often **say**, "Have a nice day." | Use the simple present tense to talk about a general truth, a habitual activity, or a custom. |
| Sarah **is sitting** in the shade now. <br> She **is writing** a letter to a friend. <br> She **is learning** a lot about American customs. | Use the present continuous tense for an action that is in progress at this moment, or for a longer action that is in progress at this general time. |

## LANGUAGE NOTES

1. *Live* in the simple present shows a person's home. In the present continuous, it shows a temporary, short-term residence.
   Sarah's family *lives* in Iran.
   Sarah *is living* in a dorm this semester.

2. "What do you do (for a living)?" asks about a job. "What are you doing?" asks about an activity now.
   What does she do for a living?
   She's a nurse.
   What is she doing?
   She's waiting for the bus.

**EXERCISE 7**  The following statements of fact or custom use the simple present tense. Take out the frequency word to tell if these things are happening now to the subject in parentheses ( ). Use the present continuous tense.

**EXAMPLES:**  Americans never study the difference between tenses. (we)
We're studying the difference between tenses now.

1. Americans often wear blue jeans. (I)

2. American men sometimes wear an earring. [Use the name of a man in this class.]

3. Americans rarely stand in class to answer the teacher's question. (I)

4. Americans sometimes make a mistake with English grammar. (I)

5. Americans often wear running shoes. (my teacher)

6. American students sometimes study a foreign language. (I)

7. American teachers sometimes sit behind the desk. (my teacher)

8. American students sometimes write in their textbooks. (I)

---

**EXERCISE 8**  Read the following statements of fact or custom. Take out the frequency word to write a question about now. Write a short answer.

**EXAMPLE:**  The teacher usually corrects the homework.
*Is the teacher correcting the homework now? No, he isn't.*

1. The teacher often gives tests.

_____

2. The students sometimes ask questions.

_____

3. You sometimes use your dictionary.

_____

4. The teacher often explains the grammar.

_____

5. You usually listen to the teacher.

_____

6. The teacher often uses the blackboard.

   _____

7. You sometimes write the answers in your book.

   _____

8. The students sometimes make mistakes.

   _____

9. The teacher sometimes stands in class.

   _____

10. You sometimes use a pencil.

   _____

## 2.5 Nonaction Verbs

| Action Verbs | Nonaction Verbs |
|---|---|
| Sarah **is watching** Americans in the park. | She **sees** some strange behaviors. |
| She **is learning** about American customs. | She **knows** that American customs are different. |
| Some people **are listening** to the radio now. | Sarah **hears** the noise. |

## LANGUAGE NOTES

1. We do not usually use the present continuous tense with certain verbs, called nonaction verbs. These verbs describe a state or condition, not an action. We use the simple present tense, even when we talk about now.

2. Nonaction verbs are:

   | believe | hear | matter | prefer | think |
   |---|---|---|---|---|
   | care | know | mean | remember | understand |
   | cost | like | need | see | want |
   | have | love | own | seem | |

Fill in the blanks with the simple present or the present
continuous tense of the verb in parentheses ( ).

EXAMPLES: Sarah _doesn't understand_ all American customs.
(not/understand)

She _is writing_ to her friend now.
(write)

1. Sarah lives in the U.S. so she _____ a little about American
(know)
customs now.

2. Sarah _____ to describe American behaviors to her friend.
(want)

3. Some of the people in the park _____ lonely to Sarah.
(seem)

4. One woman _____ on a cell phone.
(talk)

5. She _____ .
(not/relax)

6. Sarah _____ two elderly men.
(see)

7. The elderly men _____ tennis.
(play)

8. They _____ bathing suits.
(not/wear)

9. Some people in the park _____ to get a suntan. They
(want)
_____ that the sun is bad for the skin.
(not/care)

10. Sarah _____ American customs in her letter now.
(describe)

11. Sarah _____ a break from her studies.
(take)

12. She _____ to relax on Sundays.
(need)

## 2.6 *Think, Have,* and the Sense Perception Verbs

| Action | Nonaction |
|---|---|
| A) Sarah **is thinking** about her friend now. | F) Sarah **thinks** that many American behaviors are strange. |
| B) Sarah **is looking** at people in the park. <br> C) She **is smelling** the flowers. | G) Women in bathing suits **look** strange to Sarah. <br> H) The flowers **smell** nice. |

*(continued)*

| Action | Nonaction |
|---|---|
| D) Sarah **is having** new experiences in the U.S.<br>E) She **is having** a sandwich for lunch. | I) She **has** a pen and paper in her hand.<br>J) She **has** new American friends.<br>K) My friend **has** a fever now. |

## LANGUAGE NOTES

1. *Think*, *have*, and the sense perception verbs (*look*, *taste*, *feel*, *smell*) can be both action and nonaction verbs, but the meaning is different.
2. When we think about something (sentence A), *think* is an action verb. When *think* means to have an opinion about something (sentence F), *think* is a nonaction verb.
3. When the sense perception verbs describe an action (sentences B and C), they are action verbs. When they describe a state (sentences G and H), they are nonaction verbs.
4. When *have* means to experience something or to eat or drink something (sentences D and E), it is an action verb. When *have* shows possession, relationship, or illness (sentences I, J, K), it is a nonaction verb.

**EXERCISE 10** Fill in the blanks with the simple present or the present continuous form of the verb in parentheses ( ).

**EXAMPLES:** Some of the women in the park _____ *are wearing* _____ bathing suits.
<br>*(wear)*

Sarah never _____ *wears* _____ a bathing suit.
<br>*(wear)*

1. Sarah _____ in the park now.
<br>*(sit)*

2. She usually _____ in the shade because she _____
<br>*(sit)* *(not/like)*
<br>the sun. She _____ the sun is bad for the skin.
<br>*(think)*

3. Sarah _____ much about American customs.
<br>*(not/know)*

4. Some people in the park _____ magazines. They _____
<br>*(read)* *(not/talk)*
<br>to each other.

5. Sarah sometimes _____ a book in the park, but now she
<br>*(read)*
<br>_____ a letter.
<br>*(write)*

6. Some people _____ to a boom box. Sarah _____
   _(listen)_ _(hear)_
   the loud music, and she _____ it. But the people
   _(not/like)_

   _____.
   _(not/care)_

7. Sarah _____ to describe American customs to her friend.
   _(want)_

8. Her friend _____ in the U.S.
   _(not/live)_

9. Sarah _____ some American customs.
   _(not/like)_

10. Some men on the beach _____ at the women in bathing
    _(look)_
    suits now.

11. These women _____ strange to Sarah.
    _(look)_

12. A young woman _____ care of an elderly woman.
    _(take)_

13. The young woman _____ like the elderly woman's
    _(not/look)_
    daughter.

14. Sarah _____ that some Americans _____
    _(think)_ _(not/care)_
    about their elderly parents.

15. Sarah _____ her parents and _____ to take
    _(love)_ _(want)_
    care of them when they're old.

16. Her parents are in their fifties and _____ her help now.
    _(not/need)_

## 2.7 Questions with the Simple Present and the Present Continuous

Compare statements and questions that use the simple present tense.

| Wh- Word | Do/Does (+ N't) | Subject | Verb | Complement |
|---|---|---|---|---|
| | | She | **watches** | TV. |
| When | **does** | she | **watch** | TV? |
| | | My parents | **speak** | English. |
| What language | **do** | your parents | **speak?** | |
| | | Your sister | **lives** | with someone. |
| With whom | **does** | she | **live?** | |
| Who | **does** | she | **live** | with? |
| | | You | **don't like** | her. |
| Why | **don't** | you | **like** | her? |

_(continued)_

Compare statements and questions that use the present continuous tense.

| Wh- Word | Be (+ N't) | Subject | Be | Main Verb | Complement |
|----------|------------|---------|-----|-----------|------------|
|          |            | She     | is  | sitting.  |            |
| Where    | is         | she     |     | sitting?  |            |
|          |            | You     | aren't | listening | to the music. |
| Why      | aren't     | you     |     | listening | to the music? |

**EXERCISE 11** Use the words in parentheses ( ) to write a question. An answer is not necessary.

**EXAMPLES:** Sarah is watching Americans. (why)
*Why is she watching Americans?*
_____

She wants to describe American behavior. (to whom)
*To whom does she want to describe American behavior?*
_____

1. Sarah likes to sit in the park. (when)

_____

2. She doesn't like to sit in the sun. (why)

_____

3. She's very surprised by American customs. (why)

_____

4. A man is playing Frisbee. (with whom) OR (who...with)

_____

5. The people in the park seem strange to Sarah. (why)

_____

6. Some people are wearing shorts. (what/Sarah/wear)

_____

7. The sun is bad for the skin. (why)

_____

8. An elderly man is jogging. (where)

_____

9. A woman is talking on a cell phone. (who...to)

_____

10. Two men are playing tennis. (where)

_____

11. Elderly people need exercise. (why)

_____

12. A young woman is pushing an elderly woman's wheelchair. (why)

_____

**EXERCISE 12** This is a phone conversation between two friends, Patty (P) and Linda (L). Fill in the blanks with the missing words. Use the simple present or the present continuous tense.

P. Hello?

L. Hi, Patty. This is Linda.

P. Hi, Linda. What _____are you doing_____ now?
       (you/do)

L. Not much. _____ to meet for coffee?
       (1 you/want)

P. I can't. I _____ . I _____ dinner in
       (2 cook)              (3 have)

   the oven now, and I _____ for it to be finished.
                    (4 wait)

   What _____?
       (5 you/do)

L. I _____ for a test. But I _____ to take
     (6 study)                    (7 want)

   a break now. Besides, I _____ to talk to someone. I
                       (8 need)

   usually _____ to my roommate when I _____
         (9 talk)                            (10 have)

   a problem, but she _____ some friends in New York
                   (11 visit)

   now.

P. We can talk while I _____ dinner. It _____
                    (12 prepare)                (13 sound)

   like something serious _____.
                       (14 happen)

L. My boyfriend and I _____ to get married.
                   (15 plan)

P. That's wonderful! Congratulations!

L. There's one small problem. My parents _____ the
                                      (16 not/like)
   idea.

P. They don't? Why not?

L. Well, as you know, I'm a Christian. And he's a Moslem.

P. That _____.
   (17 not/matter)

L. It _____ to my family. And to his parents too.
   (18 matter)

   We _____ about getting married without telling our
   (19 think)

   parents.

P. I _____ that's such a good idea.
   (20 not/think)

L. I _____ what else to do.
   (21 not/know)

P. I'll call you later and we can talk more about it. I _____
   (22 hear)

   my husband coming in the door, and dinner is almost ready.

L. Thanks for listening. Talk to you later.

---

**Before You Read**  1.  In your native culture, who takes care of people when they get old?
                     2.  Do old people in your native culture get a lot of respect?

Read the following article. Pay special attention to future tense verbs.

---

# The Graying of America

The overall population of the U.S. is growing slowly. At the end of the twentieth century, the American population was 273 million. By the middle of this century, it **is going to be** 394 million. Even though this is not a big growth, one group is growing very fast—the elderly (65 years old and over). There are two reasons for this sudden rise in the number of older Americans. First, life expectancy is increasing. In 1900, when the life expectancy was 47, 1 in 25 Americans was elderly. In 1990, with a life expectancy of 79 for women and 73 for men, 1 in 8 was elderly.

---

The second reason for this growth is the aging of the "Baby Boomers." In the 18 years after World War II, from 1946 to 1964, a large number of babies were born—75 million. The people born during this period, known as the Baby Boomers, are now middle aged and **will** soon **be** elderly. The average age of the population **is going to increase** as the Baby Boomers get older and live longer. The median age of Americans in 1970 was 28; in 1995 it was 35.8. By 2050, it **will be** 40.3. In the middle of the twenty-first century, 1 in 5 Americans **will be** elderly.

What does this mean for America? First, more and more middle-aged people **are going to have** the responsibility of taking care of parents and other older relatives. They **will become** the "sandwich" generation, taking care of their parents as well as their children. For taxpayers, this means that they **are going to pay** more as one-fifth of the population uses one half of the resources.

It **will be** interesting to see how America **will handle** these changes.

**Did you know...?**

There are 72,000 Americans today who are 100 years old or older. By the year 2050, this number will probably be 834,000.

## 2.8 The Future Tense with *Will*

| Examples | Explanation |
|---|---|
| People **will live** longer. They **will need** help from their children. There **will be** more elderly people in 50 years. | We use *will* + the base form to form the future tense. |
| I**'ll be** 75 years old in 2050. You**'ll take** care of your parents. | We can contract *will* with the subject pronouns: *I'll, you'll, he'll, she'll, it'll, we'll, they'll.* |
| The population **will not** go down. I **won't** live with my children. | To form the negative, put *not* after *will*. The contraction for *will not* is *won't.* |

Compare statements, questions, and short answers using *will*.

| *Wh-* Word | *Will Won't* | Subject | *Will Won't* | Verb | Complement | Short Answer |
|---|---|---|---|---|---|---|
| | | She | **will** | live | with her daughter. | |
| | | She | **won't** | live | alone. | |
| | **Will** | she | | live | with her son? | Yes, she **will**. |
| Where | **will** | she | | live? | | |
| Why | **won't** | she | | live | alone? | |

# LANGUAGE NOTES

1. You can put a frequency word between *will* and the main verb.
   I will *always* help my parents.
2. Do not make a contraction for a short *yes* answer.
   Will you buy a new car soon? Yes, I *will*. (NOT: Yes, I'll.)

**EXERCISE 13** Fill in the blanks with an appropriate verb in the future tense. Use *will*.

**EXAMPLE:** In the future, people _____ *will live* _____ longer.

1. The population of old people _____.

2. There _____ more older people by the middle of the twenty-first century.

3. Where _____ you _____ when you are old?

4. _____ your children _____ care of you?

5. How old _____ you _____ in 2050?

**EXERCISE 14** A mother (M) is worried about her son (S), who is going away to college. Fill in the blanks to complete this conversation. Use the future with *will*.

M. I'm worried about you. You _____ *will be* _____ alone for the first time
   *(example)*
   in your life.

S. Don't worry, Mom. I _____ alone. There _____
   *(1)*                                    *(2)*
   a lot of people on campus.

M. Who _____ your clothes for you?
   *(3)*

S. I'll wash them myself.

M. What _____?
   *(4)*

S. I'll eat the food in the dorm.

---

The Present Continuous Tense; The Future Tense **55**

M. Make sure you eat a lot of fruits and vegetables.

S. Don't worry. I _____ (5) .

M. When _____ (6) ?

S. My classes will begin next week.

M. What _____ (7) this week?

S. This week I _____ (8) my new roommate. He's from Germany.

M. When _____ (9) ?

S. He'll probably arrive tomorrow. This week I _____ (10) my suitcases and set up my computer. Also I _____ (11) my books at the bookstore. I _____ (12) a map of the campus and learn how to get around.

M. _____ (13) enough money?

S. Yes, I'll have enough money. Remember, I have your credit card. But I _____ (14) only _____ (15) it for necessary things.

M. _____ (16) call me once a week?

S. Yes, I _____ (17) you. And I _____ (18) you e-mail too.

M. _____ (19) home for the holidays?

S. Yes, I _____ (20) . I'll come home for Thanksgiving and Christmas. But I won't come home for Labor Day.

M. Why _____ (21) for Labor Day?

S. Because I won't have enough time.

M. Drive carefully.

S. I will.

M. I _____ (22) you.

S. I'll miss you too, Mom.

# The Future Tense with *Be Going To*

| Examples | Explanation |
|---|---|
| People **are going to live** longer. They **are going to need** help from their children. There **are going to be** more elderly people in 50 years. | We use *be going to* + the base form to form the future tense. |
| I'm **not** going to live with my children. | To form the negative, put *not* after *am, is, are*. |

Compare statements, questions, and short answers with *be going to*.

| Wh- Word | Be (+ N't) | Subject | Be (Not) | Going to | Verb | Complement | Short Answer |
|---|---|---|---|---|---|---|---|
| | | She | is | going to | live | with her daughter. | |
| | | She | isn't | going to | live | alone. | |
| | Is | she | | going to | live | with her son? | No, she **isn't**. |
| Where | is | she | | going to | live? | | |
| Why | isn't | she | | going to | live | with her son? | |

## LANGUAGE NOTES

1. In informal speech, *going to* before another verb often sounds like "gonna." In formal English, we don't write "gonna." Listen to your teacher's pronunciation of *going to* in the following sentences.
   Where's he going to live?
   (Where's he "gonna" live?)
   He's going to live in a dorm.
   (He's "gonna" live in a dorm.)

2. Only *going to* before another verb sounds like "gonna." We don't pronounce "gonna" at the end of a sentence or before a noun.
   Where is he going?
   He's going to the bookstore.

3. We often shorten *going to go* to *going*.
   He's *going to go* to the supermarket.
   He's *going* to the supermarket.

4. We use the preposition *in* with the future tense to mean *after*.
   He's going return *in* an hour.

**EXERCISE 15** Fill in the blanks with an appropriate verb in the future tense. Use *be going to.*

EXAMPLE:     _____Are_____ your children _____going to take care of_____ you?

1. The cost of health care _____.

2. People _____ higher taxes.

3. How old _____ your daughter _____ in 2050?

4. _____ you _____ care of your elderly parents?

5. A lot of people _____ over 100 years old in 2050.

**EXERCISE 16** Fill in the blanks to tell what is going happen.

EXAMPLE:     My running shoes are very old. I need new shoes. _____I'm going to buy_____ a new pair.

1. The sky is getting very cloudy and dark. It looks like it _____

   _____.

2. Now it's raining. I need to go out. I _____ an umbrella with me.

3. I'm hungry. I _____ dinner.

4. My friend is arriving today at 4 o'clock. I _____ her at the airport.

5. We're almost finished with this lesson. The teacher _____ us a test soon.

6. The government needs more money. It _____ taxes.

7. My grandparents' apartment is too big for them. They _____

   _____ to a smaller apartment.

8. My grandfather is almost 65 and still working. He _____ soon and just relax.

9. My friends are coming over tomorrow, and my house is dirty.

   I _____ the house today.

10. My brother is going to Puerto Rico for vacation. He _____ me a postcard.

**EXERCISE 17** Do you have questions for the teacher about this semester, next semester, or his or her life in general? Write three questions to ask the teacher about the near or distant future.

**EXAMPLES:**   *What time are you going to leave today?*

*When are you going to give us a test?*

*Are you going to retire soon?*

1. _____

2. _____

3. _____

## 2.10   *Will* vs. *Be Going To*

| Uses | *Will* | *Be Going To* |
|---|---|---|
| Prediction | My father always exercises and eats well. I think he **will live** a long time. | I think my father **is going to live** a long time. |
| Fact | The sun **will set** at 6:43 tonight.<br><br>The population of older people **will increase**. | The sun **is going to set** at 6:43 tonight.<br><br>The population of older people **is going to increase**. |
| Scheduled event | The movie **will begin** at 8 o'clock. | The movie **is going to begin** at 8 o'clock. |
| Plan | | My grandfather **is going to move** to Florida next year.<br><br>I **am going to return** to my native country in three years. |
| Promise | I **will** always **take** care of you, Mom. | |
| Offer to help | A: This box is heavy.<br>B: **I'll carry** it for you. | |

## LANGUAGE NOTES

1. Use either *will* or *be going to* for predictions, facts about the future, and scheduled events. *Will* is more formal than *be going to*.
2. When we have a plan to do something, we usually use *be going to*.
3. When we make a promise or offer to help, we usually use *will*.

4. We sometimes use the present continuous tense with a future meaning. We can do this with planned events in the near future. We do this especially with verbs of motion.

My grandmother *is moving* into a retirement home on Friday.
I'*m helping* her move on Friday.

**EXERCISE 18** Choose *will* or *be going to* to fill in the blanks. In some cases, both are possible.

**EXAMPLE:**

1. A. Where are you going?

   B. I'm going to the park this afternoon. I ___*am going to meet*___ my
   (example: meet)
   friend and play tennis with her. I have to return some videos to the video store, but I don't have time.

   A. Give them to me. I _____ that way.
   (pass)

   I _____ them for you.
   (return)

2. A. I have to go to the airport. My sister's plane _____
   (arrive)
   at four o'clock this afternoon.

   B. I _____ with you. I _____ in the car while
   (go)                      (stay)
   you go into the airport. That way, you _____
   (not/have to)
   pay for parking.

3. A. My sister's birthday is next week.

   B. _____ her a birthday present?
   (you/give)

   A. Of course, I _____ .

   B. What _____ her?
   (you/give)

   A. She loves the theater. I _____ her tickets to a play.
   (buy)

   B. How old _____?
   (be)

   A. She _____ 21 years old.
   (be)

4. Teacher: Next week we _____ our midterm test.
   (have)

   Student: _____ hard?
   (it/be)

   Teacher: Yes, but I _____ you prepare for it.
   (help)

5. Wife: I won't have time to pick up the children this afternoon. I have to work late.

   Husband: Don't worry. I _____ them up.
   (pick)

   Wife: I won't have time to cook either.

   Husband: Just relax. I _____ dinner tonight.
   (prepare)

6. Man: I want to marry you.

   Woman: But we're only 19. We're too young.

   Man: I _____ 20 in April.
   (be)

   Woman: But you don't even have a job.

   Man: I _____ a job.
   (find)

   Woman: Let's wait a few years.

   Man: I _____ for you forever. I _____ you.
   (wait)                                    (always/love)

7. A. Do you want to watch the football game with me on Saturday?

   B. I can't. My brother _____ . I _____ him.
   (move)                                    (help)

   A. Do you need any help?

   B. We need boxes. Do you have any?

   A. No, but I _____ for boxes. I _____
   (look)                                    (go)

   to the supermarket this afternoon. I _____ boxes
   (get)

   there. I _____ them to your house.
   (bring)

   B. Thanks.

8. A. I'm so excited. I _____ a puppy.
   (get)

   B. That's a big responsibility. You're never home. How _____

   _____ care of it?
   (take)

   A. My cousin lives with me now. She doesn't have a job. She

   _____ me take care of the dog.
   (help)

   B. What about your landlord? Is it OK with him?

   A. I _____ him.
   (not/tell)

B. You have to tell him. He _____ if you have a dog.
   (know)

You _____ take the dog out three times a day.
   (have to)

And the dog _____.
   (bark)

## 2.11 The Future Tense + Time/*If* Clause

| Examples | Explanation |
|---|---|
| When my parents **are** old, I **will take** care of them. | We use the future tense only in the main clause; we use the simple present tense in the time clause and *if* clause. |
| After they **retire**, they **will move** to a warm climate. | |
| If my brother **isn't** home by six o'clock, I'm **going to eat** without him. | |
| I'm **going to do** the homework before I **go** home. | |

## LANGUAGE NOTES

Use a comma if the time or *if* clause is before the main clause.

> When my parents are old, I'll take care of them. (Use a comma.)
> I'll take care of my parents when they're old. (Don't use a comma.)

**EXERCISE 19** Connect the sentences using *if* or the time word in parentheses ( ).

**EXAMPLE:** I will retire. I will play golf. (when)

*When I retire, I will play golf.* OR *I will play golf when I retire.*

1. I will retire. I'm not going to live with my children. (when)

   _____

2. I will be old. I will take care of myself. (when)

   _____

3. My parents will need help. I'll take care of them. (if)

   _____

4. I won't be healthy. I'll live with my children. (if)

   _____

5. I won't have money. I will get help from the government. (if)

_____

6. My parents will die. I'll move to another city. (after)

_____

7. I will get a pension. I won't need to depend on my children. (if)

_____

8. I'll retire. I'm going to save my money. (before)

_____

**EXERCISE 20** Think about a specific time in your near future (when you graduate, when you get married, when you have children, when you find a job, when you return to your native country, when you are old). Write three sentences to tell what will happen at that time. Find a partner who is close to your age. Compare your answers to your partner's answers.

**EXAMPLE:** *When I have children, I won't have as much free time as I do now.*

*When I have children, I'm going to have a lot more responsibilities.*

*When I have children, my parents will be very happy.*

1. _____

2. _____

3. _____

**EXERCISE 21** A foreign student (F) is talking to an American (A) about getting old. Fill in the blanks with the correct form of the verb to complete this conversation. In many cases, you can use either *be going to* or *will*.

F. How's your grandfather?

A. He's OK. I ___'m going to visit___ him this afternoon.
    _(visit)_

F. How's he doing?

A. He's in great health. Next week he _____ to Hawaii to
    _(1 go)_
   play golf.

F. How old is he?

A. He _____ 78 next month. Did I tell you? In June, he
   (2 be)

   _____ married to a widow he met in the retirement
   (3 get)

   home.

F. That seems so strange to me. Why _____ that?
   (4 he/do)

A. Why not? They like each other, and they want to be together.

F. What _____ when he's no longer able to take care of
   (5 you/do)

   himself?

A. We never think about it. He's in such great health that we think

   he _____ healthy forever. I think he _____
   (6 be)                                      (7 outlive³)

   us all.

F. But he _____ help as he gets older.
   (8 probably/need)

A. We _____ that bridge when we come to it.⁴ Do you have
   (9 cross)

   plans for your parents as they get older?

F. They're in their 50s now. But when they _____ older,
   (10 be)

   they _____ with me and my wife. In our country, it's an
   (11 live)

   honor to take care of our parents.

A. That sounds like a great custom. But I think it's better when older
   people are independent. I'm glad that Grandpa doesn't depend on us.

   And when I _____ old, I _____ care of myself.
   (12 be)                    (13 take)

   I don't want to depend on anyone.

F. You _____ your mind when you _____ elderly.
   (14 change)                              (15 be)

A. Maybe. I have to catch my bus now. Grandpa is waiting for me.

   I _____ you later.
   (16 see)

F. Wait. I have my car. I _____ you to your grandfather's
   (17 drive)

   place.

A. Thanks.

³ To *outlive* means to live longer than other people.
⁴ This expression means *We'll worry about that problem when the problem happens, and not before.*

**EXERCISE 22** This is a conversation between two co-workers. They are talking about retirement. Fill in the blanks with the correct form and tense of the verb in parentheses ( ).

A.  I hear you're going to retire this year.

B.  Yes. Isn't it wonderful? I ___*will be*___ 65 in September.
    (be)

A.  What _____ after you _____?
    (1 you/do)                (2 retire)

B.  I'm trying to sell my house now. When I _____ my house,
    (3 sell)

    I _____ to Florida and buy a condo.
    (4 move)

A.  What _____ in Florida?
    (5 you/do)

B.  I _____ a sailboat and spend most of my time on the
    (6 buy)
    water.

A.  But a sailboat is expensive.

B.  When I _____ 65, I _____ to use my savings.
    (7 be)              (8 start)

    Also, I _____ a lot of money when I _____
    (9 get)                              (10 sell)

    my house. What _____ when you _____?
    (11 you/do)                (12 retire)

A.  I'm only 45 years old. I have another 20 years until I _____.
    (13 retire)

B.  Now is the time to start thinking about retirement. If

    you _____ your money for the next 20 years, you
    (14 save)

    _____ a comfortable retirement. But if you
    (15 have)

    _____ about it until the time _____,
    (16 not/think)                      (17 come)

    you _____ enough money to live on.
    (18 not/have)

A.  I _____ about it when the time _____. I'm
    (19 worry)                          (20 come)
    too young to worry about it now.

B.  If you _____ until you _____ 65 to think about
    (21 wait)          (22 be)

    it, you _____ a poor, old man. On Monday morning when
    (23 be)

    we _____ at work, I _____ you to a woman
    (24 be)                (25 introduce)

---

The Present Continuous Tense; The Future Tense     **65**

who can explain the company's savings plan to you. After you

_____ to her, I'm sure you _____ your mind
(26 talk)                                (27 change)

about when to worry about retirement.

# SUMMARY OF LESSON 2

## Uses of Tenses

| Simple Present Tense | |
|---|---|
| General truths, facts | Sixty percent of Americans **have** a pet.<br><br>The United States **has** 50 states. |
| Regular activities, habits, customs | I always **drink** coffee in the morning.<br><br>Sometimes I **study** in the library. |
| Place of origin | Linda **comes** from Mexico.<br><br>Maria **comes** from Guatemala. |
| In a time clause or in an **if** clause of a future statement | When I **get** home, I'll do my homework.<br><br>If I **pass** this course, I'll go on to the next level. |
| With nonaction verbs | She **knows** the answer.<br><br>I **hear** the music. |

| Present Continuous<br>(with action verbs only) | |
|---|---|
| Now | We**'re comparing** verb tenses now.<br><br>I**'m looking** at page 66 now. |
| A long action in progress at this general time | Sarah **is learning** about American customs.<br><br>She**'s keeping** a diary in the U.S. |
| A plan in the near future | I**'m driving** to California next week.<br><br>My sister **is going** with me. |
| A descriptive state | She**'s wearing** shorts.<br><br>She**'s sitting** in the park. |

## Future

| | | |
|---|---|---|
| A plan | | **I'm going to buy** a new car next month. |
| A fact | The number of old people **will increase**. | The number of old people **is going to increase**. |
| A prediction | I think you **will be** rich someday. | I think you **are going to be** rich someday. |
| A promise | I **will** always **love** you. | |
| An offer to help | Relax. **I'll cook** tonight. | |
| A scheduled event | Registration **will begin** on August 18. | Registration **is going to begin** on August 18. |

## EDITING ADVICE

1.  Always include *be* in a present continuous tense verb.

    *is*
    She ˄ working now.

2.  Don't use the present continuous tense with a nonaction verb.

    *e*
    I ~~am~~ lik~~ing~~ your new car.

3.  Don't use *be* with another verb for the future.

    I will ~~be~~ go back to my native country in five years.

4.  Include *be* in a future sentence that has no other verb.

    *be*
    He will ˄ angry.

    *be*
    There will ˄ a party soon.

5.  Don't combine *will* and *be going to*.

    He will ~~going to~~ leave.   OR   *He's going to leave.*

6.  Use the future tense with an offer to help.

    *'ll*
    The phone's ringing. I ˄ get it.

7. Don't use the future tense after a time word or *if*.

When they ~~will~~ go home, they are going to watch TV.

If I ~~will be~~ *am* late, I'll call you.

8. Use a form of *be* with *going to*.

*is*
He ^ going to help me.

9. Use correct word order in questions.

*will you*
When ~~you will~~ go back to your native country?

*isn't she*
Why ~~she isn't~~ going to buy a new car?

## LESSON 2 TEST / REVIEW

PART 1  Find the mistakes with the underlined words, and correct them. Not every sentence has a mistake. If the sentence is correct, write **C**.

EXAMPLES:  You can't move this sofa alone. <u>I'll help</u> you.    C
Where <u>will you ~~be~~ live</u> when you are old?

1. <u>He sitting</u> near the door.

2. What <u>will you do</u> after you graduate?

3. <u>I'm going to buy</u> a new car soon.

4. He's listening to the radio. <u>He's hearing</u> the news.

5. <u>She going to leave</u> on Friday.

6. <u>I'll going to watch</u> TV tonight.

7. <u>I going to do</u> my homework when I get home.

8. What <u>you going to do</u> tonight?

9. <u>I'm leaving</u> for New York on Friday.

10. <u>There will</u> a test on Friday.

11. I <u>will be know</u> English well in a few years.

12. If you don't eat dinner, you <u>will hungry</u> later.

13. She <u>won't leave</u> her family.

14. If you need something, let me know. <u>I get</u> it for you.

15. Why <u>won't you</u> tell me about your problem?

16. She's looking at the report. She <u>sees</u> the problem now.

17. Why <u>she isn't</u> going to visit her grandmother?

18. I'll cross that bridge when I <u>come</u> to it.

**PART 2**  Mary (M) is talking to her friend Sue (S) on the phone. Fill in the blanks with the correct tense and form. Use the simple present, present continuous, or future.

S.  Hi, Mary.

M.  Hi, Sue. How are you?

S.  Fine. What are you doing?

M.  I ___*am packing*___ now. We _____ next Saturday.
      (pack)                              (1 move)

S.  Oh, really? Why? You _____ such a lovely apartment now.
                          (2 have)

M.  Yes, I know we do. But I _____ a baby in four months, so we
                              (3 have)

     _____ a bigger apartment when the baby _____ .
       (4 need)                                         (5 arrive)

S.  But your present apartment _____ an extra bedroom.
                                 (6 have)

M.  Yes. But my husband _____ to have an extra room for an
                          (7 always/like)

     office. He usually _____ a lot of work home. He _____
                          (8 bring)                              (9 need)
     a place where he can work without noise.

S.  Do you need help with your packing?

M.  Not really. Bill and I _____ home this week to finish the
                             (10 stay)

     packing. And my mother _____ me now too.
                              (11 help)

S.  I _____ over next Saturday to help you move.
       (12 come)

M.  We _____ professional movers on Saturday. We don't want to
        (13 use)
     bother our friends.

S.  It's no bother. I _____ to help.
                        (14 want)

M.  Thanks. There probably _____ a few things you can help me
    (15 be)

    with on Saturday. I have to go now. I _____ Bill. He
    (16 hear)

    _____ me. He _____ me to help him in the basement.
    (17 call)          (18 want)

    I _____ you back later.
    (19 call)

S.  You don't have to call me back. I _____ you on Saturday. Bye.
    (20 see)

PART 3   Fill in the blanks with the negative form of the underlined verb.

EXAMPLE:  Mary is busy. Sue ____isn't____ busy.

1.  Sue is talking to Mary. She _____ to her husband.

2.  Mary is going to move to a bigger apartment. She _____
    to a house.

3.  Mary's husband needs an extra room. He _____ a
    big room.

4.  Sue will go to Mary's house on Saturday. She _____
    tomorrow.

5.  Mary will move the small things. She _____ the
    furniture.

6.  Her new apartment has an extra room. Her old apartment _____

    _____ an extra room.

PART 4   Write a *yes/no* question about the words in parentheses ( ).
         Then write a short answer based on the conversation in Part 2
         on pages 69–70.

EXAMPLE:  Sue is busy. (her husband)

    Is her husband busy? Yes, he is.

1.  Sue's husband is helping her pack. (her mother)

    _____

2.  Her husband works in an office. (at home)

    _____

3. Her present apartment has an extra room for an office. (for the baby)

_____

4. Professional movers will move the furniture. (her friends)

_____

5. Mary is staying home this week. (her husband)

_____

6. Mary's going to have a baby. (Sue)

_____

**PART 5**  Write a *wh-* question about the words in parentheses ( ). An answer is not necessary.

EXAMPLE:  Mary's packing now. (why)
*Why is Mary packing?*  _____

1. They're going to move to a bigger apartment. (why)

_____

2. Her husband needs an extra bedroom. (why)

_____

3. She doesn't want her friends to help her move. (why)

_____

4. She's going to have a baby soon. (when)

_____

5. Bill is calling Mary now. (why)

_____

6. They'll use professional movers. (when)

_____

# EXPANSION ACTIVITIES

1. Check (√) the activities that you plan to do soon. Form a group of 5–7 students. Ask questions about the items another student checked.

EXAMPLE:

√ move
When are you going to move?
Why are you moving?
Are your friends going to help you?
Are you going to rent a truck?
Where are you going to move to?

a. ___ send an e-mail
b. ___ visit a friend
c. ___ invite guests to my house
d. ___ buy something new
e. ___ take a vacation
f. ___ celebrate a birthday or holiday
g. ___ go to a concert or sporting event

h. ___ transfer to another college
i. ___ move
j. ___ take the citizenship test
k. ___ start a new job
l. ___ have an out-of-town visitor
m. ___ get married

2. Check (√) your predictions about the future. Form a small group and discuss your predictions with your group. Give reasons for your beliefs.

a. ___ People are going to have fewer children than they do today.

b. ___ People will live longer.

c. ___ People will have a healthier life.

d. ___ People are going to be happier.

e. ___ People will be lonelier.

f. ___ People will be more educated.

g. ___ Everyone is going to have a computer.

h. ___ There will be a cure for cancer and other serious illnesses.

i. ___ There will be a cure for the common cold.

**OUTSIDE ACTIVITIES**

1. Give the list in the above Classroom Activity 2 to an American. Find out his or her predictions. Report to the class something interesting that the American told you.

2. Keep a small notebook and a pen with you at all times for a week. Write down all the behaviors of other people that seem strange to you. Observe food, clothes, shopping, recreation, relationships between males and females, relationships between parents and children, behaviors of small children, behaviors on public transportation, behaviors at school, etc. Write what people are doing as you are observing.

EXAMPLE: A woman is standing on the bus. No one is giving her a seat.
People are eating chicken with their fingers.

## Internet Activities

1. Find a Web site for the elderly. Find out what kinds of products and services are available for senior citizens. Search under "senior citizens" or try the National Council of Senior Citizens (NCSC) or American Association of Retired Persons (AARP).

2. Look for a life expectancy calculator on the Internet. Calculate how long you will probably live.

3. On the Internet, look for *Time* magazine's article of November 8, 1999, called "Beyond 2000." Look for *Time's* February 21, 2000 issue, called "Visions of the 21st Century." What do these articles predict for the future?

## GRAMMAR

The Simple Past Tense
Habitual Past with *Used To*

## CONTEXT

Martin Luther King, Junior
Discrimination and Segregation

## LESSON FOCUS

We use the simple past tense to talk about an action
that started and finished in the past.

I *listened* carefully. I *understood* the explanation.

*Used to* + a base form shows habitual past actions.

I *used to have* a dog. Now I have a cat.

Martin Luther King, Jr. 1929–1968

1. In your native country, does the government give equality to everyone?
2. Is there one group of people that has a harder life than other groups? Which group? What kind of problems do these people have?

Read the following article. Pay special attention to simple past-tense verbs and *used to* + base form.

# Martin Luther King, Junior[1]

Today all people in the United States have equal rights under the law. But this **was** not always the case, especially for African-Americans.[2] Even though slavery in the U.S. **ended** in 1865, blacks **continued** to suffer inferior treatment. The government **did** little to improve the lives of African Americans.

Life for black people **was** especially hard in the South. Many businesses there **used to have** signs in their windows that **said**: "Blacks Not Allowed." Public restrooms **used to have** signs that **said**: "Whites Only." Black children **had to go** to separate, and often inferior, schools. Buses **used to reserve** the front seats for white people. African Americans **had** to stand or sit in the back of the bus. Martin Luther King, Jr., a black minister living in Montgomery, Alabama, **wanted** to put an end to discrimination.[3]

One evening in December of 1955, Rosa Parks, a 42-year-old African American woman, **got** on a bus in Montgomery, Alabama, to go home from work. She **was** tired when she **sat** down. When some white people **got** on the crowded bus, the bus driver **ordered** Ms. Parks to stand up. Ms. Parks **refused** to leave her seat. The bus driver **called** the police and they **came** and **arrested** Ms. Parks.

### Did you know...?

Martin Luther King, Jr., was interested in the ideas of Mahatma Gandhi of India. He studied and used Gandhi's technique of nonviolent protest.

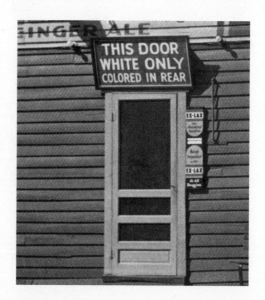

[1] When a father and son have the same name, the father uses *senior* (Sr.) after his name; the son puts *junior* (Jr.) after his name.
[2] *African-Americans*, whose ancestors came from Africa as slaves, are sometimes called "blacks."
[3] Discrimination means giving some people lower treatment than others.

When Martin Luther King, Jr., **heard** about her arrest, he **told** African Americans in Montgomery to boycott the bus company. People who **used to ride** the bus to work **decided** to walk instead. One year later, as a result of the boycott, the Supreme Court outlawed discrimination on public transportation.

During his life, King **organized** many more peaceful protests. He **was** in jail many times because of his activities, but this **did not stop** him. In 1963, he **led** a peaceful demonstration in Washington, D.C., where he **gave** his most famous speech. He **said**, "I have a dream that my four little children will one day live in a nation where they will not be judged by the color of their skin, but by the content of their character."

In 1964, Congress **passed** a new law that officially **gave** equality to all Americans. This law **made** discrimination in employment and education illegal. King **won** the Nobel Peace Prize[4] for his work in creating a better world.

In 1968, King **went** to Memphis, Tennessee, to support striking city workers. A great tragedy **occurred** there. King was shot and killed. He **was** only 39 years old.

In 1983, Martin Luther King's birthday (January 15) **became** a national holiday.

## 3.1 Past of *Be*

| Examples | Explanation |
|---|---|
| Life **was** hard for black people. King **was** in jail for his protests. Many African-Americans **were** part of the protest. Before 1964, laws **were** different. | The past of the verb *be* has two forms: *was* and *were*. I, he, she, it → was we, you, they → were |
| There **was** a bus boycott in 1955. There **were** many people in Washington in 1963. | After *there*, use *was* or *were* depending on the noun that follows. Use *was* with a singular noun. Use *were* with a plural noun. |
| King **wasn't** born in Alabama. African-Americans **weren't** happy with the segregation laws. | To make a negative statement, put *not* after *was* or *were*. The contraction for *was not* is *wasn't*. The contraction for *were not* is *weren't*. |
| King **was born** in 1929. | Always use a form of *be* with *born*. |
| King **was** married to Coretta Scott. He **was** not worried about his safety. | Use *be* with adjectives that end in *-ed*: *crowded, tired, bored, interested, worried, married, divorced, allowed, permitted.* |

*(continued)*

[4] This is a prize given once a year for great work in literature, science, and world peace.

| Wh- Word | Was/Were Wasn't/Weren't | Subject | Was/Were | Complement | Short Answer |
|---|---|---|---|---|---|
| | | King | **was** | a great leader. | |
| | | He | **wasn't** | happy with the laws. | |
| | **Was** | he | | from the North? | No, he **wasn't**. |
| Where | **was** | he | | from? | |
| Why | **wasn't** | he | | happy with the laws? | |

---

**EXERCISE 1**　　Fill in the blanks with the correct word(s).

**EXAMPLE:**　　Martin Luther King, Jr., _____*was*_____ a great American.

1. Martin Luther King, Jr., _____ born in Georgia.

2. He (not) _____ born in Alabama.

3. He and his father _____ ministers.

4. He _____ tired of discrimination of African-Americans.

5. African-Americans (not) _____ allowed to enter some restaurants in the South.

6. There _____ discrimination in public transportation.

7. _____ discrimination in employment? Yes, there

   _____ .

8. Rosa Parks was a citizen of Montgomery, Alabama. _____ an African-American? Yes, she was.

9. She was tired and took a seat on the bus. Why _____ tired?

10. African-Americans weren't allowed to sit down on a crowded bus in

    Montgomery. Why _____ to sit down?

11. King was in jail. Why _____ in jail? He _____ in jail for protesting unfair laws.

12. How old _____ when he was killed? He was 39.

13. _____ small at the time? Yes, his children were small.

| Examples | Explanation |
|---|---|
| Martin Luther King, Jr., **lived** in the South. <br> He **organized** peaceful protests. <br> In 1964, Congress **passed** a new law. <br> In 1968, someone **killed** King. | For regular verbs, the simple past tense ends in *-ed*. <br><br> BASE FORM      PAST FORM <br> live             lived <br> organize      organized <br> pass           passed <br> kill            killed |
| King **lived** in the South. <br> He **didn't live** in the North. | Use the past form in affirmative statements. Use *didn't* + the base form in negative statements. |
| He **wanted to change** certain laws. <br> Rosa Parks **refused to stand up**. | The verb after *to* does not use the past form. |

## LANGUAGE NOTES

1. The past form is the same for all persons.
   I worked.     He worked.     They worked.     You worked.

2. We often use *ago* with the simple past tense.
   Slavery ended over 100 years *ago*.
   King died more than 30 years *ago*.
   We studied about him a few minutes *ago*.

3. For a review of the spelling and pronunciation of the *-ed* past form, see Appendix A.

---

**EXERCISE 2**    Fill in the blanks with the simple past tense of the verb in parentheses ( ).

**EXAMPLE:**    King ___*lived*___ in the south.
                             *(live)*

1. Slavery _____ in 1865, but discrimination _____.
                 *(end)*                                 *(continue)*

2. King _____ equality for all people.
                *(want)*

3. King _____ as a minister.
                *(work)*

4. In many places, the law _____ whites from blacks.
                                  *(separate)*

5. Black children _____ separate schools.
                         *(attend)*

6. King _____ these laws.
   (dislike)

7. The bus driver _____ Rosa Parks to stand up, but she
   (order)

   _____.
   (refuse)

8. The bus driver _____ the police.
   (call)

9. The police _____ Ms. Parks.
   (arrest)

10. King _____ a peaceful protest.
    (organize)

11. In 1964, Congress _____ the law.
    (change)

12. In 1968, a great tragedy _____. Someone _____
    (occur)                                      (kill)
    King.

## 3.3 Simple Past Tense of Irregular Verbs

| Examples | Explanation |
|----------|-------------|
| Rosa Parks **got** on the bus and **sat** down.<br>The police **came**.<br>King **gave** a famous speech in Washington, D.C., in 1963. | Many past-tense verbs are irregular. They do not have an -*ed* ending. |
| Some African-Americans **stood** up for white people.<br>Rosa Parks **didn't stand** up. | Use the past form in affirmative statements. Use *didn't* + the base form in negative statements. |

## LANGUAGE NOTES

The following is a list of irregular past tenses. For an alphabetical list of irregular verbs, see Appendix M.

| Verbs with no change | | | | Final *d* changes to *t* | |
|---|---|---|---|---|---|
| beat | fit | put | spit | bend—bent | send—sent |
| bet | hit | quit | split | build—built | spend—spent |
| cost | hurt | set | spread | lend—lent | |
| cut | let | shut | | | |

*(continued)*

## Verbs with Vowel Changes

| | | | |
|---|---|---|---|
| feel—felt | mean—meant* | dig—dug | sting—stung |
| keep—kept | sleep—slept | hang—hung | strike—struck |
| leave—left | sweep—swept | spin—spun | swing—swung |
| lose—lost | weep—wept | stick—stuck | win—won |
| awake—awoke | speak—spoke | begin—began | sing—sang |
| break—broke | steal—stole | drink—drank | sink—sank |
| choose—chose | wake—woke | forbid—forbade | spring—sprang |
| freeze—froze | | ring—rang | swim—swam |
| | | shrink—shrank | |
| bring—brought | fight—fought | blow—blew | grow—grew |
| buy—bought | teach—taught | draw—drew | know—knew |
| catch—caught | think—thought | fly—flew | throw—threw |
| arise—arose | rise—rose | bleed—bled | meet—met |
| drive—drove | shine—shone | feed—fed | read—read** |
| ride—rode | write—wrote | flee—fled | speed—sped |
| | | lead—led | |
| sell—sold | tell—told | find—found | wind—wound |
| mistake—mistook | take—took | lay—laid | say—said*** |
| shake—shook | | pay—paid | |
| swear—swore | wear—wore | bite—bit | light—lit |
| tear—tore | | hide—hid | slide—slid |
| become—became | | fall—fell | |
| come—came | | hold—held | |
| eat—ate | | | |
| forgive—forgave | | run—ran | |
| give—gave | | sit—sat | |
| lie—lay | | see—saw | |
| forget—forgot | shoot—shot | stand—stood | |
| get—got | | understand—understood | |

## Miscellaneous Changes

| | | |
|---|---|---|
| be—was/were | go—went | hear—heard |
| do—did | have—had | make—made |

*There is a change in the vowel sound. *Meant* rhymes with *sent*.
**The past form of *read* is pronounced like the color *red*.
***Said* rhymes with *bed*.

The Simple Past Tense; Habitual Past with *Used To*    **81**

**EXERCISE 3**  Fill in the blanks with the past tense of the verb in parentheses ( ).

**EXAMPLE:**  King __*fought*__ for the rights of all people.
(*fight*)

1. King _____ born in 1929.
(*be*)

2. King _____ a minister.
(*become*)

3. He _____ married in 1953.
(*get*)

4. He _____ a job in a church in Montgomery, Alabama.
(*find*)

5. African-Americans _____ a hard time, especially in the South.
(*have*)

6. Rosa Parks was tired and _____ down on the bus.
(*sit*)

7. Some white people _____ on the bus.
(*get*)

8. The bus driver _____ Parks to stand up.
(*tell*)

9. Police _____ and arrested Parks.
(*come*)

10. King _____ about her arrest.
(*hear*)

11. In 1963, he _____ a beautiful speech in Washington, D.C.
(*give*)

12. Many people _____ to see King in Washington in 1963.
(*go*)

13. King _____ an important prize for his work.
(*win*)

14. A man _____ King in 1968.
(*shoot*)

## 3.4  Negatives and Questions with the Simple Past Tense

Compare affirmative statements, negative statements, questions, and short answers with the simple past tense.

### Regular Verb

| Wh- Word | Did Didn't | Subject | Verb | Complement | Short Answer |
|---|---|---|---|---|---|
| | | King | **wanted** | equality. | |
| | | He | **didn't want** | segregation. | |
| | **Did** | he | **want** | violence? | No, he **didn't**. |
| Why | **did** | he | **want** | equality? | |
| Why | **didn't** | he | **want** | violence? | |

*(continued)*

## Irregular Verb

| Wh- Word | Did Didn't | Subject | Verb | Complement | Short Answer |
|---|---|---|---|---|---|
| | | Black children | **went** | to separate schools. | |
| | | They | **didn't go** | to school with white children. | |
| | **Did** | they | **go** | to good schools? | No, they **didn't**. |
| Where | **did** | they | **go** | to school? | |
| Why | **didn't** | they | **go** | to school with white children? | |

## LANGUAGE NOTES

Use the past form in affirmative statements. Use *did* + the base form in negatives and questions.[5]

**EXERCISE 4**   Write the negative form of the underlined words.

**EXAMPLE:**   Slavery <u>ended</u> in 1865. Discrimination ___*didn't end*___.

1. King <u>lived</u> in the South. He _____ in the North.

2. King <u>wanted</u> equality for everyone. He _____ separate schools for blacks and whites.

3. He <u>thought</u> about the future of his children. He _____ about his own safety.

4. He <u>believed</u> in peace. He _____ in violence.

5. He <u>became</u> a minister. He _____ a politician.

6. He <u>was</u> in jail for his protests. He _____ in jail for a crime.

7. African-Americans <u>had</u> to stand on a crowded bus. White people _____ to stand.

8. African-Americans <u>rode</u> the buses in Montgomery before 1955. They _____ the buses after the arrest of Rosa Parks.

9. King <u>went</u> to Memphis in 1968. His wife _____ there.

10. He <u>died</u> violently. He _____ peacefully.

[5] For an exception to this rule, see Lesson Four, "Questions About the Subject."

**EXERCISE 5** A student is interviewing her teacher about Martin Luther King, Jr. Fill in the blanks with the correct form of the verb.

S. Do you remember Martin Luther King, Jr.?

T. Of course I do. I _____*saw*_____ him on TV many times when
(example: see)

I _____ young.
(1 be)

S. _____ him on TV when he was in Washington, D.C.?
(2 see)

T. Yes, I _____. I remember his famous speech in Washington
(3)

in 1963.

S. What _____ about?
(4 speak)

T. He _____ about equality for everyone.
(5 speak)

S. _____ to Washington?
(6 a lot of people/go)

T. Oh, yes. 250,000 _____ to Washington.
(7 go)

S. Do you remember when he died?

T. I was in high school when he _____. The principal
(8 die)

_____ to our class and _____ us the news.
(9 come)                          (10 tell)

S. What _____ when you heard the news?
(11 do)

T. At first we _____ it. Then we all started to
(12 not/believe)

_____. We _____ home from school and
(13 cry)              (14 go)

_____ the news on TV.
(15 watch)

S. Where _____ he when he died?
(16 be)

T. He _____ on the balcony of a hotel in Memphis when a
(17 be)

man _____ and _____ him. It was terrible.
(18 come)              (19 shoot)

But we should remember King for his life, not his death. We celebrate
Martin Luther King, Jr.'s birthday.

S. Really? I _____ that. When is it?
(20 not/know)

T. He _____ born on January 15. We don't have school on
(21 be)

that date.

S. _____ a holiday right after he died?
      *(22 this date/become)*

T. No. It _____ a holiday in 1985.
      *(23 become)*

S. How do you remember so much about King?

T. I _____ a paper on him when I was in college.
      *(24 write)*

---

**EXERCISE 6** A woman wrote a story about the major events in her life. Fill in the blanks with the correct form of the verb in parentheses ( ).

My name is Irina Katz. I __*was born*__ in 1938 in the former Soviet
                              *(born)*

Union in a small Ukrainian town. I _____ there until 1941. In
                                      *(1 live)*

1939 World War II _____. In 1941 the German army
                        *(2 start)*

_____ my country, and my father _____ into the
   *(3 invade)*                              *(4 go)*

army. My family _____ to leave our city. We _____
                    *(5 have)*                          *(6 go)*

to Uzbekistan. After the war _____, my family _____
                                 *(7 end)*                  *(8 return)*

to Ukraine, to the city of Lvov. My father _____ back from the
                                               *(9 come)*

army as a disabled soldier. In 1989 we _____ permission to leave
                                           *(10 get)*

our country.

There _____ a few circumstances that _____
         *(11 be)*                                *(12 lead)*

to our decision to leave our country. First, we _____ that we
                                                    *(13 think)*

would have more opportunities in the U.S. My family is Jewish and we

_____ discrimination. Second, we _____ to get
   *(14 suffer)*                             *(15 want)*

away from a bad political situation. It _____ not easy to make
                                           *(16 be)*

this decision. My father _____ to leave because he
                             *(17 not/want)*

_____ sick. However, my married daughter _____
   *(18 be)*                                         *(19 move)*

to the U.S. with her family in 1987. I _____ her very much. In
                                          *(20 miss)*

1988 my father _____, and then we _____ that
                   *(21 die)*                   *(22 realize)*

we _____ no reason to stay. However, it _____ very
      *(23 have)*                                  *(24 be)*

---

The Simple Past Tense; Habitual Past with *Used To*    **85** hard to leave behind our way of life, friends, and jobs and go to a place where the future would be uncertain.

After we _____ Ukraine, we _____ to Vienna,
            (25 leave)                        (26 go)

Austria, and then to Rome, Italy. We _____ permission to come
                                        (27 get)

to America, but some of our friends _____ permission.
                                        (28 not/receive)

We _____ to Chicago. When I _____ my daughter
     (29 come)                          (30 see)

at the airport, we both _____ to cry. I _____ happy
                          (31 start)                (32 be)

to be with my family again.

At first, everything _____ very difficult for me because
                        (33 be)

I _____ English. My children _____ English quickly,
   (34 not/understand)                      (35 learn)

and they _____ jobs. I _____ to study English at
           (36 find)                (37 begin)

Truman College. Unfortunately, I _____ English when I was in
                                    (38 not/study)

my country. I _____ German.
                (39 study)

Even though it _____ difficult to start a new life, I know
                  (40 be)

we _____ the right decision to come to the U.S.
     (41 make)

---

**EXERCISE 7**  Write the negative form of the underlined verb.

**EXAMPLE:**  I lived in a small town as a child. I ___*didn't live*___ in a city.

1. I was born in Ukraine. I _____ in Russia.

2. My father went into the army. My brother _____ into the army.

3. We got permission to leave the country in 1989. We _____ permission to come directly to the U.S.

4. There were a lot of opportunities for our children in the U.S. There _____ a lot of opportunities for them in Ukraine.

5. Our oldest daughter moved to the U.S. in 1987. We _____ to the U.S. at that time.

6. My father died in 1988. He _____ during the war.

7. It was hard to leave our country. It _____ easy to leave our friends and jobs behind.

8. We left behind our friends. We _____ a good political situation.

9. We received permission to come to the U.S. Some of our friends _____ permission.

10. My children learned English quickly. I _____ English quickly.

11. I studied English in the U.S. Unfortunately, I _____ English in Ukraine.

---

**EXERCISE 8**  Read each statement. Then write a *yes/no* question about the word(s) in parentheses ( ). Write a short answer.

**EXAMPLE:**  Irina came to the U.S. (to Los Angeles)
*Did she come to Los Angeles? No, she didn't.*

1. Irina was born in 1938. (in Moscow)

   _____

2. She lived in a small town before the war. (after the war)

   _____

3. The German army invaded Poland. (Ukraine)

   _____

4. Her family returned to Ukraine. (to their hometown)

   _____

5. She lived in Lvov until 1989. (her daughter)

   _____

6. It was hard for Irina to leave her family. (her job)

   _____

7. She went to Vienna. (to Rome)

   _____

8. She got permission to come to America. (all her friends)

   _____

9. Her children learned English quickly. (Irina)

   _____

Read each statement. Then write a *wh-* question about the word(s) in parentheses ( ). An answer is not necessary.

**EXAMPLE:**    Irina was born in 1938. (where)
*Where was she born?*

1. She left her town in 1941. (why)

_____

2. The war began in 1939. (when/the war/end)

_____

3. The German army invaded her country. (when)

_____

4. Her family went to Uzbekistan in 1941. (where/after the war)

_____

5. She wanted to leave her country in the 1980s. (why)

_____

6. She had several reasons for leaving her country. (how many)

_____

7. Her father died. (when)

_____

8. Her future was uncertain in the U.S. (why)

_____

9. She came to the U.S. in 1989. (when/her daughter)

_____

10. She saw someone in the Chicago airport. (whom)

_____

11. She didn't understand English at first. (why)

_____

**EXERCISE 10** Check (✓) the things you did this past week. Exchange books with another student. Ask the other student about the items he or she checked.

EXAMPLE:
> _✓_ I made a long-distance phone call.
> A. I made a long-distance phone call.
> B. Who(m) did you call?
> A. I called my father in Mexico.
> B. How long did you talk?
> A. We talked for about 15 minutes.

1. ___ I made a long-distance phone call.

2. ___ I shopped for groceries.

3. ___ I met someone new.

4. ___ I got together with a friend.

5. ___ I wrote a letter.

6. ___ I bought some new clothes.

7. ___ I went to the bank.

8. ___ I read something interesting (a book, an article).

9. ___ I went to the post office.

10. ___ I did exercises.

11. ___ I got a letter.

12. ___ I went to an interesting place.

**Before You Read**
1. Are you a baseball fan? Do you see many African-Americans on baseball teams?
2. Do you see many TV programs with African-American characters?
3. Do you know the people in these photos?

Jackie Robinson (1919–1972)

Bill Cosby

Read the article on the following page. Pay special attention to *used to*.

# Discrimination and Segregation

Segregation, or separation of the races, **used to be** part of American life. Many hotels, schools, and restaurants **used to be** for whites only. And many professions **used to be** limited to whites. One example of this was in major league baseball. African-Americans, unable to join the major leagues, **used to have** a separate league. That finally changed in 1947, when the manager of the Brooklyn Dodgers saw African-American Jackie Robinson play baseball and invited him to join his team. Even though Robinson was a great player, he suffered insults and even death threats.

Another profession where African-Americans suffered discrimination was in acting. They appeared in movies and on TV, but they **used to play** servants and slaves. Their characters were often lazy, stupid, or superstitious. In 1984, *The Cosby Show*, starring Bill Cosby, changed the image of African-Americans on TV. This popular show was about an upper-middle-class African-American family.

Marian Anderson (1902–1993)

Another area where African-Americans suffered discrimination was in music. Marian Anderson, a talented opera star, performed all over the U.S. and Europe. But in 1939, when a concert hall in Washington, D.C., found out that their performer was going to be a black woman, the performance was canceled.

Even though laws today prohibit discrimination, many African-Americans still feel it in their everyday life.

## 3.5 Habitual Past with *Used To*

| Examples | Explanation |
| --- | --- |
| African-Americans **used to have** their own baseball leagues. On TV and in movies, blacks **used to play** servants. | *Used to* + a base form shows a habit or custom over a past period of time. This custom no longer exists. |
| Some restaurants **didn't use to** serve African-Americans. | For negatives, omit the *d*. |

# LANGUAGE NOTES

1.  *Used to* is for past habits or customs. It is not for an action that happened once or a few times.

    Many restaurants *used to* serve white people only. (This happened over a period of time.)

    In 1946, the manager of the Dodgers *invited* Robinson to play for his team. (This happened in 1947 only.)

2.  We don't pronounce the *d* in *used to*.

**EXERCISE 11** Tell which of the following you used to do when you were a child.

**EXAMPLE:**   cry a lot
I used to cry a lot.
OR
I didn't use to cry a lot.

1.  enjoy school
2.  obey my parents
3.  attend religious school
4.  play with dolls
5.  play soccer
6.  fight with other children
7.  draw pictures
8.  have a pet
9.  tell lies
10. read mystery stories
11. live on a farm
12. eat a lot of candy
13. live with my grandparents
14. believe in Santa Claus
15. watch a lot of TV
16. read comic books

**EXERCISE 12** Name something. Practice *used to*.

**EXAMPLE:**   Name something you used to know when you were in elementary school.

I used to know the names of all the presidents (but I don't know them anymore).

1.  Name something you used to do when you were a child.

2.  Tell what kind of stories you used to enjoy when you were a child.

3.  Name something you used to believe when you were a child.

4.  Name something you used to like to eat when you were a child.

5.  Tell about some things your parents, grandparents, or teachers used to tell you when you were a child.

6.  Tell about some things you used to do when you were younger.

**EXERCISE 13** A young man is comparing how his life used to be five years ago and how his life is now. Complete his statements.

**EXAMPLE:** I used to _____be lazy_____. Now I'm hard-working.

1. I used to _____. Now I save my money.

2. I used to _____. Now I'm a serious student.

3. I used to _____. Now I live alone.

4. I used to _____. Now I almost never watch TV.

5. I used to _____. Now I come home after work and study.

6. I used to _____. Now I have short hair.

7. I used to _____. Now I have a car and drive everywhere.

8. I used to _____. Now I'm on a diet and I'm losing weight.

9. I used to _____. Now I make my own decisions.

10. I used to _____. Now I use my credit card for most of my purchases.

**EXERCISE 14** Write sentences comparing the way you used to live in your native country with the way you live now. Share your sentences with a partner or with the entire class.

**EXAMPLES:** I used to live with my whole family. Now I live alone.

I used to work in a restaurant. Now I'm a full-time student.

I didn't use to speak English at all. Now I speak English pretty well.

Ideas for sentences:
school   job   hobbies   apartment/house   family life   friends

1. _____

2. _____

3. _____

4. _____

5. _____

1. Simple Past Tense
   *Be*

   He **was** at work yesterday.

   He **wasn't** at home.

   **Was** he on time? Yes, he **was**.

   Where **was** he yesterday?

   Why **wasn't** he at home?

   Regular Verb

   She **worked** last Friday.

   She **didn't work** last Saturday.

   **Did** she **work** last night?

   Yes, she **did**.

   When **did** she **work**?

   Why **didn't** she **work** last Saturday?

   Irregular Verb

   He **bought** a new car.

   He **didn't buy** an American car.

   **Did** he **buy** a Toyota?

   Yes, he **did**.

   Where **did** he **buy** his car?

   Why **didn't** he **buy** an American car?

2. Habitual Past with *Used To*

   I **used to** live on a farm. Now I live in a city.

   I **used to** walk to work. Now I drive.

# EDITING ADVICE

1. Use *was/were* with *born*.

   *was*
   He born in Germany.
   ^

2. Don't use *was/were* with *die*.

   He ~~was~~ died two years ago.

3. Don't use a past form after *to*.

   *leave*
   I decided to ~~left~~ early.

   I wanted to go home and ~~watched~~ TV.

4. Don't use *was* or *were* to form a simple past tense.

   went
   He ~~was go~~ home yesterday.

5. Use *there* when a new subject is introduced.

   *There w*
   ~~Was~~ a big earthquake in 1906.

6. Use a form of *be* before an adjective. Remember, some *-ed* words are adjectives.

   were
   They ^ excited about their trip to America.

7. Don't use *did* with an adjective. Use *was/were*.

   were
   Why ~~did~~ you afraid?

8. Use the correct word order in a question.

   didn't you
   Why ~~you didn't~~ return?

9. Use *did* + the base form to form a question.

   did      buy
   What kind of car ^ you ~~bought~~?

10. Use the base form after *didn't*.

    He didn't work~~ed~~ yesterday.

11. Don't forget the *d* in *used to*.

    d
    She use ^ to live in Miami.

12. Don't add the verb *be* before *used to* for habitual past.

    ~~I'm~~ used to play soccer in my country.

# LESSON 3 TEST / REVIEW

<u>PART 1</u>    Write the past form of the following verbs.

**EXAMPLE:** draw ___*drew*___

1. eat _____    3. give _____    5. send _____

2. put _____    4. write _____    6. listen _____

7. read _____     12. find _____     17. make _____

8. take _____     13. stand _____     18. hear _____

9. bring _____     14. leave _____     19. feel _____

10. talk _____     15. sit _____     20. fall _____

11. know _____     16. go _____     21. get _____

**PART 2**   Find the mistakes with the underlined words, and correct them. Not every sentence has a mistake. If the sentence is correct, write **C**.

EXAMPLES:   *lost*
She ~~losed~~ her umbrella.
Did she lose her glove?       C

1. My mother borned in Italy.

2. Why you didn't eat breakfast?

3. Did you studied English in your country?

4. When arrived your uncle?

5. Were a lot of people at the airport last night.

6. Why was you late?

7. Did you afraid of the robber?

8. I enjoyed the concert.

9. Last night I read an interesting article.

10. My grandmother was died ten years ago.

11. They decided to drove to New York.

12. I excited about my trip to London last year.

13. What did she do about her problem?

14. Why he wasn't happy?

15. Where you bought your coat?

16. She use to live in Miami.

**PART 3**      Write the negative form of the underlined word.

**EXAMPLE:**    Rosa Parks <u>lived</u> in Alabama. She ___*didn't live*___ in Washington.

1.  She <u>was</u> tired when she got out of work. She _____ sick.

2.  She <u>went</u> to work by bus. She _____ to work by car.

3.  The bus driver <u>told</u> African-Americans to stand. He _____ white Americans to stand.

4.  Some African-Americans <u>stood</u> up. Rosa Parks _____ up.

5.  The police <u>came</u> to the bus. They _____ to her house.

6.  They <u>took</u> her to jail. They _____ her to her house.

7.  Martin Luther King, Jr. <u>organized</u> a protest. Rosa Parks _____ a protest.

8.  Slavery <u>ended</u> in 1865. Discrimination _____ in 1865.

9.  King <u>believed</u> in peaceful protest. He _____ in violence.

10. King <u>spoke</u> about brotherhood. He _____ about violence.

**PART 4**      Write a question beginning with the word given. (An answer is not necessary.)

**EXAMPLE:**    Martin Luther King, Jr. lived in the South.

Where ___*did he live?*___

1.  King became a minister.

    Why _____

2.  King was born in Georgia.

    When _____

3.  King didn't like segregation.

    Why _____

4.  Black children went to separate schools.

    Why _____

5.  Some restaurants didn't permit black people to eat there.

    Why _____

6. King was in jail many times because of his protests.

How many times _____

7. King won the Nobel Prize.

When _____

8. Rosa Parks worked in Montgomery.

Where _____

9. She was tired.

Why _____

10. She went home by bus.

How many times _____

11. She lived in the South.

Where _____

12. She didn't want to obey the law.

Why _____

13. The police took her to jail.

Why _____

**PART 5**

Write two sentences with *used to* comparing your life in your native country with your life in the U.S.

1. _____

2. _____

## EXPANSION ACTIVITIES

**CLASSROOM ACTIVITIES**

1. Check (√) the sentences that are true for you. Find a partner and exchange books. Give each other more information about the things you checked. Ask each other questions about these activities.

a) _____ I bought a CD in the past week.

b) _____ I worked last Saturday.

c) _____ I rode a bike this past week.

d) —— I went to a party last weekend.

e) —— I got a driver's license in the past year.

f) —— I took a trip in the past year.

g) —— I got married in the last two years.

h) —— I found a job this month.

i) —— I spent more than $50 today.

j) —— I received some money this week.

k) —— I was born in March.

l) —— I ate pizza in the past month.

m) —— I bought a car in the past year.

n) —— I came to the U.S. alone.

2.  Who did it?

    Teacher: Pass out an index card to each student.

    Students: Write something you did last weekend. It can be something unusual or something ordinary. (Examples: I went fishing. I baked a pie. I did my laundry.)

    Teacher: Collect the cards. Pull out one card at a time and read the sentence to the class. The students have to guess who wrote the card.

3.  Who used to do it?

    Teacher: Pass out an index card to each student.

    Students: Think of some things you used to be, wear, do, etc. when you were in high school. Think of things that other students would not guess about you. Write two or three of these things on the card.

    Teacher: Collect the cards. Pull out one card at a time and read the sentences to the class. The students have to guess who wrote the card.

**EXAMPLES:**
    I used to hate studying a foreign language.
    I used to have very long hair.
    I used to be a terrible student.

4.  Bring in a picture of yourself when you were younger. Describe yourself at that time and compare yourself to now.

**EXAMPLE:**
    I used to play soccer all day with my friends. Now I don't have time for it.

5.  Fill in the blank. Discuss your answers in a small group or with the entire class.
    Before I came to the U.S., I used to believe that _____
    _____, but now I know it's not true.

**DISCUSSION** In a small group or with the entire class, discuss the following:

1. Changes in daily life: Compare how life used to be when you were younger with how it is now.

2. Fashions: Talk about different styles or fashions in the past.

**EXAMPLE:** In the 1960s, men used to wear their hair long.

**WRITING** Choose one of the following topics to write a short composition.

1. Write a paragraph or paragraphs telling about your childhood.

2. Write a paragraph or paragraphs to tell about changes in your native country. Compare how life used to be with how it is now.

3. If you are married, write a paragraph or paragraphs comparing your life as a married person with your life as a single person.

4. Write a short composition about your life. Use the composition in Exercise 6 as your model. Answer the following questions as part of your composition.

   a. Where were you born?

   b. What was your life like in your native country?

   c. Why did you decide to leave your native country?

   d. What happened immediately after you left your native country?

   e. How was your life in your first few months in the U.S.?

**OUTSIDE ACTIVITY** Interview an American. Ask this person to tell you about changes he or she sees in American society. Ask this person to compare how he or she used to live with how he or she lives now. Report some interesting information to the class.

## Internet Activities

1. Find information about one of the people below. Tell the class why this person was (or is) famous.

   George Wallace            James Earl Ray

   Jesse Jackson             Jesse Owens

   Malcolm X                 Nat Turner

   John Wilkes Booth         Rodney King

   Mohandas Gandhi

2. At a search engine, type in "I Have a Dream" to find Martin Luther King, Jr.'s most famous speech.

## GRAMMAR
Subject and Object Pronouns
Possessive Forms
Reflexive Pronouns

## CONTEXT
An American Wedding
His Story/Her Story

## LESSON FOCUS
We use subject and object pronouns to take the place of subject and object nouns.

Steve likes Debbie because *she* is good to *him*.

We can use possessive forms to show ownership or relationship.

*Steve's* wedding was big. *My* wedding was small.

If the subject and the object of the sentence are the same, we use a reflexive pronoun for the object.

I see *myself*.     They can take care of *themselves*.

1. Where do people get married in your native culture?
2. What kind of clothes do the bride and groom wear in your native culture?
3. At what age do people usually get married in your native culture?

Read the following article. Pay special attention to object pronouns.

# An American Wedding

veil

bride    groom    bouquet

Many American young couples consider their wedding to be one of the most important days of their life. They save for **it** and often spend a year planning for **it**: finding a place, selecting a menu, buying a wedding dress, ordering invitations and sending **them** to friends and relatives, choosing bridesmaids and ushers, selecting musicians, and much more.

When the day arrives, the groom doesn't usually see the bride before the wedding. It is considered bad luck for **him** to see **her** ahead of time. The guests wait with excitement to see **her** too. When the wedding begins, the groom enters first. Then the bridesmaids and ushers enter. When the bride finally enters, everyone turns around to look at **her**. Often the bride's father or both her parents walk **her** down the aisle to the groom's side.

During the ceremony, the bride and groom promise to love and respect each other for the rest of their lives. They answer questions about love and respect by saying "I do." The groom's "best man" holds the rings for **them** until they are ready to place **them** on each other's fingers. At the end of the ceremony, the groom lifts the bride's veil and kisses **her**.

There is a party after the ceremony. People make toasts, eat dinner, and dance. The bride and groom usually dance the first dance alone. Then guests join **them**.

Before the bride and groom leave the party, the bride throws her bouquet over her head, and the single women try to catch **it**. It is believed that the woman who catches **it** will be the next one to get married.

The newlyweds[1] usually take a trip, called a honeymoon, immediately after the wedding.

## Did you know...?

The average cost of a wedding in the U.S. with 200 guests is $15,000. These costs include the bridal dress, the flowers, the rings, the dinner, the cake, the invitations, the reception hall, the musicians, the photographer, and the limousine.

---

[1] For a short time after they are married, the bride and groom are called *newlyweds*.

| Examples | Explanation |
|---|---|
| The bride wears a veil. The groom lifts **it** to kiss **her**. | We use object pronouns to take the place of nouns that follow the verb. |
| When the bride enters, everyone turns around to look at **her**. | An object pronoun can follow a preposition. |

## LANGUAGE NOTES

1.  The object pronouns are: *me, you, him, her, it, us, them.* Compare subject and object pronouns:

| Subject | Object | Examples: S | V | O |
|---|---|---|---|---|
| I | me | You | love | me. |
| you | you | I | love | you. |
| he | him | She | loves | him. |
| she | her | He | loves | her. |
| it | it | I | love | it. |
| we | us | They | love | us. |
| they | them | We | love | them. |

2.  We use *them* for plural people and things.
    Do you know the bride's parents? Yes, I know *them.*
    Do you like the flowers? Yes, I like *them.*

**EXERCISE 1**  Fill in the blanks with an object pronoun in place of the underlined word.

**EXAMPLE:**  The groom doesn't walk down the aisle with the bride. Her father walks with ____her____ .

1.  The bride doesn't enter with the groom. He waits for _____, and she goes to _____ .

2.  The groom takes the ring. He puts _____ on the bride's hand.

3.  The bride wears a veil. The groom lifts _____ to kiss _____ .

4.  The bride doesn't throw the bouquet to all the women. She throws _____ to the single women only.

5. People make toasts to <u>the bride and groom</u>. They wish _____ health and happiness.

6. <u>The groom</u> promises to love the bride, and the bride promises to love _____ .

7. The bride and groom receive <u>gifts</u>. They usually open _____ at home.

<table>
<tr><td>**4.2**</td><td>*Say* and *Tell*</td></tr>
</table>

| Examples | Explanation |
|---|---|
| The bride and groom **say** "I do." <br> The newlyweds **said** "thank you" to the guests. | We *say* something. <br> We *say* something to someone. |
| The newlyweds **told** their friends about their honeymoon. <br> They **told** the musicians to start the music. | We *tell* someone something. <br> We *tell* someone to do something. |

## LANGUAGE NOTES

1. *Say* and *tell* have the same meaning, but we use them differently. We say something. (*Say* has a direct object.) We tell someone something. (*Tell* has an indirect object and a direct object.)
   COMPARE:
   The teacher *said* the answer.
   The teacher *told* us the answer.

2. We use *tell* in a few expressions without an indirect object:
   tell the truth     tell a secret
   tell a lie         tell time
   tell a story      tell (all) about something

3. There are other verbs like *tell* that have an indirect object and a direct object. For verbs followed by an indirect and a direct object, see Appendix I.

   | | INDIRECT OBJECT | DIRECT OBJECT |
   |---|---|---|
   | I gave | the newlyweds | a present. |
   | They sent | the guests | thank-you notes. |

**EXERCISE 2** Fill in the blanks with the correct form of *say* or *tell*.

**EXAMPLES:** The teacher usually ___*says*___ hello when he enters the room.

The teacher ___*told*___ the class about the meeting.

1. The teacher _____ us her name on the first day of class.

2. The teacher tries to _____ the students' names correctly.

3. Don't _____ your classmates the answers during a test.

4. If you know that you're going to be absent, _____ the teacher.

5. Children shouldn't _____ a lie.

6. Some people _____ a prayer before they go to bed.

7. You must _____ the truth in court.

8. I had to _____ goodbye to many friends before I left my country.

9. When you need to interrupt a conversation, you should _____, "Excuse me."

10. Some people can't _____ no.

11. He _____, "Sit down."

12. The teacher _____ us to write a short composition.

## 4.3 Possessive Forms of Nouns

We use possessive forms to show ownership or relationship.

| Noun | Ending | Examples |
|------|--------|----------|
| Singular Noun:<br>bride<br>groom | Add apostrophe + **s** | The **bride's** dress is white.<br>The **groom's** tuxedo is black. |
| Plural noun ending in -**s**:<br>parents<br>guests | Add apostrophe only | She got married in her **parents'** house.<br>The **guests'** coats are in the coat room. |
| Irregular Plural Noun:<br>men<br>women | Add apostrophe + **s** | The **men's** suits are black.<br>The **women's** dresses are beautiful. |
| Names that end in **s**:<br>Charles | Add apostrophe only<br>OR<br>Add apostrophe + **s** | Do you know **Charles'** wife?<br>OR<br>Do you know **Charles's** wife? |

# LANGUAGE NOTES

1. We use the possessive form for people and other living things.
   *Jack's* wife is very nice.
   The *dog's* name is Pee-Wee.
2. For inanimate objects, we usually use "the _____ of _____."
   *The name of the church* is Saint Mary's.
3. We can use a possessive noun and a possessive adjective together.
   *My mother's* brother lives in Washington, D.C.

---

**EXERCISE 3**   Fill in the blanks to make the possessive form of the noun.

**EXAMPLE:**   The bride___'s___ grandfather looked very handsome.

1. The groom_____ mother is very nice.

2. The bride_____ flowers are beautiful.

3. The bridesmaids_____ dresses are blue.

4. They invited many guests to the wedding. They didn't invite the guests_____ children.

5. The women_____ dresses are very elegant.

6. Charles_____ sister was a bridesmaid.

7. The newlyweds_____ picture is in the newspaper.

8. Do you know the children_____ names?

---

**EXERCISE 4**   Fill in the blanks with the two nouns in parentheses ( ). Put them in the correct order. Use the possessive form of one of the nouns, except with non-living things.

**EXAMPLES:**   ___The dog's name___ is Pee-Wee.
               (name/the dog)

I don't like the ___color of your car.___
                  (your car/color)

1. The _____ lives far away.
       (bride/grandmother)

2. The _____ are not very big.
       (offices/teachers)

3. The _____ are very small.
       (windows/the rooms)

4. The _____ are in the basement.
       (children/toys)

5. The _____ is King College.
       (name/this school)

6.  Barbara and Sally are _____ .
    _(names/women)_

7.  I'm studying English in _____ .
    _(Mr. Harris/class)_

8.  My _____ is not very far.
    _(house/parents)_

## 4.4    Possessive Adjectives

We can use possessive adjectives to show possession. Compare the subject pronouns and the possessive adjectives.

| Subject Pronoun | Possessive Adjective | Examples |
|---|---|---|
| I | my | I'm wearing **my** white dress. |
| you | your | You're wearing **your** new dress. |
| he | his | He's wearing **his** blue suit. |
| she | her | She's wearing **her** new necklace. |
| it | its | The church has **its** own reception hall. |
| we | our | We're attending **our** cousin's wedding. |
| they | their | The newlyweds opened **their** gifts. |

## LANGUAGE NOTES

Be careful with _his_ and _her_.

I have a married brother. _His_ wife is very nice.

The bride looks beautiful. _Her_ father looks proud.

**EXERCISE 5**    Fill in the blanks with a possessive adjective.

**EXAMPLE:**    I love _____*my*_____ parents.

1.  I have one sister. _____ sister got married five years ago.

2.  She loves _____ husband very much.

3.  He's an accountant. He has _____ own business.

4.  They have one child. _____ son's name is Jason.

5.  They bought a house last year. _____ house isn't far from my house.

6. My sister and I visit _____ parents once a month. They live two hours away from us.

7. My sister said, "My car isn't working this week. Let's visit them in _____ car."

8. You don't know what's in a book by looking at _____ cover.

---

**EXERCISE 6**   Fill in the blanks with a possessive adjective.

A. What are you going to wear to ___*your*___ sister's wedding?
                                    (example)

B. I'm going to wear _____ new blue dress.
                        (1)

A. Did your sister buy a new dress for her wedding?

B. No, she's going to borrow _____ best friend's dress.
                                (2)

A. Will the wedding be at your house?

B. Oh, no. We live in an apartment. _____ apartment is too small.
                                        (3)
We're going to invite over 200 guests. The wedding is going to be at a church. Afterward, we're going to have a dinner in a restaurant.

The restaurant has _____ own reception hall.
                        (4)

A. Are the newlyweds going on a honeymoon after the wedding?

B. Yes. They have friends who have a cottage.

They're going to stay at _____ friends'
                            (5)
cottage in the country for a week.

cottage

A. Is the groom's mother a nice woman?

B. I don't know _____ mother. I'll meet her at the wedding for the
                    (6)
first time.

## 4.5   Questions with *Whose*

| *Whose* + Noun | Auxiliary Verb | Subject | Verb | Answer |
|---|---|---|---|---|
| **Whose** dress | did | the bride | borrow? | She borrowed her sister's dress. |
| **Whose** last name | will | the bride | use? | She'll use her husband's last name. |
| **Whose** flowers | are | those? | | They're the bride's flowers. |

---

# LANGUAGE NOTES

*Whose* + a noun asks a question about possession.

**EXERCISE 7**  Write a question with *whose*. The answer is given.

**EXAMPLE:**  ___Whose flowers are these_____? They're the bride's flowers.

1. _____? That's my father's car.

2. _____? Those are my brothers' toys.

3. _____? I listen to the Beatles' music.

4. _____? I'm using my friend's bike.

5. _____? I like my mother's cooking.

6. _____? The bride borrowed her sister's dress.

## 4.6  Possessive Pronouns

| Examples | Explanation |
|---|---|
| You forgot your book today. You can borrow **mine**. | *Mine* = my book |
| My car is old. **Yours** is new. | *Yours* = your car |

# LANGUAGE NOTES

1.  When we use a possessive pronoun, we omit the noun.
    COMPARE: Her dress is white.
    Your dress is blue. OR *Yours* is blue.

2.  Compare the three forms below:

| Subject Pronoun | Possessive Adjective | Possessive Pronoun |
|---|---|---|
| I | my | mine |
| you | your | yours |
| he | his | his |
| she | her | hers |
| it | its | — |
| we | our | ours |
| they | their | theirs |
| who | whose | whose |

3. After a possessive noun, we can omit the noun.
   The groom's parents look happy.
   The bride's parents do too. OR The *bride's* do too.

4. *Whose* can be a possessive adjective or a possessive pronoun.
   This is my coat.
   Whose coat is that? OR *Whose* is that?

---

**EXERCISE 8**  In each sentence below, choose either the possessive pronoun or the possessive adjective.

**EXAMPLE:**  Can I borrow ((your,) yours) car?

1. (My, Mine) is in the shop.

2. My sister has a car, but (her, hers) car needs a new battery.

3. My parents have a car. (Their, Theirs) doesn't have air conditioning.

4. My wife and I have a car. (Our, Ours) car is a Chevy.

5. Your car is old. (My, Mine) car is new.

6. My car has a new battery. (Your, Yours) has an old battery.

7. My parents have an American car. (Your, Yours) parents have a Japanese car.

---

**EXERCISE 9**  Fill in the blanks with *I, I'm, me, my,* or *mine*.

1. _____ a student.

2. _____ live in an apartment near school.

3. _____ apartment is on the first floor.

4. _____ parents often visit _____ .

5. They don't have a computer. They use _____ .

---

**EXERCISE 10**  Fill in the blanks with *we, we're, us, our,* or *ours*.

1. _____ classroom is large.

2. _____ study English here.

3. _____ foreign students.

4. The teacher helps _____ learn English.

5. The teacher brings her book, and we bring _____ .

---

**EXERCISE 11** Fill in the blanks with *you, you're, your,* or *yours*. Pretend you are talking directly to the teacher.

1. _____ the teacher.

2. _____ come from the U.S.

3. My first language is Polish. _____ is English.

4. _____ pronunciation is very good.

5. We see _____ every day.

**EXERCISE 12** Fill in the blanks with *he, he's, his,* or *him.*

1. I have a brother. _____ name is Paul.

2. _____ married.

3. _____ has four children.

4. My apartment is small. _____ is big.

5. I see _____ on the weekends.

**EXERCISE 13** Fill in the blanks with *she, she's, her,* or *hers.*

1. I have a sister. _____ name is Marilyn.

2. I visit _____ twice a week.

3. _____ lives in a suburb.

4. _____ a teacher. _____ husband is a doctor.

5. My children go to private school. _____ go to public school.

**EXERCISE 14** Fill in the blanks with *it, it's,* or *its.*

1. The school has a big library. _____ comfortable and clean.

2. _____ has many books and magazines.

3. _____ hours are from 8 a.m. to 8 p.m.

4. I use _____ every day.

5. _____ on the first floor.

Fill in the blanks with *they, they're, them, their,* or *theirs*.

1. My parents rent _____ apartment.

2. My apartment is small, but _____ is big.

3. _____ very old now.

4. _____ live in a suburb.

5. I visit _____ on the weekends.

## 4.7 Questions About the Subject

Compare these statements and related questions:

| Wh- Word | Do/Does Did | Subject | Verb | Complement |
|---|---|---|---|---|
| What | does | The bride | throws | something. |
| | | she | throw? | |
| | | Someone | caught | the bouquet. |
| | | Who | caught | the bouquet? |
| What | did | The guests | brought | something. |
| | | they | bring? | |
| | | Some guests | brought | gifts. |
| | | How many guests | brought | gifts? |
| Why | do | Some women | try | to catch the bouquet. |
| | | they | try | to catch the bouquet? |
| | | Which women | try | to catch the bouquet? |
| | | Something | happened | next. |
| | | What | happened | next? |

## LANGUAGE NOTES

1. Questions about the subject are different from other questions. They don't include *do, does,* or *did*.

2. We usually answer a subject question with a subject and an auxiliary verb.
    Who wears a white dress? The bride *does*.
    Who caught the bouquet? The bride's cousin *did*.
    How many people came to the wedding? One hundred fifty people *did*.

3. *What happened* is a subject question. We usually answer with a different verb.

> *What happened* after the wedding?
> The bride and groom *went* on a honeymoon.

4. After *who*, use the **-s** form for the simple present tense. After *how many*, use the base form. After other questions, use either the base form or the **-s** form.

> Who *has* the prettiest dress?
> How many people *want* to dance?
> Which woman *has* the prettiest dress?
> Which women *have* the prettiest dresses?

5. In a question about the object, *whom* is very formal. Informally, many Americans say *who*.

> FORMAL:   *Whom* did your brother marry?
> INFORMAL: *Who* did your brother marry?

---

**EXERCISE 16** Use the simple present tense of the verb in parentheses ( ) to ask a question about this class. Any student may volunteer an answer.

**EXAMPLES:**  Who (ride) a bike to school?
A. Who rides a bike to school?
B. I do.

How many students (have) the textbook?
A. How many students have the textbook?
B. We all do.

1. Who (explain) the grammar?

2. How many students (speak) Spanish?

3. Who usually (sit) near the door?

4. What usually (happen) after class?

5. Who (want) to repeat this course?

6. Who (need) help with this lesson?

7. Who (have) a computer?

8. How many students (live) in a dorm?

9. Who (have) a cell phone?

10. Who (live) alone?

---

**EXERCISE 17** Use the simple past tense of the verb in parentheses ( ) to ask a question. Any student may volunteer an answer.

**EXAMPLE:**   Who (buy) a used textbook?
A. Who bought a used textbook?
B. I did.

   1. Who (move) last year?

   2. Who (understand) the explanation?

   3. Who (take) a trip recently?

   4. Who (bring) a dictionary to class today?

   5. Who (pass) the last test?

   6. Which students (come) late today?

   7. Which student (arrive) first today?

   8. How many students (do) today's homework?

   9. How many students (study) English in their countries?

 10. How many students (bring) a cell phone to class?

**EXERCISE 18** Read each statement. Then write a question about the words in parentheses ( ). No answer is necessary.

**EXAMPLE:**   Someone takes the bride to the groom. (who)
*Who takes the bride to the groom?*

   1. Someone dances the first dance. (who)

   2. Someone holds the rings. (who)

   3. Two people say "I do." (how many people/"congratulations")

   4. The bridesmaids sometimes wear matching dresses.[2] (which woman/ a white dress)

   5. The bride pays for her white dress. (who/the bridesmaids' dresses)

[2] *Matching dresses* are all the same color.

Read each statement. Then write a question about the words in parentheses ( ). Some of the questions are about the subject. Some are not. No answer is necessary.

**EXAMPLES:** The bride wears a white dress. (what/the groom)

*What does the groom wear?*
_____

The bride enters last. (who/first)

*Who enters first?*
_____

1.  The bride throws the bouquet. (when)

_____

2.  Some women try to catch the bouquet. (which women)

_____

3.  The groom puts the ring on the bride's finger. (on which hand) OR (which hand . . . on)

_____

4.  The band plays music. (what kind of music)

_____

5.  Someone dances with the bride. (who)

_____

6.  Guests give presents. (what kind of presents)

_____

7.  Some people cry at the wedding. (who)

_____

8.  There's a dinner after the ceremony. (what/happen/after the dinner)

_____

**EXERCISE 20** In the conversation below, two women are talking about their families. Fill in the blanks to complete the questions. Some of the questions are about the subject. Some are about the object.

A. How do you have time to work, go to school, and take care of a family?

B. I don't have to do everything myself.

A. Who _____*helps you*_____?
      *(example)*

B. My husband helps me.

A. I usually cook in my house. Who _____?
                                              *(1)*

B. Sometimes my husband cooks; sometimes I cook. We take turns.

A. I usually clean. Who _____?
                                  *(2)*

B. I usually clean the house.

A. How many _____?
                      *(3)*

B. I have five children.

A. How many _____?
                      *(4)*

B. Three children go to school. The younger ones stay home.

A. Do you send them to public school or private school?

B. One of my sons goes to private school.

A. Which _____?
                *(5)*

B. The oldest does. He's in high school now.

A. It's hard to take care of so many children. How do you find the time to go to class?

B. As I said, my husband helps me a lot. And sometimes I use a babysitter.

A. I'm looking for a sitter. Who(m) _____?
                                              *(6)*

B. I recommend our neighbor, Susan. She's 16 years old, and she's very good with our children.

A. Maybe she's too busy to help me. How many families _____
   _____?
          *(7)*

B. I think she works for only one other family. I'll give you her phone number. If she's not busy, maybe she can work for you too.

A. Thanks. I can use some help.

**EXERCISE 21** Fill in the blanks with *who, whom, who's,* or *whose.*

1. _____ your English teacher? Cindy Kane is my teacher.
2. _____ do you live with? I live with my sister.
3. _____ has the right answer? I have the right answer.
4. There's no name on this book. _____ is it?
5. _____ parents speak English? My parents do.

## 4.8 Reflexive Pronouns—Forms

| Subject | Verb | Reflexive Pronoun |
|---------|------|-------------------|
| I | see | myself. |
| You | see | yourself. |
| He | sees | himself. |
| She | sees | herself. |
| It | sees | itself. |
| We | see | ourselves. |
| You | see | yourselves. |
| They | see | themselves. |

## LANGUAGE NOTES

If the subject and object are the same, we use a reflexive pronoun as the object. COMPARE:

I see you. (object pronoun)
I see myself. (reflexive pronoun)

**Before You Read**
1. What kind of problems do married people usually have?
2. How can married people solve their problems?

Read the following stories. Pay special attention to reflexive pronouns.

# His Story/Her Story

Frank and Sylvia are like many American couples. They have problems balancing their relationship, their children, their careers, their families, and other responsibilities. Read each one's story.

*Sylvia's story:*
Now that I'm married, I don't have time for **myself** anymore. We used to spend time with each other. Now that we have kids, we never have time

for **ourselves**. We both work, but Frank doesn't help me with housework or with the kids. I have to do everything all by **myself**. My husband only thinks of **himself**. When he wants something, like a new CD player or new software, he buys it. He never buys me flowers or other presents anymore. I tell **myself** that he still loves me, but sometimes I'm not so sure. Sometimes I think the problem is his fault, but sometimes I blame **myself**.

*Frank's story:*

Sylvia never has time for me anymore. We used to do things together. Now I have to do everything **myself**. If I want to go to a movie, she says that she's too busy or too tired or that the kids are sick. I rarely go to the movies, and if I do, I go by **myself**. It seems that all I do is work and pay bills. Other married people seem to enjoy **themselves** more than we do. She says she wants me to help her with the housework, but she really prefers to do everything **herself** because she doesn't like the way I do things. She wants us to see a marriage counselor, but I don't like to tell other people about my problems. I like to solve my problems **myself**.

## 4.9  Using Reflexive Pronouns

| Examples | Explanation |
|---|---|
| Sylvia sometimes blames **herself**. (D.O.) <br><br> I tell **myself** that he loves me. (I.O.) <br><br> He only thinks of **himself**. (O.P.) | A reflexive pronoun can be a direct object (D.O.), an indirect object (I.O.), or the object of a preposition (O.P.) |
| He goes to the movies **by himself**. <br><br> She has to do everything **all by herself**. | We often use a reflexive pronoun to mean alone. We often add (*all*) *by* before the reflexive pronoun. |

## LANGUAGE NOTES

1.  After an imperative, use *yourself* or *yourselves*.
       Enjoy *yourself*.
       Here's $50. Buy *yourselves* a nice present.
       Be good to *yourself*.

2.  We use reflexive pronouns in a few idiomatic expressions:
       When you are a guest in someone's house and the host wants you
           to feel comfortable, he may say, "Make *yourself* at home."
       When you are invited to take food at the dinner table, the hostess
           may say, "Help *yourself*."

**EXERCISE 22** Fill in the blanks with the correct reflexive pronoun.

**EXAMPLE:**   Sylvia and Frank are talking about ___*themselves*___.

1. I don't have enough time for _____.

2. Are both of you serious or can you laugh at _____?

3. They can't solve the problem by _____.

4. Frank doesn't like to talk about _____.

5. What does Sylvia tell _____?

6. We sometimes blame _____ for our problems.

7. Do you ever go to the movies by _____?

8. Maybe you expect too much of marriage, Frank. Don't be so hard on
   _____.

9. I have to take care of the children. They can't take care of _____
   _____.

10. We have a new electric coffee maker. It turns _____ on
    in the morning.

11. We enjoyed _____ on our honeymoon.

12. A. Did your mother teach you to cook or did you teach _____
       _____?

    B. I taught _____.

13. A. My parents have a great marriage.

    B. Don't compare _____ to your parents. Times are
       different.

14. Don't just look at the problems. Give _____ credit for the
    good things you do too.

**EXERCISE 23** Write two sentences telling about things you like to do by yourself. Write two sentences telling about things you don't like to do by yourself.

**EXAMPLES:**  *I like to shop by myself.*

*I don't like to eat by myself.*

_____

_____

_____

_____

**EXERCISE 24** Answer these questions.

1. Do you like to talk about yourself in class?

2. Do you ever do something special for yourself? What do you do?

3. What kind of problems do most married people have today? Do you think American married couples have the same problems as couples in your native country?

4. Do you think married couples can solve their problems by themselves? At what point should they go to a marriage counselor?

5. Do you think married people should spend most of their time together, or should they spend time by themselves?

6. Do you think young people are realistic about marriage? How can they prepare themselves for the reality of marriage?

7. Some people go on TV in the U.S. and talk about themselves and their personal problems. Does this happen in your native country?

8. What do you think Sylvia and Frank should do?

**EXERCISE 25** Combination Exercise. Fill in the blanks with the correct pronoun or possessive form.

Frank and Sylvia used to do a lot of things together. __*They*__
                                                        *(example)*

went to movies, went out to restaurants, and took vacations together. But

now _____ are always too busy for each other. _____
        *(1)*                                              *(2)*

have two children and spend most of _____ time taking care
                                           *(3)*

of _____ .
       *(4)*

Frank and Sylvia bought a house recently and spend _____
                                                          *(5)*

free time taking care of _____. It's an old house and needs a
                             (6)
lot of work.

When Frank and Sylvia have problems, _____ try to solve
                                           (7)

_____ by _____. But sometimes Sylvia goes
     (8)                (9)

to _____ mother for advice. Frank never goes to _____
      (10)                                                    (11)

mother. He doesn't want to bother _____ with _____
                                       (12)              (13)

problems. Frank often complains that Sylvia cares more about the kids and

the house than about _____.
                          (14)

Sylvia wants to go to a marriage counselor, but Frank doesn't want to

go with _____. He always says to Sylvia, "We don't need a
            (15)

marriage counselor. We can solve _____ problems by _____.
                                      (16)                      (17)

You just need to pay more attention to _____. If you want to
                                            (18)

see a counselor, you can go by _____. I'm not going." Sylvia
                                    (19)

feels very frustrated. She thinks that the marriage isn't going to get better

by _____.
       (20)

# SUMMARY OF LESSON 4

1.   Pronouns and Possessive Forms

| Subject Pronoun | Object Pronoun | Possessive Adjective | Possessive Pronoun | Reflexive Pronoun |
|---|---|---|---|---|
| I | me | my | mine | myself |
| you | you | your | yours | yourself |
| he | him | his | his | himself |
| she | her | her | hers | herself |
| it | it | its | — | itself |
| we | us | our | ours | ourselves |
| you | you | your | yours | yourselves |
| they | them | their | theirs | themselves |
| who | whom | whose | whose | — |

Examples:

Robert and Lisa are my friends.
**They** come from Canada.
I like **them**.
My country is small. **Theirs** is big.
**Their** children are grown.
They live by **themselves**.

**Who** has a new car?
With **whom** do you live?
(FORMAL)
**Who** do you live with?
(INFORMAL)
**Whose** book is that?
This is my dictionary. **Whose** is that?

2. Possessive Form of Nouns

Singular Nouns
the **boy's** name
my **father's** house
the **child's** toy
the **man's** hat
**Charles'** wife/**Charles's** wife

Plural Nouns
the **boys'** names
my **parents'** house
the **children's** toys
the **men's** hats

3. *Say* and *Tell*
He **said** his name.
He **told** me his name.

He **said** goodbye to his friends.
He **told** them to write often.

4. Questions About the Subject

Simple Present:
Someone knows the answer.
Who knows the answer?
How many students know the answer?
Which student knows the answer?
Which students know the answer?

Simple Past:
Someone killed Martin Luther King, Jr.
Who killed King?
Which man killed King?
What happened to this man?

# EDITING ADVICE

1. Don't confuse *you're* (you are) and *your* (possessive form).

~~Your~~ You're late.

~~You're~~ Your class started ten minutes ago.

2. Don't confuse *he's* (he is) and *his* (possessive form).

~~His~~ He's married.

~~He's~~ His wife is a friend of mine.

3. Don't confuse *it's* (it is) and *its* (possessive form).

This college is big. ~~Its~~ *It's* a state university.

*It's* ~~Its~~ library has many books.

4. Don't confuse *his* (masculine possessor) and *her* (feminine possessor).

   My sister loves ~~his~~ *her* son.

   My brother loves ~~her~~ *his* daughter.

5. Don't confuse *my* and *mine*.

   I don't have ~~mine~~ *my* book today.

6. Don't confuse *they're* and *their*.

   ~~They're~~ *Their* last name is Williams.

7. Use the correct pronoun (subject or object).

   I have a daughter. I love ~~she~~ *her* very much.

8. For a compound subject, use "another person and I." Don't use *me* in the subject position.

   My father and ~~me~~ *I* like to go fishing.

   ~~Me and my father~~ *My father and I* like to go fishing.

9. For a compound object, use "another person and me." Don't use *I* in the object position.

   My parents gave my brother and ~~I~~ *me* a present.

10. Don't use *the* with a possessive form.

    ~~The~~ *M*~~my~~ wife's mother is very nice.

11. Don't use an apostrophe to make a plural form.

    They invited many ~~guest's~~ *guests* to the wedding.

12. Don't use an auxiliary verb in a question about the subject.

    Who ~~does~~ speak*s* Spanish?

13. Don't separate *whose* from the noun.

    Whose~~ is this ⟨book⟩?~~

14. Don't confuse *whose* and *who's*.

    *Whose*
    ~~Who's~~ coat is that?

15. Use the correct word order for possession.

    *My wife's mother*
    ~~Mother my wife~~ helps us a lot.

16. Put the apostrophe after the **s** of a plural noun that ends in **s**.

       *parents'*
    My ~~parent's~~ house is small.

17. The **s** in a possessive pronoun is not for a plural.

    Theirs parents live in Canada.

18. Don't use a form of *be* with *what happened*.

    What ~~was~~ happened to your new car?

# LESSON 4 TEST / REVIEW

**PART 1**    Find the mistakes with the underlined words, and correct them. Not every sentence has a mistake. If the sentence is correct, write **C**.

**EXAMPLES:**  The bride's ~~the~~ parents are very proud.
    They are going to get married in <u>their parents' house</u>.    C

1. Do you like <u>the bridesmaid's</u> dresses?

2. The groom puts the ring on the <u>brides'</u> left hand.

3. The bride throws <u>his</u> bouquet to the single women.

4. The groom dances with <u>her</u> new wife.

5. When will they open <u>their friends</u> gifts?

6. <u>They're</u> car has a sign that says "Just Married."

7. <u>The groom's friend's</u> often make a party for <u>him</u> before the wedding.

8. Your wedding was very beautiful.

9. She married his best friend's brother.

10. Her husband's mother's friend is wearing a beautiful dress.

11. Do you like your mother-in-law? I don't like mother my husband.

12. The womens' dresses are very elegant.

13. My sister's the wedding will be in March.

14. Your name is different from your husband's name.

15. She visits hers parents once a week.

16. The groom graduated from college. His an accountant now.

17. Our friends invited my wife and me to their wedding.

18. My wife and me went to a beautiful wedding.

19. Who did get married in a church?

20. Whose mother is that? I think it's mother the bride.

21. How many people brought gifts to the wedding?

22. Who throw the bouquet at an American wedding? The bride does.

23. Theirs dresses are green. Mine is black.

24. The your wedding was lovely.

25. What was happened after the wedding?

## PART 2
Choose the correct word to complete each sentence.

EXAMPLE:  Do you like _____*C*_____ neighbors?

    a. you      b. you're    c. your    d. yours

  1. Where do your parents live? _____ live in Colombia.

      a. My      b. Mine     c. Mine's     d. Mines

  2. _____ coat is that?

      a. Whose     b. Who's     c. Who     d. Whom

3. _____ is usually white.

   a. The bride's dress         c. The brides' dress
   b. Dress the bride           d. The dress of bride

4. My sister's daughter is 18. _____ son is 16.

   a. His        b. Her        c. Hers        d. Her's

5. What's _____?

   a. the name your son         c. the name your son's
   b. your son's name           d. your the son's name

6. Look at those dogs. Do you see _____?

   a. they        b. its        c. them        d. it's

7. We have your phone number. Do you have _____?

   a. us        b. our        c. ours        d. our's

8. What is _____?

   a. that building name        c. the name of that building
   b. the name that building    d. the name's that building

9. _____

   a. Whose is this sweater?    c. Who's is this sweater?
   b. Whose sweater is this?    d. Who's sweater is this?

10. _____ knows the correct answer?

   a. Who        b. Whom        c. Whose        d. Who's

11. They have my address, but I don't have _____.

   a. their        b. them        c. they're        d. theirs

12. We did it by _____.

   a. self        b. oneself        c. ourself        d. ourselves

13. They can help _____.

   a. theirself        b. theirselves        c. themself        d. themselves

14. I know _____ very well.

   a. myself        b. mineself        c. meself        d. self

15. My teacher speaks Spanish. My _____ teacher doesn't.

   a. husbands        b. husbands'        c. husband's        d. the husband's

**PART 3**      Fill in the blanks with *said* or *told*.

1. She _____, "Excuse me."

2. She _____ them to study.

3. She _____ him the truth.

4. She _____ hello to her neighbor.

5. She _____ the answers.

6. She _____ us about her trip.

7. She _____ an interesting story.

8. She _____ them her name.

**PART 4**      Complete the question. Some of these questions ask about the subject. Some do not. (The answer is underlined.)

**EXAMPLES:** What _*does the bride wear*_____?
The bride wears <u>a white dress and a veil</u>.

Who _*usually cries at the wedding*_____?
<u>The bride's mother</u> usually cries at the wedding.

1. When _____?
She throws the bouquet <u>at the end of the wedding party</u>.

2. Which women _____?
<u>The single women</u> try to catch the bouquet.

3. On which hand _____?
The groom puts the ring <u>on the bride's left hand</u>.

4. Whom _____?
The groom kisses <u>the bride</u>.

5. Whose _____?
<u>The bride's ring</u> has a diamond.

6. Whose _____?
The bride uses <u>her husband's last name</u>.

7. Who _____?
<u>A professional photographer</u> took pictures at my wedding.

8. Whose _____?
I borrowed <u>my sister's dress</u>.

9. Whose _____, yours or your sister's?
   My sister's wedding was bigger.

10. How many people _____?
    Over 250 people came to the wedding.

11. Who _____?
    The bride and groom cut the cake.

**PART 5**  Fill in the blanks with a reflexive pronoun.

**EXAMPLE:** She likes to talk about ____*herself*____.

1. I made the cake all by _____.

2. The bride made her dress _____.

3. They prepared _____ financially before getting married.

4. We helped _____ to another piece of cake.

5. The groom bought _____ a new pair of shoes.

6. All of you should help _____ to more cake and coffee.

7. Did you go to the wedding by _____ or did your wife go with you?

# EXPANSION ACTIVITIES

**CLASSROOM ACTIVITIES**

1. Form a small group. The group should have people from different countries, if possible. Talk about weddings and marriages in your native countries.

   a. Who chooses a husband for a woman?

   b. Who pays for the wedding?

   c. What happens at the wedding?

   d. What happens after the wedding?

   e. Do the guests bring gifts to the wedding? What kind of gifts do they give? Where do the bride and groom open the gifts?

   f. How many people attend a wedding?

   g. Where do people get married?

   h. Do people dance at a wedding?

i. Who takes pictures?

j. What color dress does the bride wear?

k. At what age do people usually get married?

2. In a small group, interview one person who is married. Ask this person questions about his or her wedding.

EXAMPLES:
Where did you get married?
How many people did you invite?
How many people came?
Where did you go on your honeymoon?

3. According to an American tradition, the bride should wear:
Something old,
Something new,
Something borrowed,
Something blue.
Do you have any traditions regarding weddings in your native country?

4. Do you have a video of a wedding in your family? If so, can you bring it to class and tell the class about it? The teacher may have a video of an American wedding to show the class.

5. Write some advice for newlyweds in each of the following categories. Discuss your sentences in a small group.

| | |
|---|---|
| home | problem solving |
| children | mother-in-law |
| housework | money |
| careers | time together/time apart |
| family obligations | |

## WRITING

1. Write about a typical wedding in your native country, or describe your own wedding.

2. Write about a problem you once had or have now. Tell what you did (or are doing) to help yourself solve this problem or how others helped you (or are helping you).

## Internet Activities

1. Do a search on "bridal registry" on the Internet. Make a list of the types of wedding gifts people give in the U.S.

2. Do a search on "weddings" on the Internet. Find out how Americans plan for a wedding.

## GRAMMAR

Singular and Plural
Noncount Nouns
*There + Be*
Quantity Words

## CONTEXT

Pilgrims, American Indians, and Thanksgiving
Taking the Land from the American Indians

## LESSON FOCUS

Some nouns have a singular and plural form. These
are called count nouns.

I ate one *apple*. She ate two *apples*.

Some nouns have no plural form. These are called
noncount nouns.

I ate some *soup*. I drank some *water*.

We can use *there + be* to introduce count and
noncount nouns.

*There are* some apples on the table.

*There's* some milk in the refrigerator.

We can use quantity words with count and noncount
nouns.

I bought *a little* coffee. I bought *a few* bananas.

The Mayflower

1.  What do you know about American Thanksgiving?
2.  Do you have a day of thanks in your native culture?

Read the following article. Pay special attention to singular and plural nouns.

# Pilgrims, American Indians,[1] and Thanksgiving

Pilgrims

Americans celebrate Thanksgiving on the fourth Thursday in November. At this time, they get together with family and **friends**, eat a traditional big **meal**, and give thanks for all the good **things** in their **lives**. What is the origin of this special day?

In 1620, a group of 120 **men**, **women**, and **children** left England for America on a ship called the Mayflower. They came to America in search of religious **freedom**. They started their new life in a deserted[2] Indian village in what is now the state of Massachusetts. But half of the Pilgrims did not survive their first cold, hard winter. In the spring, two American **Indians** found the **people** from England in very bad condition. They didn't have enough **food**, and they were in bad **health**. Squanto, an English speaking American Indian, stayed with them for several **months** and taught them how to survive in this new place. He brought them deer **meat** and animal **skins**; he showed them how to grow **corn** and other **vegetables**; he showed them how to use **plants** as **medicine**; he explained how to use **fish** for fertilizer[3]—he taught them many **skills** for survival in their new land.

squash

By the time their second fall arrived, the Pilgrims had enough **food** to get through their second winter. They were in better **health**. They decided to have a thanksgiving **feast**[4] to celebrate their good **fortune**. They invited Squanto and neighboring Indian **families** of the Wampanoag tribe to come to their dinner. The Pilgrims were surprised when 90 Indians showed up. The Pilgrims did not have enough **food** for so many people. Fortunately, the Indian **chief** sent some of his people to bring food to the celebration. They brought five **deer**, **fish**, **beans**, **squash**, corn **bread**, **berries**, and many wild **turkeys**. The feast lasted for three **days**. There was a short time of **peace** and **friendship** between the Indians and the Pilgrims.

Now on Thanksgiving Day in the U.S., we eat some of the traditional **foods**, such as **turkey**, **sweet potatoes**, and **cranberries**, that the Indians shared with the Pilgrims.

---

[1] The natives of America are called American Indians, Indians, or Native Americans.
[2] *Deserted* means empty of people.
[3] We put fertilizer in the earth to help plants grow. Fertilizer is made of natural things.
[4] A *feast* is a large dinner.

## 5.1 Noun Plurals

### Regular Noun Plurals

| Word Ending | Example Noun | Plural Addition | Plural Form |
|---|---|---|---|
| Vowel | bee<br>banana | + s | bees<br>bananas |
| s, ss, sh, ch, x, z | church<br>dish<br>box<br>watch<br>class | + es | churches<br>dishes<br>boxes<br>watches<br>classes |
| Voiceless consonants | cat<br>lip<br>month | + s | cats<br>lips<br>months |
| Voiced consonants | card<br>pin | + s | cards<br>pins |
| Vowel + y | boy<br>day | + s | boys<br>days |
| Consonant + y | lady<br>story | y̸ + ies | ladies<br>stories |
| Vowel + o | video<br>radio | + s | videos<br>radios |
| Consonant + o | potato<br>hero | + es | potatoes<br>heroes |
| EXCEPTIONS: photos, pianos, solos, altos, sopranos, autos, avocados | | | |
| f or fe | leaf<br>knife | f̸ + ves | leaves<br>knives |
| EXCEPTIONS: beliefs, chiefs, roofs, cliffs, chefs, sheriffs | | | |

*(continued)*

## Irregular Noun Plurals

| Singular | Plural | Examples | Explanation |
|---|---|---|---|
| man<br>woman<br>mouse<br>tooth<br>foot<br>goose | men<br>women<br>mice<br>teeth<br>feet<br>geese | **Men** and **women** came to America from England. | Vowel change |
| sheep<br>fish<br>deer | sheep<br>fish<br>deer | The Indians brought five **deer**. | No change |
| child<br>person | children<br>people (or persons)<br>NOTE: *People* is more commonly used than *persons*. | The Pilgrims brought their **children** to America.<br><br>Many **people** came to the celebration. | Different word form |
| | pajamas<br>clothes<br>pants/slacks<br>(eye)glasses<br>scissors | Your **clothes** are dirty.<br><br>My **glasses** are broken. | No singular form |
| news<br>politics | | The **news** is not good.<br>**Politics** is interesting for me. | Singular form ends in *-s*. No plural form. |

# LANGUAGE NOTES

1. We use the plural to talk about more than one. Regular noun plurals end in *-s* or *-es*. Some noun plurals are irregular.
   > One hundred twenty *men*, *women*, and *children* came from England. Two *Indians* found these people.
2. Exact numbers use the singular form.
   > The U.S. has over 270 *million* people.
3. Inexact numbers use the plural form.
   > *Millions* of Indians live in America.
   > *Hundreds* of Europeans came to America in the 1600s.
   > My grandfather is in his *seventies*.
4. We use the plural form in the following expressions: *one of* (*the, my, his, her*, etc.).
   > One of the *Indians* spoke English.
5. We use a singular noun and verb after *every*.
   > Every *person needs* love and attention.
6. Don't make an adjective plural.
   > We have many *good* things in our lives.

**EXERCISE 1**    Write the plural form of each noun.

**EXAMPLE:**    hour ____*hours*____

1. American _____
2. family _____
3. leaf _____
4. child _____
5. deer _____
6. city _____
7. language _____
8. cloud _____
9. potato _____
10. valley _____

11. butterfly _____
12. man _____
13. fish _____
14. wolf _____
15. donkey _____
16. fox _____
17. country _____
18. month _____
19. goose _____
20. woman _____

**EXERCISE 2**    Find the mistakes with the underlined words, and correct them. Not every sentence has a mistake. If the sentence is correct, write **C**.

**EXAMPLES:**    Five ~~man~~ *men* left early.

Mathematics ~~are~~ *is* my favorite subject.

I saw two <u>deer</u> in the forest.      *C*

1. She has two <u>childrens</u>.

2. One of her <u>daughter</u> is a doctor.

3. Eleven <u>millions peoples</u> died in the war.

4. The <u>news are</u> on TV at 6 o'clock.

5. His <u>pants is</u> very expensive.

6. Five <u>women</u> in this class speak French.

7. <u>Every students want</u> to pass this course.

8. Math is one of my favorite <u>subject</u> in school.

9. <u>Everyone want</u> to have a good life.

10. Many Americans <u>own</u> a home.

11. <u>Hundreds</u> of people saw the accident.

12. My mother is in her <u>sixties</u>.

**EXERCISE 3**  Fill in the blanks with the correct form of the word in parentheses ( ).

EXAMPLE:    ___*Americans*___ celebrate Thanksgiving in November.
            *(American)*

1. One hundred twenty _____ came to America on the
   *(person)*
   Mayflower.

2. _____, _____, and _____ came to
   *(Man)*        *(woman)*           *(child)*
   America on the Mayflower.

3. They had very hard _____ in America.
   *(life)*

4. _____ of Indians lived in America before the arrival of
   *(Million)*
   the Pilgrims.

5. Squanto taught the Pilgrims _____ to live in America.
   *(skill)*

6. He stayed with the Pilgrims for several _____.
   *(month)*

7. Indians used _____ for fertilizer.
   *(fish)*

8. Many Indian _____ came to celebrate with the Pilgrims.
   *(family)*

9. They brought five _____ and many wild _____.
   *(deer)*                    *(turkey)*

10. The feast lasted for three _____.
    *(day)*

## 5.2  Using the Singular and Plural for Generalizations

| Examples | Explanation |
| --- | --- |
| A child needs love.<br>  Children need love. | When we make a generalization, we say that something is true of the noun in general. |
| A big city has a lot of traffic.<br>  Big cities have a lot of traffic. | To make a generalization, we use a singular noun after *a* or *an*, or the plural noun with no article. |

**EXERCISE 4**  Make a generalization about the following nouns. Use the plural form. (You may work with a partner.)

EXAMPLE:    American teachers ___*are very informal.*___

1. American children _____

2. American colleges _____

3. Buses in this city _____

4. Elderly Americans _____

5. American cities _____

6. American doctors _____

7. American women _____

8. American men _____

---

**EXERCISE 5**  Make a generalization about these professions. Use the singular form. (You may work with a partner.)

**EXAMPLE:**  A taxi driver *has a dangerous job.* _____

1. A teacher _____

2. A doctor _____

3. A nurse _____

4. A garbage collector _____

5. A lawyer _____

6. A musician _____

7. A librarian _____

8. A movie star _____

9. An accountant _____

10. A newspaper reporter _____

## 5.3  Noncount Nouns

There are several types of noncount nouns:

| **Group A.** Nouns that have no distinct, separate parts. We look at the whole. | | | |
|---|---|---|---|
| milk | wine | bread | electricity |
| oil | yogurt | meat | lightning |
| water | pork | butter | thunder |
| coffee | poultry[5] | paper | cholesterol |
| tea | soup | air | blood |
| **Group B.** Nouns that have parts that are too small or insignificant to count | | | |
| rice | hair | sand | |
| sugar | popcorn | corn | |
| salt | snow | grass | |

*(continued)*

[5] Poultry includes domestic birds that we eat, such as chickens and turkeys.

**Group C.** Nouns that are classes or categories of things. The members of the category are not the same.

money or cash (nickels, dimes, dollars)

food (vegetables, meat, spaghetti)

furniture (chairs, tables, beds)

clothing (sweaters, pants, dresses)

mail (letters, packages, postcards, fliers)

fruit (cherries, apples, grapes)

makeup (lipstick, rouge, eye shadow)

homework (compositions, exercises, reading)

jewelry (necklaces, bracelets, rings)

**Group D.** Nouns that are abstractions

| | | | | |
|---|---|---|---|---|
| love | happiness | nutrition | music | information |
| life | education | intelligence | art | nature |
| time | experience | unemployment | work | help |
| truth | crime | pollution | health | noise |
| beauty | advice | patience | trouble | energy |
| luck | knowledge | poverty | fun | friendship |

**Group E.** Subjects of study

| | | |
|---|---|---|
| history | grammar | biology |
| chemistry | geometry | math (mathematics*) |

*NOTE: Even though *mathematics* ends with *s*, it is not plural.

# LANGUAGE NOTES

1. We classify nouns into two groups: count nouns and noncout nouns. A count noun is something we can count. It has a singular and plural form. We can put a number before a count noun.

   one potato      five potatoes

   one apple      ten apples

2. A noncount noun is something we don't count. It has no plural form. We cannot put a number before a noncount noun. With a noncount noun, we use a unit of measure, which we can count.

   one cup of coffee      five cups of coffee

3. Count and noncount nouns are grammatical terms, but they are not always logical. Rice is very small and is a noncount noun. Beans and peas are also very small but are count nouns.

4. Some nouns can be either count or noncount. *Food* and *fruit* can be count nouns when they mean categories of food or fruit. COMPARE:

   She eats a lot of *fruit* every day. (noncount noun)

   Oranges and grapefruits are *fruits* that contain vitamin C. (count noun)

   She bought a lot of *food* for the party.

   Traditional *foods* on Thanksgiving are turkey and sweet potatoes. (count noun)

   For a list of nouns that can be count or noncount, see Appendix G.

5. When referring to whole turkeys or other birds, these words are count nouns. When referring to a part of the bird, these are noncount nouns.

The Indians brought many *turkeys* to the feast.
We eat *turkey* on Thanksgiving.

6.  Some nouns that have a plural form in other languages are noncount in English. *Advice, information, knowledge, equipment, furniture,* and *homework* are always noncount nouns in English.

---

**EXERCISE 6**  Go back to the article about Indians, Pilgrims, and Thanksgiving on page 132. Mark the nouns in the article with **C** for count noun or *NC* for noncount noun.

**EXAMPLES:**  Indians = *C*
freedom = *NC*

---

**EXERCISE 7**  Decide if the noun in parentheses ( ) is count or noncount. If it is a count noun, change it to the plural form. If it is a noncount noun, do not use the plural form.

**EXAMPLE:**  <u>    Education    </u> is expensive in an American college.
            *(Education)*

Besides the tuition, you have to pay for your <u>  books  </u>.
                                              *(book)*

1.  American Indians have a lot of respect for <u>            </u>. They
                                                *(nature)*

    love <u>          </u>, <u>          </u>, <u>          </u>, and
         *(flower)*        *(tree)*         *(bird)*

    <u>          </u>.
    *(fish)*

2.  Thanksgiving is a celebration of <u>        </u> and <u>          </u>.
                                       *(peace)*          *(friendship)*

3.  On Thanksgiving, Americans eat a lot of <u>        </u> and sometimes
                                              *(food)*

    gain weight.

4.  Squanto gave the Pilgrims a lot of <u>            </u> about planting
                                         *(advice)*

    <u>        </u> and other <u>            </u>. He had a lot of
    *(corn)*                  *(vegetable)*

    <u>            </u> about the land.
    *(knowledge)*

5.  The Pilgrims didn't have any <u>            </u> with American food.
                                   *(experience)*

6.  On the first Thanksgiving, Indians brought <u>                </u>,
                                                 *(meat)*

    <u>          </u>, <u>          </u>, and <u>          </u>.
    *(bean)*           *(bread)*             *(berry)*

7.  The Pilgrims celebrated because they had a lot of good

    <u>            </u>.
    *(fortune)*

8.  American Indians use <u>            </u> for <u>            </u>.
                           *(plant)*             *(medicine)*

---

Singular and Plural; Noncount Nouns; *There + Be*; Quantity Words    **139**

9. My friends went to the Southwest last summer. They bought

American Indian _____, such as _____ and
     (jewelry)                                    (ring)

_____.
     (necklace)

10. Do you have a lot of _____ about American
                              (information)

_____?
     (holiday)

## 5.4  Quantities with Count and Noncount Nouns

Ways we see noncount nouns:

| By container | By portion | By measurement | By shape or whole piece | Other |
|---|---|---|---|---|
| a bottle of water<br>a carton of milk<br>a jar of pickles<br>a bag of flour<br>a can of soda (pop)<br>a cup of coffee<br>a glass of water<br>a bowl of soup | a slice (piece) of bread<br>a piece of meat<br>a piece of cake<br>a strip of bacon<br>a piece (sheet) of paper<br>a slice of pizza<br>a scoop of ice cream | an ounce of sugar<br>a quart of oil<br>a pound of meat<br>a gallon of milk<br>a pint of cream | a loaf of bread<br>an ear of corn<br>a piece of fruit<br>a head of lettuce<br>a candy bar<br>a roll of film<br>a tube of toothpaste<br>a bar of soap | a piece of mail<br>a piece of furniture<br>a piece of advice<br>a piece of information<br>a work of art<br>a homework assignment |

## LANGUAGE NOTES

1. We cannot put a number before a noncount noun. With a noncount noun, we use a unit of measure, which we can count.
   one cup of coffee       five cups of coffee

2. For a list of conversions from the American system of measurement to the metric system, see Appendix D.

**EXERCISE 8**  Fill in the blanks with a specific quantity.

**EXAMPLE:**  I drink three ___*glasses of*___ water a day.

1. You should take a few _____ film on your vacation.

2. I'm going to buy two _____ meat to make dinner for the family.

3. _____ milk is heavy to carry.

4. She drinks two _____ coffee every morning.

5. Buy _____ bread for dinner.

6. He eats _____ fruit a day.

7. Some Americans carry a _____ water with them.

8. I ate two _____ cake.

9. Let me give you _____ advice before you apply to colleges.

10. How many _____ gas did you buy at the gas station?

---

**Before You Read**
1. Who were the original inhabitants of your native country?
2. Are there any ethnic minorities in your native country? Do they have the respect of the majority population?

Read the following article. Pay special attention to *there* + a form of *be*.

# Taking the Land from the Native Americans

Before the arrival of Europeans, **there were** between 10 and 16 million Native Americans in America. Today **there are** fewer than 2 million. What happened to these natives of America?

The friendship between the Indians and Europeans did not last for long. As more English people came to America, they did not need the help of the Indians, as the first group of Pilgrims did. The white people started to take the land away from the Indians. As Indians fought to keep their land, many of them were killed. Also, **there were** many deaths from diseases that Europeans brought to America. In 1830, President Andrew Jackson took the Indians' lands and sent them to live on reservations. Indian children had to learn English. Often they were punished for speaking their own language. As a result, **there are** very few Indians today who speak the language of their ancestors.[6]

Today **there are** about 500 tribes in the U.S., each with its own traditions. **There are** about 300 reservations, but only 22 percent of American Indians live on this land. **There is** a lot of unemployment and poverty on many reservations. As a result, many Indians move to big cities to find work. Many return to their reservations only for special celebrations such as Pow-Wows, when Indians wear their traditional clothing and dance to traditional music.

**Did you know...?**

Many place names in the U.S. are American Indian names. Chicago, for example, comes from an Indian word meaning smelly onion.

[6] *Ancestors* are grandparents, great-grandparents, etc.

---

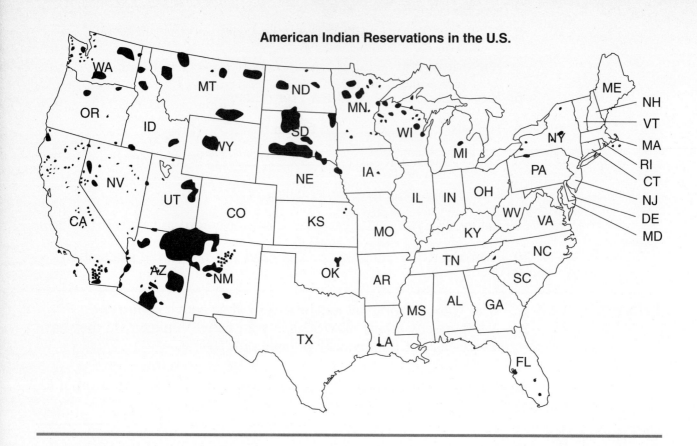

**American Indian Reservations in the U.S.**

## 5.5 *There* + A Form of *Be*

|  | *There* | *Be* | Article/ Quantity | Noun | Place/Time |
|---|---|---|---|---|---|
| COUNT | There | is | a | reservation | in Wyoming. |
|  | There | are | about 500 | Indian tribes | in the U.S. |
|  | There | are | a lot of | jobs | in a big city. |
|  | There | will be | some | rain | tomorrow. |
| NONCOUNT | There | is | a lot of | unemployment | on some reservations. |
|  | There | was |  | peace | at first. |

## LANGUAGE NOTES

1.  We use *there* + a form of *be* to introduce a new noun, either count or noncount. A sentence that begins with *there* often gives a place or a time.
2.  If two nouns follow *there*, use a singular verb (*is*) if the first noun is singular. Use a plural verb (*are*) if the first noun is plural.

    There *is one* Korean student and three Mexican students in this class.

There *are three* Mexican students and one Korean student in this class.

3. In conversation, you will sometimes hear *there's* with plural nouns.
   INFORMAL: *There's* a lot of reservations in California.
   FORMAL:   *There are* a lot of reservations in California.
4. After we introduce a noun with *there*, we can continue to speak of this noun with a pronoun.
   There are over 500 tribes of Native Americans in the U.S. *They* each have their own traditions.
   There is a Navajo reservation in Arizona. *It's* very big.
   There's a Navajo woman in my chemistry class. *She* comes from Arizona.
5. Observe the word order in questions with *there*.
   *Is there* unemployment on some reservations? Yes, there is.
   *Are there* any reservations in California? Yes, there are.
   How many Navajo Indians *are there* in Arizona?
6. We don't use a specific noun after *there*.
   WRONG: There's the Sears Tower in Chicago.
   RIGHT:   The Sears Tower is in Chicago.
   WRONG: There's Paris in France.
   RIGHT:   Paris is in France.

---

EXERCISE 9    Fill in the blanks with the correct form and tense.

EXAMPLE:    There ____*are*____ a lot of Indians in Oklahoma.

1. There _____ a lot of reservations in California.

2. There _____ more American Indians 200 years ago than there

   _____ today.

3. In the beginning, there _____ peace between the Indians and the Pilgrims.

4. Later there _____ wars between the Indians and the white people who took their land.

5. _____ _____ enough food to eat at the first Thanksgiving? Yes, there was.

6. How many people _____ _____ at the first Thanksgiving celebration?

7. Next week there _____ _____ a test on noncount nouns.

8. How many questions _____ _____ _____ on the test?

**EXERCISE 10** Fill in the blanks with a time or place.

EXAMPLE: There was a war *in my country from 1972 to 1975.*

1. There will be a test _____

2. There are a lot of problems _____

3. There's a lot of snow _____

4. There are a lot of people _____

5. There is a lot of crime _____

6. There are a lot of reservations _____

7. There was a presidential election _____

8. There are a lot of students _____

9. There was a war in my country _____

## 5.6 Quantity Expressions—Overview

We can use quantity expressions to talk about the quantity of count and noncount nouns.

**Examples**

There are about **two million** American Indians today.
The Pilgrims had **very little** food during the first winter.
The American Indians had **a lot of** knowledge about the land.
The Pilgrims didn't have **much** knowledge about the land.
**Many** Indians died from disease.
**Some** Indians today live on reservations.
**Very few** Indians today speak their native language.

**EXERCISE 11** Fill in the blanks to complete these statements.

EXAMPLE: There are 500 _____*tribes*_____ of American Indians in the U.S.

1. Before the arrival of the white people from Europe, there were at

   least _____ American Indians.

2. After the first cold winter in America, the Pilgrims didn't have much _____ .

3. Many Pilgrims _____ during the first winter.

4. Some _____ helped the Pilgrims.

5. The Indians taught them many _____ to help them survive.

6. The second year in America was much better. They had a lot of _____ .

7. As more white people came to America, many _____ lost their land.

8. Many Indians can't find work on their reservations. There is a lot of _____ on a reservation.

## 5.7 *Some, Any, A, No*

| | Singular Count | Plural Count | Noncount |
|---|---|---|---|
| Affirmative | There's **a** clock in the kitchen. | There are (**some**) windows in the kitchen. | There's (**some**) rice in the kitchen. |
| Negative | There isn't **a** clock in the kitchen. | There aren't (**any**) windows in the kitchen. | There isn't (**any**) rice in the kitchen. |
| | There's **no** clock in the kitchen. | There are **no** windows in the kitchen. | There's **no** rice in the kitchen. |
| Question | Is there **a** clock in the kitchen? | Are there (**any**) windows in the kitchen? | Is there (**any**) rice in the kitchen? |

## LANGUAGE NOTES

1. We use *a* or *an* with singular count nouns.
2. We can use *some* for affirmative statements, with both noncount nouns and plural count nouns. *Some* can be omitted.
    I have *some* time.
    I have time.

3. We can use *any* for questions and negatives, with both noncount nouns and plural count nouns. *Any* can be omitted.
    Do you have *any* change?
    Do you have change?

4. *Some* can also be used in questions.
    Do you have *some* change?

5.   Use an affirmative verb before *no*. COMPARE:
      There *is no* time.
      There *is no** answer to your question.
      There *isn't any* time.
      There *isn't an* answer to your question.
    *NOTE: Don't use the indefinite article after *no*.

6.   You will sometimes see *any* with a singular count noun.
      Which pen should I use for the test? You can use *any* pen.
    *Any*, in this case, means whichever you want. It doesn't matter which pen.

---

**EXERCISE 12**  Use *there* + the words given to tell about your hometown. (If you use *no*, delete the article.) You can add a statement to give more information.

**EXAMPLES:**   a mayor
There's a mayor in my hometown. He's a young man.

a subway
There's no subway in my hometown.

| | |
|---|---|
| 1.  a university | 6.  a river |
| 2.  a subway | 7.  a jail |
| 3.  an English language newspaper | 8.  an art museum |
| 4.  an airport | 9.  an English language institute |
| 5.  a soccer team | 10.  a cemetery |

---

**EXERCISE 13**  Fill in the blanks with *some, any, a, an*, or *no*.

**EXAMPLES:**   I have ___*some*___ money in my pocket.

Do you have ___*any*___ time to help me?

Do you have ___*a*___ new car?

I have ___*no*___ experience as a babysitter.

1.  Do you have _____ questions about this exercise?

2.  Do you have _____ dictionary with you?

3.  Did you have _____ trouble with the homework?

4.  If we have _____ extra time, we'll go over the homework.

---

5. The teacher can't help you now because he has _____ time.

6. The teacher can't help you now because he doesn't have _____ time.

7. I'm confused. I need _____ answer to my question.

8. I have _____ questions about the last lesson. Can you answer them for me?

9. I understand this lesson completely. I have _____ questions.

10. I understand this lesson completely. I don't have _____ questions.

11. I work hard all day and have _____ energy late at night.

12. I don't have _____ computer.

## 5.8 *A Lot Of, Much, Many*

| | Plural Count | Noncount |
|---|---|---|
| Affirmative | He has **many** friends.<br>He has **a lot of** friends. | He has **a lot of** time. |
| Negative | He doesn't have **many** friends.<br>He doesn't have **a lot of** friends. | He doesn't have **much** time.<br>He doesn't have **a lot of** time. |
| Question | Does he have **many** friends?<br>Does he have **a lot of** friends?<br>How **many** friends does he have? | Does he have **much** time?<br>Does he have **a lot of** time?<br>How **much** time does he have? |

## LANGUAGE NOTES

1. *Much* is rare in affirmative statements. It is more common to use *a lot of* in affirmative statements.

2. In conversation, *of* is often pronounced /ə/. Listen to your teacher pronounce the above sentences.

3. When the noun is omitted, we say *a lot*, not *a lot of*.
   Do you get *a lot of* mail?
   No, I don't get *a lot*.

4. In conversation, many people say "lots of" or "plenty of" for both noncount and plural count nouns:
   He has *lots of time*. He has *plenty of friends*.

**EXERCISE 14** Fill in the blanks with *much, many,* or *a lot (of).* Avoid *much* in affirmative statements. In some cases, more than one answer is possible.

**EXAMPLES:** You don't need _____*much*_____ time to do this exercise.

I have _____*a lot of (or many)*_____ friends.

1. Busy people don't have _____ free time.

2. Was there _____ snow last winter?

3. _____ American Indians prefer to live in big cities.

4. There's _____ crime in a big city.

5. There isn't _____ traffic in a small town.

6. There aren't _____ schools in a small town.

7. How _____ coffee do you drink in the morning?

8. I like coffee, but I don't drink _____ because it keeps me awake at night.

9. There are _____ Japanese cars in the U.S.

10. How _____ students in this class come from Korea?

## 5.9 *A Lot Of* vs. *Too Much/Too Many*

| *A lot of* = Large quantity No problem is presented | *Too much/many* = Excessive quantity A problem is presented |
|---|---|
| **A lot of** American Indians live in Oklahoma. | My friend left the reservation because there was **too much** unemployment and she couldn't find a job. |
| I have **a lot of** homework. | I don't have time to talk to you. I have **too much** homework. |
| I have **a lot of** cousins. | I have no time to study. I have **too many** family responsibilities. |

# LANGUAGE NOTES

1.  *A lot of* has a neutral tone. It shows a large quantity but doesn't present a problem. *Too much* or *too many* usually presents a problem or has a complaining tone.

2.  Use *too much* with noncount nouns. Use *too many* with count nouns.
    I have *too much* work.
    I have *too many* responsibilities.

3.  We can put *too much* at the end of a verb phrase.
    She can't buy that car because it costs *too much*.

---

**EXERCISE 15** Use *a lot of, too much*, or *too many* to fill in the blanks in the story below. In some cases, more than one answer is possible.

Coleen Finn

My name is Coleen Finn. I'm a Ho-chunk Indian. My tribal land is in Wisconsin. But I live in Chicago because there is ___too much___ unemployment on my tribal land, and I can't find a good job there. There are _____ (1) opportunities in Chicago, and I found a job as a secretary in the English Department at Truman College. I like my job very much. I have _____ (2) responsibilities and I love the challenge.

I like Chicago, but I miss my land, where I still have _____ (3) relatives and friends. I often go back to visit them whenever I get tired of life in Chicago. My friends and I have _____ (4) fun together, talking, cooking our native food, walking in nature, and attending Indian ceremonies, such as Pow-Wows. I need to get away from Chicago once in a while to feel closer to nature. Even though there are _____ (5) nice things about Chicago, there are _____ (6) cars and trucks in the big city and there is _____ (7) pollution. A weekend with my tribe gives me time to relax and smell fresh air.

---

**EXERCISE 16** Fill in the blanks after *too* with *much* or *many*. Then complete the statement.

EXAMPLE:    If I drink too __*much*__ coffee, __*I won't be able to sleep tonight.*__

1.  If I try to memorize too _____ words, _____

2.  If I make too _____ mistakes on my homework, _____
    _____

3.  If I spend too _____ money on clothes, _____

4.  If I drink too _____ coffee, _____

5.  If I spend too _____ time with my friends, _____

6.  If I stay up _____ late, _____

## 5.10   *A Few, Several, A Little*

| Count | Noncount |
|-------|----------|
| I have **a few** questions. | I need **a little** help. |
| I have **several** mistakes on my composition. | I need **a little** more time. |

## LANGUAGE NOTES

1.  Use *a few* or *several* with count nouns.
2.  Use *a little* with noncount nouns.

**EXERCISE 17** Fill in the blanks with *a few*, *several*, or *a little*.

EXAMPLES:    He has __*a few*__ problems with his car.

He has __*a little*__ experience as a teacher.

1.  Every day we study _____ grammar.

2.  We do _____ exercises in class.

3.  I have _____ knowledge about computers.

4.  _____ students are absent today.

5.  I have _____ cash with me.

6.  I have _____ dollars in my pocket.

7. I bought _____ furniture for my apartment.

8. I have _____ chairs in my living room.

9. I had _____ mistakes on my composition.

10. I need _____ help with my composition.

## 5.11 *A Few* vs. *Few; A Little* vs. *Little*

| Positive Emphasis | Negative Emphasis |
|---|---|
| I have **a few** good friends. I'm happy. | I have **few** good friends. I'm lonely. |
| I have **a little** money. Let's go to the cafeteria and get something to eat. | I have **very little** money. I can't buy anything today. |
| There are **a few** American Indian students in my biology class. | **Few** young American Indians speak the language of their ancestors. |

## LANGUAGE NOTES

1.  When we omit **a** before *few* and *little*, we are emphasizing the negative quantity. We are saying the quantity is not enough.

2.  We often use *very few* or *very little* to emphasize a negative quantity.

3.  Whether something is enough or not enough does not depend on the quantity. It depends on the perspective of the person.
    Is the glass half empty or half full?

    ☺ One person may say the glass is half full. He sees something positive about the quantity of water in the glass: The glass has *a little* water.

    ☹ Another person may say the glass is half empty. He sees something negative about the quantity of water in the glass: The glass has *(very) little* water.

**EXERCISE 18** Fill in the blanks with *a little*, *very little*, *a few*, or *very few*.

**EXAMPLES:**  He has ___*a little*___ extra money. He's going to buy a sandwich.

He has ___*very little*___ extra money. He can't buy anything.

1. I have _____ food in my refrigerator. Let's make dinner at my house.

2. In some countries, people have _____ food, and many people are starving.[7]

3. That worker has _____ experience. He probably can't do that job.

4. That worker has _____ experience. He can probably do that job.

5. I eat _____ meat every day because I want protein in my diet.

6. I want to bake cookies, but I can't because I have _____ sugar in the house.

7. When there is _____ rain, plants can't grow.

8. Tomorrow there may be _____ rain, so you should take an umbrella.

9. Twenty-five years ago, home computers were very rare. _____ people had a home computer.

10. Before I bought my computer, I talked to _____ people about which computer to buy.

11. There are _____ monkeys in the zoo. Let's go to see them.

12. There are _____ gray whales in the world. These animals are an endangered species.[8]

13. If you want to study medicine, I can give you a list of _____ good medical schools in the U.S.

whale

14. _____ high schools teach Latin. It is not a very popular language to study anymore.

15. I want to say _____ words about my country. Please listen.

16. My father is a man of _____ words. He rarely talks.

17. English is the main language of _____ countries.

18. Women are still rare as political leaders. _____ countries have a woman president.

---

[7] To *starve* means to suffer or die from not having enough food.
[8] An *endangered species* is a type of living thing that is becoming more and more rare. The species is in danger of disappearing completely if it is not protected.

**EXERCISE 19** Ask question with *"Are there . . . ?"* and the words given about another student's hometown. The other student will answer with an expression of quantity. Practice count nouns.

EXAMPLE:    museums
A. Are there any museums in your hometown?
B. Yes. There are a lot of (a few, three) museums in my hometown.
   OR
   No. There aren't any museums in my hometown.

1. department stores          6. open markets
2. churches                   7. hospitals
3. synagogues                 8. universities
4. skyscrapers                9. mosques
5. supermarkets              10. bridges

**EXERCISE 20** Ask a question with *"Are there any . . . ?"* or *"Are there many . . . ?"* and the words given about another student's native country. The other student will answer with an expression of quantity. Practice count nouns.

EXAMPLE:    single mothers
A. Are there many single mothers in your country?
B. There are very few.

1. homeless people            5. American businesses
2. working women             6. nursing homes
3. fast-food restaurants      7. rich people
4. factories                  8. good universities

**EXERCISE 21** Ask a question with *"Is there . . . ?"* and the words given about another student's native country. The other student will answer with an expression of quantity. Practice noncount nouns.

EXAMPLE:    petroleum/in your native country
A. Is there much petroleum in your native country?
B. Yes. There's a lot of petroleum in my native country.
   OR
   No. There isn't much petroleum in my native country.

In Your Native Country        In Your Hometown
1. petroleum                  5. traffic
2. industry                   6. rain
3. agriculture                7. pollution
4. tourism                    8. noise

---

Singular and Plural; Noncount Nouns; *There + Be*; Quantity Words    **153**

Ask a student a question with *"Do you have . . . ?"* and the words given. The other student will answer. Practice both count and noncount nouns.

EXAMPLE:     American friends
A. Do you have any American friends?
B. Yes. I have many (or a lot of) American friends.
OR
No. I don't have many American friends.

EXAMPLE:     free time
A. Do you have a lot of free time?
B. Yes. I have some free time.
OR
No. I have very little free time.

1. problems in the U.S.

2. American friends

3. relatives in New York

4. time to relax

5. brothers and sisters (siblings)

6. experience with computers

7. questions about American customs

8. trouble with English pronunciation

9. information about points of interest in this city

10. knowledge about computer programming

EXERCISE **23** Cross out the phrase that doesn't fit and fill in the blanks with an expression of quantity to make a **true** statement about your native country. Discuss your answers.

EXAMPLE:     ~~There's~~/There isn't ____*much*____ unemployment in my native country.

1. There's/There isn't _____ opportunity to make money in my native country.

2. There are/There aren't _____ divorced people in my native country.

3. There are/There aren't _____ foreigners in my native country.

4. There's/There isn't _____ freedom in my native country.

5. There are/There aren't _____ American cars in my native country.

6. There are/There aren't _____ political problems in my native country.

7. There is/There isn't _____ unemployment in my native country.

8. There is/There isn't _____ crime in my hometown.

## SUMMARY OF LESSON 5

1. Study the words that we use before count and noncount nouns.

| Singular Count | Plural Count | Noncount |
|---|---|---|
| a tomato | some tomatoes | some coffee |
| no tomato | no tomatoes | no coffee |
| | any tomatoes | any coffee |
| | (with questions and negatives) | |
| | a lot of tomatoes | a lot of coffee |
| | many tomatoes | much coffee |
| | | (with questions and negatives) |
| | a few tomatoes | a little coffee |
| | several tomatoes | |
| | How many tomatoes? | How much coffee? |

2. Sentences with *There*
    Count
        **There's a** Vietnamese student in this class.
        **There are** some Chinese students in this class.
    Noncount
        **There's** some rain in my hometown in the winter.
        How much rain **is there** in the spring?

3. *Too Much/Too Many/A Lot Of*
    • *A lot of* + count or noncount noun (no problem is presented)
        She's a healthy woman. She gets **a lot of** exercise.
        She walks **a lot of** miles.
    • *Too much* + noncount noun (a problem is presented)
        She doesn't qualify for financial aid because her parents make **too much** money.
    • *Too many* + count noun (a problem is presented)
        There are **too many** students in the class. The teacher doesn't have time to help everyone.

1.  Some plural forms are irregular and don't take -*s*.

    She has two children~~s~~.

2.  Use a singular noun and verb after *every*.

    Every child~~ren~~ need*s* love.

3.  Use the plural form after *one of*.

    One of my sister*s* is a lawyer.

4.  Don't use *a* or *an* before a plural noun.

    She bought *(some)* ~~a~~ new socks.

5.  Don't put *a* or *an* before a noncount noun.

    I want to give you *some OR a piece of* ~~an~~ advice.

6.  A noncount noun is always singular.

    I have *a lot of* ~~many~~ homeworks to do.

    She bought three *pieces of* furniture~~s~~.

7.  Use *there* to introduce a noun.

    *There a* ~~Are~~ a lot of people in China.

8.  Be careful with *there* and *they're*. They sound the same.

    *There* ~~They're~~ are many problems in the world.

9.  Don't use a specific noun after *there*.

    ~~There's~~ *T*~~t~~he Golden Gate bridge *is* in San Francisco.

10. Include *of* with a unit of measure.

    He bought three rolls *of* film.

11. Omit *of* after *a lot* when the noun is omitted.

I have a lot of time, but my brother doesn't have a lot ~~of~~.

12. Use *a little/a few* for a positive meaning. Use *little/few* for a negative meaning.

He can't help you because he has *(very)* ~~a~~ little time.

13. Don't use *too much* or *too many* if the quantity doesn't present a problem.

He's a lucky man. He has *a lot of* ~~too many~~ friends.

14. Don't use a double negative.

He doesn't have *any* ~~no~~ money.
*or He has no money.*

# LESSON 5 TEST / REVIEW

PART 1 Find the mistakes with the underlined words, and correct them. Not every sentence has a mistake. If the sentence is correct, write **C**.

**EXAMPLES:** How *much* ~~many milks~~ did you drink?

How <u>much</u> time do you have?     C

1. He doesn't have <u>no</u> job.

2. One of my <u>friend</u> moved to Montana.

3. I can't go out tonight because I have <u>too much</u> work.

4. Three <u>womens</u> came into the room.

5. I had a lot of friends in my country, but in the U.S. I don't have <u>a lot of</u>.

6. <u>A lot of American</u> own a computer.

7. A person can be happy if he has <u>a few</u> good friends.

8. I have <u>much</u> information about my country.

9. Every <u>workers</u> in the U.S. pays taxes.

10. Are there <u>any</u> mistakes in this sentence?

11. My mother gave me a lot of <u>advices</u>.

12. You need <u>a luck</u> to win the lottery.

13. <u>There's the White House</u> in Washington, D.C.

14. I can help you on Saturday because I'll have <u>too much</u> time.

15. <u>Are</u> a lot of students in the cafeteria, and I can't find a seat.

16. A few of my <u>teacher</u> speak English very fast.

17. Did you buy <u>a new furniture</u> for your apartment?

18. Some <u>man</u> are very polite.

19. I have <u>many</u> problems with my landlord.

20. Did you have <u>much fun</u> at the party?

21. I have <u>a</u> new dishes in my kitchen.

22. Several <u>students</u> in this class speak French.

23. I have a dog. I don't have <u>any</u> cat.

24. <u>Many</u> people like to travel.

25. He doesn't need <u>any</u> help from you.

26. I have <u>a little</u> time. I can help you.

27. I have <u>a little</u> time. I can't help you.

28. He bought three <u>pounds meat</u>.

29. How <u>much</u> apples did you eat?

30. How many <u>cup of coffees</u> did you drink?

31. <u>They're are</u> four Mexican students in the class.

32. I want to give you <u>an</u> advice about your education.

Fill in the blanks with the singular or plural form of the word in parentheses ( ).

EXAMPLE:   The Pilgrims didn't have a lot of ___*experience*___ with American land.
(experience)

1.   The Indians had many _____ with white _____
(war)                    (person)
over their lands.

2.   Some _____ have a big problem with _____ and
(reservation)                        (unemployment)
_____. There aren't enough _____ for everyone.
(poverty)                              (job)

3.   My father gave me a lot of _____. He told me that there are
(advice)
more _____ in big _____ than on the reservations.
(job)                  (city)

4.   We like to visit the art museum. We like to see the _____
(sculpture)
and _____ by famous _____. We like all kinds
(painting)                    (artist)
of _____.
(art)

5.   My brother likes all kinds of _____. He has a large collection
(music)
of _____ and _____.
(CD)                  (tape)

Fill in the blanks with an appropriate measurement of quantity. In some cases, several answers are possible.

EXAMPLE:   I bought a ___*loaf*___ of bread.

1.   I drank a _____ of tea.

2.   She drank a _____ of milk.

3.   I usually put a _____ of sugar in my coffee.

4.   There's a _____ of milk in the refrigerator.

5.   I'm going to buy a _____ of furniture for my living room.

6.   The teacher gave a long homework _____.

7.   My father gave me an important _____ of advice.

8.   I took three _____ of film on my vacation.

9.   I need a _____ of paper to write my composition.

10.   We need to buy a _____ of soap.

**Read this composition by an American Indian. Choose the correct words to complete the composition.**

My name is Joseph Falling Snow. I'm (*an*, *@*, *any*) Native American from a Sioux[9] reservation in South Dakota. I don't live in South Dakota anymore because I couldn't find (*a*, *any*, *no*) job. There's (*a little*, *a few*, *very little*, *very few*) work on my reservation. There's (*much*, *a lot of*, *many*) poverty. My uncle gave me (*a*, *an*, *some*, *any*) good advice. He told me to go to Minneapolis to find (*a*, *an*, *some*) job. Minneapolis is a big city, so there are (*much*, *many*, *any*) job opportunities here. It was easy for me to find a job as a carpenter. I had (*no*, *not*, *any*) trouble finding a job because I have (*a lot of*, *many*, *much*) experience.

My native language is Lakota, but I know (*any*, *a few*, *very few*) words in my language. Most of the people on my reservation speak English. (*A few*, *Any*, *A little*) older people still speak Lakota, but the language is dying out as the older people die.

(*A few*, *A little*, *Few*, *Little*) times a year, I go back to the reservation for a Pow-Wow. We wear our native costumes and dance our native dances. It gets very crowded at these times because (*much*, *any*, *a lot of*) people from our reservation and nearby reservations attend this celebration. We have (*much*, *many*, *a lot of*) fun.

[9] *Sioux* is pronounced /su/.

# EXPANSION ACTIVITIES

**CLASSROOM ACTIVITIES**

1. Work with a partner. Imagine that you have to spend a few weeks alone on a deserted island. You can take 15 things with you. What will you need to survive? Give reasons for each item.

**EXAMPLE:**
> I'll take a lot of water because I can't drink ocean water. It has salt in it.

2. Complete the following sentence in as many ways as you can. Compare your answers with a partner or in a small group.

Happiness is _____ .

**EXAMPLES:**
> Happiness is sleeping until ten o'clock in the morning.
> Happiness is helping an elderly person.
> Happiness is an air conditioner on a hot day.

3. Complete the following sentence in as many ways as you can. Compare your answers with a partner or in a small group.

Life is _____ .

**EXAMPLES:**
> Life is too short.
> Life is a gift.

4. Game: Where am I? Teacher: Write these words on separate index cards: at the airport, downtown, at the library, at a supermarket, at a department store, on the highway, at the zoo, at church, at the beach, at home, on an elevator, on a bus, on an airplane, at the post office, in the school cafeteria. Students: One student picks an index card with a place name and says, "Where am I?" Other students have to guess where he/she is by asking questions.

**EXAMPLES:**
> Are you indoors or outdoors?
> Are there a lot of cars in this place?
> Is it noisy in this place?
> Are there a lot of people in this place?

5. Find a partner. Take something from your purse, pocket, book bag, or backpack. Say, "I have _____ with me." Then ask your partner if he or she has this. If you're not sure if the item is a count or noncount noun, ask the teacher.

**EXAMPLES:**
> I have a comb in my pocket. Do you have a comb in your pocket?
> I have some makeup in my purse. Do you have any makeup in your purse?
> I have some money from my country in my pocket. Do you have any money from your country?

## DISCUSSION  Read the following quotes and discuss what they mean to you.

1. Once I was in a big city and I saw a very large house. They told me it was a bank and that the white men place their money there to be taken care of, and that by and by they got it back with interest. We are Indians and we have no such bank. When we have plenty of money or blankets, we give them away to other chiefs and people, and by and by they return them with interest, and our hearts feel good. Our way of giving is our bank.
    —Chief Maquinna, Nootka tribe

2. Treat the earth well. It was not given to you by your parents; it was loaned to you by your children.

3. "Today is a time of celebrating for you—a time of looking back to the first days of white people in America. But it is not a time of celebrating for me. It is with a heavy heart that I look back upon what happened to my people. When the Pilgrims arrived, we, the Wampanoags, welcomed them with open arms, little knowing that it was the beginning of the end. . . . Let us always remember, the Indian is and was just as human as the white people." From a speech by a Wampanoag Indian given on Thanksgiving in 1970 in Massachusetts, at the 350th anniversary of the Pilgrim's arrival in America.

## WRITING

1. Write about an ethnic minority in your native country. Where and how do they live? Use expressions of quantity.

2. Write a paragraph telling about the advantages or disadvantages of living in this city. You may write about pollution, job opportunities, weather, traffic, transportation, and crime. Use expressions of quantity.

## Internet Activities

1. Search for American Indian Web sites. Find the names and locations of three tribes.

2. Search for more information about the Pilgrims. Why did they leave England? Where did they go before coming to America?

## GRAMMAR
Adjectives
Noun Modifiers
Adverbs
*Too* and *Enough*

## CONTEXT
Exercise, Diet, and Weight
Overweight Children

## LESSON FOCUS

An adjective describes a noun.
> I ate an *excellent* dinner.

A noun can also describe a noun.
> I need a *soup* spoon.

An adverb describes a verb (phrase).
> They prepared the dinner *lovingly*.

We can use *too* and *enough* with adjectives, adverbs, and nouns.
> The soup is *too* hot to eat.
> The soup has *too* much salt.
> I don't have *enough* time to prepare dinner.

1. Do you ever eat at fast-food restaurants?
2. What kind of food commercials do you see on TV?

Read the following article. Pay special attention to adjectives, noun modifiers, and adverbs.

# Exercise, Diet, and Weight

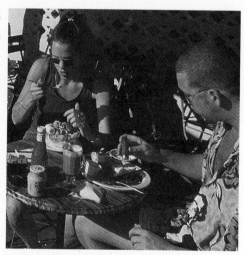

Americans are **concerned** about their weight. Everyone knows that it's important to eat **well** and exercise **regularly**. We see **beautiful, thin** fashion models and want to look like them. We see commercials for **exercise** machines showing **fit, thin** people exercising. **Health** clubs are full of people trying to get in shape. Sales of **diet** colas and low-calorie foods indicate that Americans want to be **thin**. However, 50 percent of Americans are **overweight**. Why is this so?

First, today's lifestyle does not include enough **physical** activity. When the U.S. was an agricultural society, farmers ate a **big, heavy** meal, but they burned off the calories by doing **hard physical** labor. Today, most people don't get enough exercise. Instead of walking, Americans drive almost everywhere, even when the trip is close to home. When people get home from work, they're usually too **tired** to exercise **regularly**. After dinner, they just watch TV. They have no chance to burn off calories.

Another reason why Americans don't lose weight is that they eat **poorly**. They are influenced by commercials and ads for **fatty** foods, **soft** drinks, candy, and **sugary** cereals that look **good**. Even though most people know that these foods aren't **healthy**, many don't have enough time to eat a **well-balanced** diet. It's **easy** to stop at a **fast-food** restaurant to pick up a **greasy** burger and fries. These foods are **high** in fat, carbohydrates, sodium, and calories. People eat them **quickly** and in **large** quantities—triple burgers, **extra-large** colas, **large** orders of fries.

Eating a high-fat diet and not getting enough exercise will result in **heart** disease for many people.

## Did you know...?

Thirty-five percent of the money Americans spend on food is spent outside the home.

| Examples | Explanation |
|---|---|
| We ate a **big** meal.<br>I don't like to eat **fatty** foods. | An adjective describes a noun. An adjective can come before a noun. |
| Fast food is **inexpensive**.<br>Models are **thin**.<br>You look **healthy**.<br>Burgers taste **delicious**. | An adjective can come after the verb *be* and the sense-perception verbs: *look, seem, sound, smell, taste, feel.* |
| Are you **concerned** about your weight?<br>I'm **tired** after work.<br>The health club is **located** near my house. | Some *-ed* words are adjectives: *tired, worried, crowded, located, married, divorced, excited, disappointed, finished, frightened.* |
| He did exercises and got **tired**.<br>I ran for three miles and got **thirsty**.<br>If you eat too much candy, you're going to **get** sick. | An adjective can follow *get* in these expressions: *get tired, get worried, get hungry, get sleepy, get thirsty, get married, get divorced, get sick, get angry.* In these expressions, *get* means *become.* |

## LANGUAGE NOTES

1. We do not make adjectives plural.
   | | |
   |---|---|
   | a *thin* model | *thin* models |
   | a *big* glass | *big* glasses |

2. *Very, quite,* and *extremely* can come before adjectives.
   You are *very* healthy.
   They are *extremely* tired.

3. Conversational words that come before adjectives are *pretty, sort of, kind of,* and *real.*
   I was *kind of* tired after work.
   We had a *real* delicious meal.
   I had a *pretty* hard day.

4. After an adjective, we can substitute a singular noun with *one* and a plural noun with *ones.*
   Do you want a big pizza or a small *one*?
   The first lessons were easy. The last *ones* are hard.

Fill in the blanks with an appropriate word.

EXAMPLE:   Burgers and fries are _____ *high* _____ in calories.

1.  Fries are cooked in oil. They are very _____.

2.  I ate a terrible meal and I got _____.

3.  Do you want a large cola or a small _____?

4.  She's very _____ about her children's health because they prefer candy to fruit.

5.  I didn't sleep at all last night. I'm very _____ today.

6.  Have a piece of fresh apple pie. I just had a piece. It _____ good.

EXERCISE 2   Find the mistakes with the underlined words and correct them. Not every sentence has a mistake. If the sentence is correct, write C.

EXAMPLE:   *excited*
I'm very ~~excite~~ about my trip to Italy.

He got sleepy while he was driving and had to stop.      C

1.  I didn't get enough sleep last night and I'm very tire today.

2.  She has two wonderfuls children and a great husband.

3.  This T-shirt is too small for me. I need a big.

4.  This turkey sandwich tastes quite good.

5.  When did you get marry?

6.  The park was very crowded.

7.  The park located near the lake.

8.  You look beautiful today.

## 6.2 Noun Modifiers

| Examples | Explanation |
|---|---|
| Do you have an **exercise machine**?<br><br>A **farm worker** gets a lot of exercise. Some people eat at a **fast-food restaurant**.<br><br>I joined a **health club**. | A noun can modify (describe) another noun. The second noun is more general than the first. An exercise machine is a machine. A leg exercise is an exercise. |
| I bought new **running** shoes.<br>Do you ever use the **swimming** pool? | Sometimes a gerund describes a noun. It shows the purpose of the noun. |
| My five-year-**old** son prefers candy to fruit.<br>**Potato** chips have a lot of grease.<br>My new shoes are in the **shoe** box. | The first noun is always singular. A five-year-old son is a son who is five **years** old. |
| Do you have your **driver's** license?<br>I can't understand the **owner's** manual for my new VCR. | Sometimes a possessive form describes a noun. |

## LANGUAGE NOTES

When a noun describes a noun, the first noun usually receives the greater emphasis in speaking. Listen to your teacher pronounce the following:

I wear my *running* shoes when I go to the *health* club and use the *exercise* machines.

---

**EXERCISE 3** Fill in the blanks by putting the words in parentheses ( ) in the correct order. Remember to remove the *s* from plural noun modifiers.

**EXAMPLES:** People need a ___winter coat___ in December.
<br>(coat/winter)

He bought a ___beautiful car.___
<br>(beautiful/car)

1. In the supermarket, we put our things in a _____
<br>(cart/shopping)

2. I need a _____ to stir my tea.
<br>(tea/spoon)

3. To fry eggs, you need a _____
<br>(pan/frying)

4. A _____ drives a taxi.
<br>(taxi/driver)

5. The school is closed during _____ .
   *(spring/break)*

6. She took a _____ .
   *(vacation/very/long)*

7. A _____ has a _____ .
   *(factory/worker)*          *(hard/job)*

8. Many _____ use robots.
   *(factories/automobiles)*

9. _____ buy their _____ at the _____ .
   *(college/students)*        *(books/text)*              *(store/books)*

10. I had a _____ with my boss.
    *(meeting/pretty/long)*

11. Some people prefer to shop in a _____ store.
    *(food/health)*

12. Does your building have a _____ ?
    *(swimming/pool)*

## 6.3 Adverbs of Manner

| Examples | Explanation |
|---|---|
| I choose my food **carefully**. Some people eat **poorly**. | An adverb of manner tells how or in what way a person does something. We form most adverbs of manner by putting *-ly* at the end of an adjective. |
| Do you eat **well**? | The adverb for *good* is *well*. |
| He worked **hard** and came home **late**. Don't eat so **fast**. | Some adverbs of manner do not end in *-ly*. The adjective and adverb are the same. |

## LANGUAGE NOTES

1. Some adjectives end in *-ly: lovely, early, friendly, lively, ugly, lonely.* They have no adverb form. We use an adverbial phrase to describe the action.

   She is a friendly person.
   She behaves *in a friendly manner.*
   He is a lively person.
   He danced *in a lively way.*

2. *Hard* and *hardly* are both adverbs, but they have completely different meanings.

   He worked very *hard.* = He put a lot of effort into his work.
   He *hardly* worked. = He did very little work.

3. *Late* and *lately* are both adverbs, but they have completely different meanings.

> He came home *late*. He missed dinner.
> *Lately*, he never comes home on time. (*Lately* means "recently.")

4. An adverb of manner usually follows the verb phrase.

> She ate her lunch *quickly*.
> You speak English *well*.

5. *Very*, *extremely*, and *quite* can come before an adverb.

> They work *very slowly*.
> She drives *extremely well*.
> You speak English *quite fluently*.

---

**EXERCISE 4**  Write the adverb form of the word in parentheses ( ). Then check (√) the activities that you do in this way. Make statements telling how you do these activities.

**EXAMPLES:**

√ shop ___carefully___
(careful)

I shop carefully. I always try to buy healthy food for my family.

___ dance ___well___
(good)

I don't dance well. I never learned.

1. ___ answer every question _____
(honest)

2. ___ drive _____
(fast)

3. ___ cook _____
(good)

4. ___ talk _____
(constant)

5. ___ work _____
(hard)

6. ___ study _____
(hard)

7. ___ speak Spanish _____
(fluent)

8. ___ type _____
(fast)

9. ___ type _____
(accurate)

10. ___ choose my food _____
(careful)

---

Adjectives; Noun Modifiers; Adverbs; *Too* and *Enough*  **169**

11. ____ live _____
     (dangerous)

12. ____ love _____
     (passionate)

13. ____ meditate _____
     (quiet)

14. ____ sleep _____
     (sound[1])

15. ____ learned a second language _____
     (easy)

16. ____ lived _____ in my country
     (comfortable)

## 6.4 Adjective vs. Adverb

| Adjective | Adverb |
| --- | --- |
| Jim looks **serious**.<br>(*Serious* describes Jim.) | Jim is looking at his mistakes **seriously**.<br>(*Seriously* tells how he is looking at his mistakes.) |
| The music sounds **good**.<br>(*Good* describes the music.) | The singer sings **well**.<br>(*Well* describes the singing.) |
| Your composition looks **good**.<br>(*Good* describes the composition.) | You wrote it **well**.<br>(*Well* describes how you wrote it.) |
| My father got **angry**.<br>(*Angry* describes my father.) | He spoke **angrily** to his children.<br>(*Angrily* tells how he spoke.) |

## LANGUAGE NOTES

1.  An adjective describes a noun. An adverb describes a verb (phrase).
2.  Use an adjective after the following verbs if you are describing the subject. Use an adverb if you are telling how the action (the verb) is done:

       smell       sound       seem       feel

       taste       look       appear

    She looks *happy*.
    She is looking at the contract *carefully*.

3.  Use an adjective, not an adverb, in expressions with *get*.
    He got *sleepy* after drinking a glass of warm milk.
    He got *hungry* after working all morning.

[1] When a person sleeps *soundly*, she doesn't wake up easily.

4. For health, use *well*.

   > He's sick. He doesn't look *well* today.

   In conversational English, people often use *good* for health.

   > He's sick. He doesn't look *good* today.

5. Use the adjective, not the adverb, in the expression *as usual*.
   COMPARE:

   > As *usual*, he worked last Saturday.
   > He *usually* works on Saturday.

6. An adverb can come before an adjective in phrases such as these:

   | | | |
   |---|---|---|
   | completely right | extremely important | pleasantly surprised |
   | well known | perfectly clear | absolutely wrong |

---

**EXERCISE 5**  Fill in the blanks with the correct form of the word—adjective or adverb.

Last week I had my first job interview in the U.S. I wanted to do
_____*well*_____. A _____ friend of mine told me about a
   *(good)*       *(1 good)*
résumé service. He told me that this service helps you prepare your résumé
_____. I wanted my résumé to look _____. I never
 *(2 careful)*          *(3 professional)*
wrote a résumé before, so I used this service. I wanted to have a
_____ résumé.
 *(4 perfect)*

A few days before the interview, I worked very _____ to
      *(5 hard)*
prepare answers to possible questions. The night before the interview, I chose
my clothes _____ and ironed them. I wanted to appear
    *(6 careful)*
_____. My friend told me that it's best to look _____,
 *(7 neat)*          *(8 conservative)*
so I chose my dark-blue suit. I went to bed _____, as
      *(9 early)*
_____, but I didn't sleep _____ because I was
 *(10 usual)*       *(11 good)*
_____.
 *(12 extreme/nervous)*

The interview was _____ because I had trouble answering
    *(13 difficult)*
many of the questions. The interviewer was _____, but she didn't
      *(14 friendly)*
speak _____. I couldn't understand her pronunciation. I could
 *(15 clear)*
_____ understand some of the questions.
 *(16 hard)*

I probably won't get this job. But it was _____ practice to
      *(17 good)*
have this interview. It prepared me _____ for the next interview.
    *(18 good)*

---

1. Do you see a lot of overweight children in the U.S.?
2. Do you think American children have a healthy lifestyle?

Read the following article. Pay special attention to *too* and *enough*.

# Overweight Children

In the United States, at least one in five children is overweight. Over the past 20 years, this number has increased by more than 50 percent. Why are so many children overweight?

First, many children don't get **enough** physical exercise. Only one-third of children who live within a mile of their school walk to school. When children get home from school, they spend **too much** time watching TV and playing video games. The average American child spends 24 hours a week watching TV. In addition, many children have unhealthy eating habits. Children eat **too much** food that is high in calories and fat. Eight percent of the calories children take in are from sodas.

Genetics is also a factor. Children with overweight parents may be at risk for becoming overweight. However, if families develop good eating and exercise habits early, they can prevent their children from becoming overweight.

## 6.5 *Too* and *Enough*

| *Too* + Adjective/Adverb<br>*Too* + *Much/Many* + Noun | Adjective/Adverb +<br>*Enough* | *Enough* + Noun |
|---|---|---|
| I'm **too tired** to exercise.<br>It's never **too late** to change your habits.<br>Children eat **too much food** that is high in calories.<br>They spend **too many hours** in front of the TV. | A diet of colas and burgers is not **good enough**.<br><br>I walked **quickly enough** to raise my heart rate. | Children don't get **enough exercise**.<br><br>I don't have **enough time** to exercise. |

## LANGUAGE NOTES

1. *Too* indicates a problem. The problem is stated or implied.

2. Put *too* before the adjective or adverb: *too old, too tired, too slowly, too dangerously.*

3. Use *too much* before noncount nouns. Use *too many* before count nouns.
   | | |
   |---|---|
   | *too much time* | *too many calories* |
   | *too much grease* | *too many sodas* |

4. *Too much* can come at the end of the sentence.
   He got sick because he ate *too much.*

5. Put *enough* after the adjective or adverb. Put *enough* before the noun.
   *old enough, tall enough, slowly enough*
   *enough money, enough time, enough books*

6. An infinitive phrase can follow a phrase with *too* and *enough.*
   He's too young *to understand* life.
   You're old enough *to drive.*

7. *Too good to be true* shows a positive surprised reaction.
   I just won a million dollars. It's *too good to be true.*

---

**EXERCISE 6**    Fill in the blanks to complete these statements.

**EXAMPLE:**    People drive everywhere. They don't _____*walk*_____ enough.

1. Children eat too _____, so they get fat.

2. Children shouldn't drink so much soda because it contains too many

   _____.

---

3. Most Americans don't get enough _____ .

4. Many people say, "I don't have enough _____ to do all the things I need to do."

5. Some students have too _____ responsibilities and can't handle all of them.

6. _____ takes too much time, so I rarely do it.

7. _____ costs too much, so I don't have one.

8. It's never too _____ to change your bad habits.

9. His clothes don't fit him anymore because he got too

   _____ .

10. You're never too old to _____ .

---

**EXERCISE 7** Read the conversation between a husband (H) and a wife (W). Fill in the blanks with *too* or *enough* plus the word in parentheses ( ).

H. I'm tired of my job. Let's retire and go live in Hawaii.

W. But we're only 57 years old. We're __*too young*__ to retire.
   (young)

H. I'd like to buy a very big house with a swimming pool.

W. But our house is _____ for us. Besides, we don't have
   (1 big)

   _____ for a bigger house.
   (2 money)

H. And I'd like to travel around the world.

W. But that's _____ .
   (3 expensive)

H. And I'd like our daughter to go with us.

W. She's 23 years old! She's _____ to make her own decisions.
   (4 old)

H. And I'd like to spend the next 50 years on a sailboat.

W. The next 50 years? You're kidding! We don't have _____ .
   (5 time)

   We're already 57 years old!

H. I'm just dreaming. You take me _____ .
   (6 seriously)

**EXERCISE 8**  Complete each statement with an infinitive.

**EXAMPLES:**   I'm too young ___*to retire*___ .

I'm not strong enough ___*to move a piano.*___

1.   I'm not too old _____ .

2.   I'm too young _____ .

3.   I'm not tall enough _____ .

4.   I have enough money _____ .

5.   I don't have enough time _____ .

6.   I don't speak English well enough _____ .

**EXERCISE 9**  Use the words given to write questions to ask another student. The other student will answer.

**EXAMPLES:**   old enough
*Are you old enough to retire soon?*

too tired
*Are you too tired to do the homework?*

1.   too busy _____

2.   too hard _____

3.   enough time _____

4.   strong enough _____

5.   enough experience _____

**EXERCISE 10**  Fill in the blanks with *too*, *too much*, or *too many*. A person is complaining about the big city where she lives.

**EXAMPLE:**   This city has ___*too much*___ crime.

1. It's _____ noisy.

2. It's _____ dirty.

3. There are _____ people.

4. There's _____ traffic.

5. There's _____ unemployment.

6. There's _____ pollution.

7. It's _____ big.

8. Life is _____ fast.

9. There are _____ problems.

10. Apartments are _____ expensive.

## 6.6 *Too* and *Very*

| Subject | Verb | *Very/Too* | Adjective/Adverb |
|---|---|---|---|
| My grandmother | is | **very** | old, but she's in great health. |
| My 14-year-old brother | is | **too** | old to get into the movie theater at half price. |
| I | was | **very** | tired, but I went to work. |
| I | was | **too** | tired to exercise after work. |
| She | drives | **very** | slowly. |
| She | drives | **too** | slowly for highway traffic. She might get a ticket. |

## LANGUAGE NOTES

Don't confuse *very* and *too*. *Too* always indicates a problem in a specific situation. The problem can be stated or implied. *Very* is a neutral word.

**EXERCISE 11** Fill in the blanks with *too* or *very*.

**EXAMPLES:** My sister is ___*very*___ beautiful.

I'm ___*too*___ short to touch the ceiling.

1. My grandfather is in _____ good health. He runs five miles a day.

2. I'm _____ sick to go to work today. I'll just stay in bed.

3. I can't believe I won first prize. It's _____ good to be true!

4. She found a great job. She's _____ happy.

5. She should be in an easier English class. This class is _____ hard for her.

6. That meal was delicious. You're a _____ good cook.

7. He is a _____ good person. He always helps his friends and neighbors.

8. My son is only six years old. He's _____ young to stay home alone.

9. Yesterday I saw a _____ beautiful sunset.

10. I can't reach those boxes on that shelf. It's _____ high for me.

1. Adjectives and Adverbs

| ADJECTIVES | ADVERBS |
|---|---|
| She has a **beautiful** voice. | She sings **beautifully**. |
| She has a **late** class. | She arrived **late**. |
| She is a **good** driver. | She drives **well**. |
| She looks **serious**. | She looked at the contract **seriously**. |
| As **usual**, she woke up early. | She **usually** wakes up early. |

2. Adjective Modifiers and Noun Modifiers

| ADJECTIVE MODIFIER | NOUN MODIFIER |
|---|---|
| a **new** machine | an **exercise** machine |
| **old** shoes | **running** shoes |
| a **short** vacation | a **two-week** vacation |
| a **valid** license | a **driver's** license |

3. *Very/Too/Enough/Too Much/Too Many*

He's **very** healthy.

He's **too** young to retire.

You're old **enough** to understand life.

I have **enough** money to take a vacation.

I can't go to the movies with you. I have **too much** homework.

She doesn't eat ice cream because it has **too many** calories.

One of my neighbors bothers me because she talks **too much**.

# EDITING ADVICE

1. Adjectives are always singular.

   I had two importants meetings last week.

2. Certain adjectives end with *-ed*.

   He was tire<sub>d</sub> after his trip.

3. Put an adjective before the noun.

   *very intelligent girl*
   She is a ~~girl very intelligent~~.

4. Use *one(s)* after an adjective to take the place of a noun.

   *one*
   He has an old dictionary. She has a new.

5. Put a specific noun before a general noun.

   She made a ~~call phone~~. *phone call*

6. A noun modifier is always singular.

   She took a three-week~~s~~ vacation.

7. An adverb describes a verb. An adjective describes a noun.

   The teacher speaks English fluent*ly*.

   The teacher looks serious~~ly~~.

8. Don't put the *-ly* adverb between the verb and the object.

   He opened (carefully) the envelope.

9. Adverbs of manner that don't end in *-ly* follow the verb phrase.

   He (late) came home.

10. *Too* indicates a problem. If there is no problem, use *very*.

    Your father is ~~too~~ *very* intelligent.

11. *Too much/too many* is followed by a noun. *Too* is followed by an adjective or adverb.

    She's too ~~much~~ old to take care of herself.

12. Put *enough* after the adjective.

    He's ~~enough old~~ *old enough* to get married.

13. Don't use *very* before a verb.

    He ~~very~~ likes his job *very much*.

14. Don't confuse *hard* and *hardly*.

    I'm tired. I worked hard~~ly~~ all day.

PART **1**          Find the mistakes with the underlined words, and correct them. Not every sentence has a mistake. If the sentence is correct, write **C**.

EXAMPLES:     When did you get your ~~license~~ driver's? *license*

He gets up early and walks the dog.     C

1.  Do you know where I can find the shoes department in this store?

2.  She doesn't feel well today.

3.  The language English is very different from my language.

4.  I'm very tire because I worked hard all week.

5.  Your answer seems wrongly.

6.  My grandfather is too much old to work.

7.  I don't like red apples. I like yellows ones.

8.  The singer's voice sounds sweet.

9.  I wrote carefully my name.

10.  She bought a car very expensive.

11.  I'm too happy to meet you.

12.  He stayed in the library late to finish his class project.

13.  She looked beautiful when she got marry.

14.  You speak English very fluently.

15.  He's not old enough to work.

16.  I like your new shoes very much.

17.  He hardly speaks a word of English. He just came to the U.S.

18.  She's going to take her driving test. She looks nervously.

19.  I'm completely surprised by the news of your marriage.

20.  I very like your new apartment.

Adjectives; Noun Modifiers; Adverbs; *Too* and *Enough*     **179**

21. If you spend <u>too much</u> time in front of the TV, you'll get fat.

22. You have <u>too many</u> friends. You're a lucky person.

**PART 2**    Fill in the blanks with the correct form, adjective or adverb, of the word in parentheses ( ).

EXAMPLES: She has _____*clear*_____ pronunciation. She pronounces very _____*clearly*_____.
                      *(clear)*                                              *(clear)*

1. You need to find time to eat _____. Don't eat food that is
                                    *(good)*

   _____ for you.
        *(bad)*

2. Don't drive _____. It's important to arrive _____.
                    *(fast)*                                      *(safe)*

3. I can't understand you. Could you speak more _____, please?
                                                      *(slow)*

4. Some people learn languages _____.
                                    *(easy)*

5. Some people think that math is _____, but it's
                                        *(hard)*

   _____ for me.
        *(easy)*

6. As _____, we will have a test at the end of the lesson.
        *(usual)*

7. She spoke _____, and I couldn't hear her _____.
                  *(soft)*                                    *(good)*

8. I need to learn English _____.
                                *(quick)*

9. Do you exercise _____ or are you _____?
                        *(regular)*                      *(lazy)*

10. You seem _____ today.
                  *(tired)*

11. I'm very _____.
                  *(busy)*

12. She works very _____, but she's _____ with her job.
                        *(hard)*                      *(happy)*

13. She is a _____ woman. She's very _____.
                  *(lovely)*                            *(friendly)*

14. John sounds _____, but he's not angry. He just talks
                      *(angry)*

    _____.
        *(loud)*

15. You speak English _____ well. You have _____
                            *(extreme)*                      *(perfect)*

    pronunciation. Everything you say is _____ _____.
                                              *(absolute)*      *(clear)*

**CLASSROOM ACTIVITIES**

1. Make a list of things that you ate in your native country that you don't eat in the U.S. Make a list of things that you eat in the U.S. that you didn't eat in your native country. Form a small group and compare your lists.

| Things I eat in the U.S. that I didn't eat before: | Things I ate in my native country that I don't eat now: |
|---|---|
|  |  |

2. Make a list of lifestyle changes for you and your family in the U.S. Find a partner from a different country, if possible. Compare your lists with your partner's lists. Which of these activities affect your health?

| Things I do (or don't do) in the U.S.: | Things I did (or didn't do) in my native country: |
|---|---|
| EXAMPLES: | EXAMPLES: |
| *I watch TV more often.* | *I hardly ever watched TV.* |
| *I shop once a week.* | *I shopped almost every day.* |
| *My children play with video games.* | *My children usually played outside.* |

3. Bad habits. Make a list of bad habits that you or someone in your family has.

**EXAMPLES:**    I don't get enough exercise.
My daughter talks on the phone too much.

4. Game: One student thinks of the name of a food. Other students try to guess what it is by asking questions.

> Sample questions:
> Is it a fruit?
> Is it soft?
> Do people eat it for breakfast?
> Is it good for your health?

5. Take something from your purse, pocket, or bag, but don't show it to anyone. Describe it. Another student will try to guess what it is.

6. Game: "In the manner of"
Teacher: Write these adverbs on separate pieces of paper or on index cards: gladly, suddenly, slowly, comfortably, simply, steadily, foolishly, efficiently, accurately, quietly, surprisingly, excitedly, promptly, fearlessly, fearfully, indecisively, carefully, carelessly, neatly, smoothly, repeatedly. Make sure the students know the meaning of each of these adverbs. Ask one student to leave the room. The other students pick one adverb. When the student returns to the room, he/she asks individuals to do something by giving imperatives. The others do this task in the manner of the adverb that was chosen. The student tries to guess the adverb.

**EXAMPLES:**

> Edgar, write your name on the blackboard.
> Sofia, take off one shoe.
> Maria, open the door.
> Elsa, walk around the room.
> Nora, give me your book.

7. In some colleges, students evaluate teachers. Work with a partner and write an evaluation form for teachers at this college or for another profession you are familiar with.

**EXAMPLES:**

|  | Strongly Agree | Agree | Disagree | Strongly Disagree |
|---|---|---|---|---|
| 1. Begins class promptly. |  |  |  |  |
| 2. Treats students with respect. |  |  |  |  |
| 3. Explains assignments clearly. |  |  |  |  |

1. In a small group or with the entire class, discuss what kind of food you usually eat. Do you think people eat healthful food in your native culture?

2. Americans often say, "You are what you eat." What do you think this means?

**WRITING**

1. Think of a place in this city (a museum, a government office, a park, a shopping center, the airport, etc.). Write a brief description of this place.

2. Write a paragraph about your hometown (or a specific place in your hometown). Use descriptions.

3. Write a short composition comparing food in your native country to food in the U.S.

4. Write a short composition telling how your eating and exercise habits are different in the U.S.

## Internet Activities

1. In a search engine, type in "food guide pyramid" to see what the U.S. Department of Agriculture recommends as a healthy daily diet. Or you can find the pyramid and more information about food by going to the U.S. Department of Agriculture Web site. Fill out the form called "How to Rate Your Diet." Bring a copy of the pyramid to class.

2. At a search engine, type in "height weight." Find a copy of a height/weight chart. Print it. See if you are the right weight for your height.

3. Find a conversion chart from the metric system to the English system. See how much you weigh in pounds.

# Lesson Seven

## GRAMMAR
Time Words and Time Clauses
The Past Continuous Tense

## CONTEXT
Ellis Island
Albert Einstein

## LESSON FOCUS

We use time words to introduce words and clauses of time.

I studied German *for* ten years.
I studied German *when* I lived in my country.

We use the past continuous tense to show the relationship of a longer past action to a shorter past action.

She *was driving* to work when she had a flat tire.
I *was climbing* a tree when I fell and broke my arm.

Ellis Island, New York

1.  Are you the first member of your family to come to the U.S.?
2.  How did you or your family come to the U.S.?
3.  Was the process of entering the country difficult for you? How was it difficult?

Read the following article. Pay special attention to time words.

# Ellis Island

**For** many years, Ellis Island, an island in New York harbor, was the main door through which millions of immigrants entered the United States. **From** the time it opened **in** 1892 **until** the time it closed **in** 1924, the U.S. Bureau of Immigration used Ellis Island to receive and process new arrivals. **During** this time, 12 million foreigners passed through this door with the hope of becoming Americans. They came from Italy, Poland, Russia, Germany, China, and many other countries. Sometimes more than 10,000 people passed through the registry room in one 24-hour period. New arrivals often waited **for** many hours **while** inspectors checked to see if they met legal and medical standards. Most did not speak English, and they were tired, hungry, and confused. Two percent (250,000 people) did not meet the requirements to enter the U.S. and had to return to their countries.

**After** Congress passed an immigration law that limited the number and nationality of new immigrants, immigration slowed down and Ellis Island was closed as an immigration processing center. It remained abandoned **until** 1965, **when** President Lyndon Johnson decided to restore it as a monument. Restoration of Ellis Island was finished **by** 1990. Now visitors to this monument can see the building as it looked **from** 1918 **to** 1920. In addition, they can see a wall with the names of many of those who passed through on their way to becoming American citizens.

## Did you know...?

The largest number of immigrants in the U.S. between 1820 and 1996 came from Germany. The largest number between 1991 and 1996 came from Mexico.

## 7.1    *When, While, Until*

| Examples | Explanation |
| --- | --- |
| **When** my grandfather arrived, he passed through Ellis Island. | *When* means "at that time" or "after that time." *Until* means "before that time." |
| **Until** he came to the U.S., he lived in Poland. | |
| Ellis Island was closed **until** 1990. | |
| **When** it opened, visitors could see the history of immigration. | |

*(continued)*

| Examples | Explanation |
|---|---|
| New arrivals waited **while** inspectors checked their documents.<br>**While** they waited, they were often tired, confused, and hungry. | *While* means "during that time." |

## LANGUAGE NOTES

We can sometimes use *when* in place of *while*.

> *While* (or *when*) he was on the ship coming to America, he thought about his uncertain future.
> *While* (or *when*) I was in Paris, I studied French.

**EXERCISE 1**    Fill in the blanks with *when, while,* or *until*. In some cases, more than one answer is possible.

**EXAMPLE:**    My grandfather came to the U.S. ____*when*____ he was 25 years old.

1. _____ he lived in Poland, he had a hard life.

2. _____ he left Poland, he didn't speak English at all.

3. _____ he was at Ellis Island, he had to wait for hours. He was nervous _____ he waited.

4. He was nervous _____ he got permission to enter the country. Then he felt more relaxed.

5. _____ he passed the inspection, he entered the country.

6. In Poland, he didn't study English. He didn't speak a word of English _____ he started to work in the U.S. Then he learned a little.

7. _____ he worked, he saved money to bring his wife and children to America.

8. My grandmother couldn't come to the U.S. _____ my grandfather had enough money to send for her and their children.

9. My grandfather lived in the U.S. _____ he died in 1968.

**EXERCISE 2**  Add a main clause to complete each statement.

**EXAMPLE:**  Before I got to class today, _I finished all my homework._

1. While I was in high school, _____

2. When I finished high school, _____

3. When I left my country, _____

4. Until I came to this city/school, _____

5. When I arrived in the U.S., _____

6. Until I came to America, _____

**EXERCISE 3**  Finish the time expression to complete each statement.

**EXAMPLE:**  I stayed in my country until _a civil war broke out._

1. I decided to come to the U.S. when _____

2. I found my apartment/house after _____

3. I enrolled in this English class after _____

4. I didn't understand English until _____

5. I got married/found a job/bought a car (*choose one*) when _____

**EXERCISE 4**  Name something you never . . . until you came to the U.S.

**EXAMPLE:**  Name something you never had.
I never had a car until I came to the U.S.

1. Name something you never did.

2. Name something or someone you never heard of.

3. Name something you never saw.

4. Name something you never thought about.

5. Name something you never had.

6. Name something you never ate.

7. Name something you never knew.

## 7.2  *When* and *Whenever*

| Examples | Explanation |
| --- | --- |
| **When** she read the book, she learned a lot about American history. | *When* means "at that time" or "after that time." |
| **Whenever** she reads, she uses glasses. | *Whenever* means any time or every time. |

# LANGUAGE NOTES

With the general present, *when* and *whenever* have about the same meaning.

> *Whenever* I have free time, I like to play tennis.
> *When* I have free time, I like to play tennis.

---

**EXERCISE 5**   Add a main clause to complete each statement. Use the general present.

**EXAMPLE:**   Whenever I take a test, _____ *I feel nervous.* _____

1. Whenever I feel sad or lonely, _____

2. Whenever I get angry, _____

3. Whenever I need advice, _____

4. Whenever I receive a present, _____

5. Whenever I get a letter from my family, _____

6. Whenever I'm sick, _____

7. Whenever the weather is bad, _____

8. Whenever the teacher explains the grammar, _____

_____

---

**EXERCISE 6**   Finish each sentence with a time clause.

**EXAMPLES:**   I feel nervous _____ *before I take a test.* _____
I feel nervous _____ *whenever I have to speak in class.* _____

1. I feel relaxed _____

2. I get angry _____

3. I get bored _____

4. I can't concentrate _____

5. I'm happy _____

6. I'm in a bad mood _____

7. I sometimes daydream[1] _____

8. Time passes quickly for me _____

---

[1] To *daydream* means to dream while you are awake. Your mind does not stay in the present moment.

## 7.3 *For, In, During, By, Ago*

| Time Word | Examples | Explanation |
|---|---|---|
| for | My grandfather waited at Ellis Island **for** many hours. | *For* tells how long. |
| in | Ellis Island closed **in** 1924.<br><br>I'll go back to my country **in** two years.<br><br>He finished the test **in** ten minutes. | Use *in* with a specific year or month.<br><br>Use *in* to mean after or within a period of time. |
| during | He thought about his future **during** his trip to the U.S.<br><br>**During** his interview, he answered many questions. | Use *during* with an activity. |
| by | Restoration of Ellis Island was finished **by** 1990.<br><br>Please finish the test **by** 8:30. | *By* means no later than. |
| ago | One hundred years **ago**, new arrivals passed through Ellis Island. | *Ago* means before now. |

## LANGUAGE NOTES

1. Compare *before* and *ago*.
   She got married *before* she graduated.
   She got married three years *ago*.

2. Compare *during* and *for*.
   She fell asleep *during* the movie.
   She slept *for* two hours.

3. Compare *after* and *in*.
   I'll come back *in* an hour.
   I'll come back *after* I go to the post office.

4. Compare *before* and *by*.
   I have to return my library books *before* Friday. (Friday is not included.)
   I have to return my library books *by* Friday. (Friday is included.)

---

**EXERCISE 7** Choose the the correct time word to fill in the blanks.

**EXAMPLE:** He lived with his parents (*during* (*until*) *by*) he was 19 years old.

1. (*When* *During* *Whenever*) he was a child, he lived with his grandparents.

2. (*During* *For* *While*) several years, he lived with his grandparents.

3. (*For   While   During*) his childhood, he lived with his grandparents.

4. (*While   Until   When*) he got married, he lived with his grandparents. Then he found an apartment with his wife.

5. (*Whenever   While   When*) he was ten years old, his grandparents gave him a bike.

6. (*While   During   Whenever*) he was in elementary school, he lived with his grandparents.

7. She worked for her father (*during   while   whenever*) she was in college.

8. She worked for her father (*for   during   while*) her free time.

9. She worked for her father (*during   whenever   when*) she was single.

10. She worked for her father (*for   during   while*) three years.

11. She worked for her father full time (*while   when   during*) her summer vacation.

12. She worked for her father (*when   until   while*) she got married. Then she quit her job to take care of her husband and children.

13. She worked for her father 12 years (*before   ago   after*).

14. (*Until   Whenever   During*) her husband needs help in his business, she helps him out.

15. She can't help you now. She's busy. She'll help you (*by   ago   in*) an hour.

16. Please finish this exercise (*by   in   until*) 8:30.

17. Please finish this exercise (*by   before   until*) you go home. The teacher wants it today.

18. Please finish this exercise (*in   after   by*) ten minutes.

19. He'll retire (*after   in   by*) two years.

20. He'll retire (*when   while   until*) he's sixty-five years old.

21. He'll work (*when   while   until*) he's sixty-five years old. Then he'll retire.

22. I'm not going to eat dinner (*when   while   until*) my wife gets home. Then we'll eat together.

---

Time Words and Time Clauses; The Past Continuous Tense    **191**

| Examples | Explanation |
|---|---|
| In 1998, I **was living** in the U.S. <br> In 1998, my parents **were living** in the Ecuador. | To form the past continuous tense, we use *was* or *were* + verb-*ing*. <br> I, he, she, it → *was* <br> you, we, they → *were* |
| In 1998, I **wasn't living** in my country. <br> My parents **weren't living** with me. | To form the negative, put *not* after *was* or *were*. The contraction for *was not* is *wasn't*. The contraction for *were not* is *weren't*. |

**Before You Read**

1. What famous immigrants to the U.S. do you know?
2. Did anyone from your native culture become famous in the U.S.?

Read the following article. Pay special attention to past continuous and simple past tense verbs.

# Albert Einstein

Of the many immigrants who came to the U.S., one will always be remembered throughout the world: Albert Einstein. Einstein changed our understanding of the universe. When people think of the word "genius," Einstein's name often comes to mind. However, in Einstein's early years, he was not successful in school or at finding a job.

**Did you know...?**

After Einstein died, Princeton University kept his brain in a jar to study how the brain of a genius is different from an ordinary brain.

Einstein was born in Germany in 1879 of Jewish parents. He loved math and physics, but he disliked the discipline of formal German schooling. Because of his poor memory for words, his teachers believed that he was a slow learner. Einstein left school before receiving his diploma and tried to pass the exam to enter the Swiss Polytechnic Institute, but he failed on his first attempt. On his second attempt, he passed. He graduated in 1900. He **was planning** to become a teacher of physics and math, but he could not find a job in this field. Instead, he went to work in a patent office as a third class technical expert from 1902 to 1909. While he **was working** at this job, he **wrote** in his spare time. In 1905, when he was only 26 years old, he published three papers that explained the basic structure of the universe. His theory of relativity explained the relationship of space and time. Einstein was finally respected for his brilliant discovery. He returned to Germany to accept a research position at the University of Berlin. However, in 1920, while he **was lecturing** at the university, anti-Jewish groups often **interrupted** his lectures, saying they were "un-German."

In 1920, Einstein visited the United States for the first time. During his visits, he talked not only about his scientific theories, but also about world peace. While he **was visiting** the U.S. again in 1933, the Nazis **came** to power in Germany. They took his property, burned his books, and removed him from his university job. The U.S. offered Einstein a home. In 1935, he became a permanent resident of the U.S., and in 1940, he became a citizen. He received many offers of jobs from all over the world, but he decided to accept a position at Princeton University in New Jersey. He lived and worked there until he died in 1955.

## 7.5 The Past Continuous Tense—Forms

Compare statements, questions, and short answers using the past continuous tense.

| Wh-Word | Was/Wasn't Were/Weren't | Subject | Was/Wasn't Were/Weren't | -ing Form | Complement | Short Answer |
|---|---|---|---|---|---|---|
| | | Einstein | **was** | **living** | in the U.S. | |
| | | He | **wasn't** | **living** | in Germany. | |
| | **Was** | he | | **living** | in New Jersey? | Yes, he **was**. |
| Where | **was** | he | | **living?** | | |
| Why | **wasn't** | he | | **living** | in Germany? | |
| | | Who | **was** | **living** | in Germany? | |

Fill in the blanks with the correct form.

EXAMPLE: In 1889, Einstein was ____*studying*____ in the Swiss Polytechnic Institute.

1. Einstein _____ plan_____ to become a teacher.

2. He _____ _____ to become a doctor.

3. In 1907, he _____ _____ in a patent office.

4. In 1933, he was _____ the U.S.

5. What _____ he do_____ in the U.S.?

6. _____ he planning to go back to Germany? Yes, he _____.

7. Where _____ you _____ in January, 1999?

8. _____ you sleep_____ at midnight last night?
   No, I _____ .

9. Why_____ _____ sleeping? I wasn't sleeping because I wasn't tired.

10. Who _____ _____ TV at 9:15 last night?

## 7.6 The Past Continuous Tense—Uses

| Examples | Explanation |
|---|---|
| Einstein **was working** in a patent office in 1905. | We use the past continuous tense to show what was in progress at a specific moment in the past.<br><br>1905<br>↓<br>←- - - - -x- - - - - -↑ - - - - - - →<br>⎣ was working ⎦ |
| Einstein **was living** in Switzerland when he **developed** his theory of relativity.<br>While Einstein **was visiting** the U.S., the Nazis **took** his property.<br>Einstein **was living** in New Jersey when he **died**. | We use the past continuous tense with the simple past to show the relationship of a longer past action to a shorter past action.<br><br>developed<br>↓<br>←- - - - - -x- - - - - -↑ - - - - →<br>⎣ was living ⎦ |

## LANGUAGE NOTES

1. You can show the relationship of a longer past action to a shorter past action two ways:

- Use *when* + the simple past with the shorter action.
- Use *while* + the past continuous with the longer action.

COMPARE:

Einstein was living in Switzerland *when* he *developed* his theory of relativity.

Einstein developed his theory of relativity *while* he *was living* in Switzerland.

2. If the time clause precedes the main clause, separate the two clauses with a comma.

| MAIN CLAUSE | TIME CLAUSE |
|---|---|
| He was living in New Jersey | when he died. |

| TIME CLAUSE | MAIN CLAUSE |
|---|---|
| While he was living in New Jersey, | he worked at Princeton University. |

3. In a question with two clauses, only the verb in the main clause is in a question form.

Where *was Einstein living* when the Nazis *took* his home?

4. We don't use the continuous form with the verb *be*, but it can have a continuous meaning.

While she *was* at work, her husband called.

While Einstein *was* in Switzerland, he developed his theory.

---

EXERCISE **9**  Tell if the following things were happening in January, 1999.

EXAMPLE:  go to school
I was (not) going to school in January, 1999.

1. work
2. go to school
3. study English

4. live in the U.S.
5. live with my parents

---

EXERCISE **10** Ask a question with "What were you doing?" at these specific times. Another student will answer.

EXAMPLE:  at 6 o'clock this morning
A. What were you doing at 6 o'clock this morning?
B. I was sleeping.

1. at 10 o'clock last night
2. at 4 o'clock this morning
3. at 5 o'clock yesterday afternoon

4. at this time yesterday
5. at this time last year[2]

---

[2] *At this time last year* does not refer to a specific hour, but is very general.

---

**EXERCISE 11** Decide which of these two verbs has longer action. Fill in the correct tense (simple past or past continuous) of the verb in parentheses ( ) and *when* or *while*.

**EXAMPLES:**  She ___*was taking*___ a shower ___*when*___ the telephone ___*rang*___.
(take)                                    (ring)

It ___*started*___ to rain ___*while*___ I ___*was walking*___ to
(start)                        (walk)
school.

1. _____ the teacher _____ on the blackboard,
(write)

   she _____ the chalk.
   (drop)

2. He _____ and _____ his arm _____
   (fall)              (break)

   he _____ a tree.
   (climb)

3. Mary _____ in a department store _____ she
   (shop)

   _____ her purse.
   (lose)

4. I _____ my homework _____ my friend
   (do)

   _____ over.
   (come)

5. She _____ her husband _____ she _____
   (meet)                                    (attend)
   college.

6. _____ I _____ to work, I _____
   (drive)                        (run)
   out of gas.[3]

7. _____ he _____ at the airport, his friends
   (arrive)

   _____ for him.
   (wait)

8. They _____ dinner _____ someone
   (eat)

   _____ on the door.
   (knock)

9. _____ I _____ a test, my pencil point
   (take)

   _____.
   (break)

10. The baby _____ me _____ I _____
    (interrupt)                      (talk)
    to a friend.

[3] To *run out of* means to use up everything.

11. I _____ my tooth _____ I _____
       (break)                                    (eat)
    a nut.

12. I _____ an old friend _____ I _____
       (meet)                                    (walk)
    in the park.

13. She _____ dinner _____ the smoke alarm
          (cook)

    _____ off.[4]
       (go)

14. He _____ snow _____ he _____
        (shovel)                         (lose)
    his glove.

15. I _____ a fuse _____
       (blow)

    I _____ .
       (iron)

16. She _____ _____ the baby
          (sleep)

    _____ to cry.
       (start)

17. She _____ her favorite plate _____ she
         (break)

    _____ the dishes.
       (wash)

fuse

---

**EXERCISE 12** Fill in the blanks with the simple past or the past continuous form of the verb in parentheses ( ) in the following conversations.

**Conversation 1**, between a wife (W) and husband (H)

W.  Look what I found today! Your favorite watch!

H.  Where ___*did you find*___ it?
            (example: find)

W.  In your top drawer. I _____ away your socks when
                            (1 put)

    I _____ it.
       (2 find)

H.  I wonder how it got there.

W.  Probably while you _____ something in that drawer,
                          (3 put)

    it _____ off your wrist.
       (4 fall)

---

[4] When an alarm *goes off*, it starts to sound.

**Conversation 2**, between a wife (W) and husband (H)

H. What happened? I _____ TV when I _____
$\quad$ (1 watch) $\hspace{5.5cm}$ (2 hear)
$\quad$ a loud crash in the kitchen.

W. I _____ to get something off the top shelf when
$\quad$ (3 try)

$\quad$ I _____ a vase.
$\quad\quad$ (4 drop)

H. Why didn't you ask me to help you?

W. You _____ TV, and I _____ to disturb
$\quad\quad$ (5 watch) $\hspace{4cm}$ (6 not/want)
$\quad$ you.

**Conversation 3**, between a son (S) and mother (M)

S. I _____ through some old boxes when
$\quad$ I
$\quad$ (1 look) $\hspace{5cm}$ _____
$\hspace{8cm}$ (2 find)
$\quad$ this picture of you and Dad when you were young. By the way,

$\quad$ how _____ you _____ Dad?
$\quad\quad\quad$ (3 meet)

M. One day I _____ in the park when he _____
$\hspace{3.5cm}$ (4 walk) $\hspace{5cm}$ (5 stop)

$\quad$ me to ask what time it was. We _____ to talk, and then
$\hspace{7cm}$ (6 start)

$\quad$ he _____ me to go out with him.
$\quad\quad$ (7 ask)

S. Did you get married right away?

M. No. At that time, there was a war going on. We _____ for
$\hspace{10.5cm}$ (8 date)

$\quad$ about five months when he _____ drafted.[5] He had to
$\hspace{6cm}$ (9 get)

$\quad$ serve in the army. While he _____ in the army,
$\hspace{7cm}$ (10 serve)

$\quad$ he _____ me a beautiful letter. He asked me to marry
$\quad\quad$ (11 write)
$\quad$ him as soon as he returned from military service.

S. Did you marry him when he _____ home?
$\hspace{7cm}$ (12 get)

M. Not right away. When he _____ home, I _____
$\hspace{5.5cm}$ (13 come) $\hspace{4cm}$ (14 study)

$\quad$ at the university, and I wanted to graduate first. We _____
$\hspace{11cm}$ (15 get)

$\quad$ married ten days after my graduation.

[5] When a person *gets drafted,* the government chooses him to serve in the military.

| Was/Were going to (THE PLAN) | but . . . (WHY THE PLAN DIDN'T HAPPEN) |
|---|---|
| Einstein **was going to** return to Germany, | but the Nazis came to power. |
| I **was going to** buy a new car, | but I lost my job. |
| I **was going to** call you, | but I lost your phone number. |

## LANGUAGE NOTES

We use *was/were going to* + the base form to describe a plan that we didn't carry out. It means the same thing as *was/were planning to*.

> I *was going to* call you, but I lost your phone number.
> I *was planning to* call you, but I lost your phone number.

**EXERCISE 13** Fill in the blanks to tell what prevented a plan from happening.

**EXAMPLE:** I was going to call you, but ___*I got busy and forgot about it.*___

1. We were going to have a picnic, but _____

   _____

2. I was going to finish that book last night, but _____

   _____

3. We were going to buy a house, but _____

   _____

4. They were going to leave for vacation on Monday, but _____

   _____

5. She was going to marry her boyfriend, but _____

   _____

6. They were going to drive to Canada, but _____

   _____

7. I was going to cook dinner, but _____

   _____

| Examples | Explanation |
|---|---|
| (A) She **was eating** dinner when he arrived. | In sentence (A), the man's arrival happened during the time of the woman's dinner. |
| (B) She **ate** dinner when he arrived. | In sentence (B), the woman ate dinner after the arrival of the man. |
| (C) Einstein **was living** in the U.S. when he died.<br><br>(D) Einstein **lived** in the U.S. when he lost his German citizenship. | In sentence (C), his death occurred during the time he was living in the U.S.<br><br>In sentence (D), he started to live in the U.S. after he lost his German citizenship. |
| (E) While my son **did** his homework, I **cooked** dinner.<br><br>(F) While my son **was doing** his homework, I **was cooking** dinner. | *While* can connect two past actions that happened in the same time period. You can use either the simple past (E) or the past continuous (F) in both clauses. |

**EXERCISE 14** A fable is an old story that teaches us a lesson about life. Fables often use animals to represent people. Here is a fable about an ant and a grasshopper. Fill in the blanks with the past or past continuous of the verb in parentheses ( ) to complete this story. In some cases, you may use either tense.

grasshopper

ant

During the summer, the ant ___was working (or worked)___ very hard
(work)

trying to gather the food that she would need for the long, cold winter. While

the ant _____, her neighbor, the grasshopper, _____
         (1 work)                                                      (2 have)

a good time. He _____ and _____ himself all summer.
                   (3 sing)          (4 enjoy)

When winter _____, the ant had plenty of food to eat. However,
               (5 come)

the grasshopper _____ nothing to eat. The grasshopper _____
                   (6 have)                                        (7 go)

to the ant's house one day to ask for food. The ant _____
                                                        (8 prepare)

a delicious meal when he _____ the grasshopper knock on the door.
                            (9 hear)

When she _____ the door, the grasshopper _____,
            (10 open)                                   (11 say)

"Please give me some food." The ant asked him, "What _____ you

_____ all summer while I _____?" The grasshopper
   (12 do)                         (13 work)

_____, "I _____ all summer." "Then go and dance now,"
   (14 reply)           (15 sing)

the ant _____ him.
           (16 tell)

## 7.9   Time with Present Participles

### Examples

Einstein left high school **before he finished** his studies.
Einstein left high school **before finishing** his studies.
**After Einstein left** high school, he studied mathematics and physics.
**After leaving** high school, Einstein studied mathematics and physics.

## LANGUAGE NOTES

When the main clause and the time clause have the same subject, we can delete the subject of the time clause and use a present participle (verb + *-ing*.)

EXERCISE **15**  Change these sentences. Use a present participle after the time word.

EXAMPLE:     After ~~Einstein entered~~ the university, ~~he~~ developed his theory.
                        *entering*                        *Einstein*

1.   Einstein passed an exam before he entered the university.

2.   He left high school before he received his diploma.

3.   After Einstein developed his theory of relativity, he became famous.

4. He became interested in physics after he received books on science.

5. After Einstein came to the U.S., he got a job at Princeton.

6. Before you begin a test, you should read the instructions carefully.

7. You shouldn't talk to another student while you are taking a test.

8. After children finish kindergarten, they go to first grade.

# SUMMARY OF LESSON 7

1. Time Words

| Time Word | Examples |
|---|---|
| When | **When** immigrants came to America, they passed through Ellis Island. |
| While | They waited **while** inspectors checked their health. |
| Until | Ellis Island remained closed **until** 1990. |
| Before | **Before** 1920, many immigrants came to America. |
| After | **After** 1920, Congress limited the number of immigrants. |
| From . . . to | **From** 1892 **to** 1924, Ellis Island was an immigrant processing center. |
| During | **During** this time, 12 million immigrants passed through Ellis Island. |
| For | New arrivals had to wait **for** hours. |
| In | **In** 1905, Einstein wrote about relativity. |
| | We will finish the test **in** an hour. |
| By | Restoration of Ellis Island was finished **by** 1990. |
| Ago | One hundred years **ago**, new arrivals passed through Ellis Island. |

2. Uses of the past continuous tense:
   A. To describe a past action that was in progress at a specific moment:
      He **was sleeping** at 6 o'clock this morning.
      Where **were** you **living** in December 1991?
   B. With the past tense, to show the relationship of a longer past action to a shorter past action:
      He **was sleeping** when the telephone **rang**.
      While she **was eating** lunch in the park, it **started** to rain.
      Martin Luther King, Jr., **was standing** on the balcony of a motel when a man **shot** and **killed** him.
   C. To show past intentions:
      I **was going to call** you, but I lost your phone number.
      She **was going to cook** dinner, but she didn't have time.

1.  Put the subject before the verb in all clauses.

    *the teacher entered*
    When ~~entered the teacher~~, the students stood up.

2.  Use *when*, not *while*, if the action has no duration.

    *When*
    ~~While~~ she spilled the milk, she started to cry.

3.  Don't confuse *during* and *for*.

    *for*
    He watched TV ~~during~~ 3 hours.

4.  Don't confuse *until* and *when*.

    *when*
    She will eat dinner ~~until~~ her husband comes home.

5.  Don't confuse *before* and *ago*.

    *ago*
    They came to the U.S. three years ~~before~~.

6.  After a time word, use an *-ing* form, not a base form.

    *finding*
    After ~~find~~ a job, he bought a car.

## LESSON 7 TEST / REVIEW

**PART 1**    Find the mistakes with the underlined words, and correct them. Not every sentence has a mistake. If the sentence is correct, write C.

**EXAMPLES:**   She came to the U.S. two weeks ~~before~~. *ago*

While I <u>was walking</u> in the park, I saw my friend.     C

1.  When he arrived, he <u>ate</u> dinner with his family.

2.  After <u>leaving</u> my country, I went to Thailand.

3.  When <u>arrived the teacher</u>, the students had a test.

4.  I graduated <u>until</u> I finished all my courses.

5.  While she <u>was washing</u> the dishes, she dropped the glass.

---

Time Words and Time Clauses; The Past Continuous Tense    **203**

6. <u>While</u> she dropped the glass, it broke.

7. He studied English <u>until</u> he became fluent.

8. She served dinner <u>when</u> her guests arrived.

9. Einstein lived in the U.S. <u>until he died</u>.

10. They went home <u>until</u> the movie was over.

11. I'll be back <u>in</u> ten minutes.

12. <u>During</u> three weeks, he was on vacation.

13. Please return your library books <u>by</u> Friday.

14. She found a job three weeks <u>before</u>.

15. He was sick <u>for</u> a week.

16. I ate dinner an hour <u>ago</u>.

17. Einstein was in the U.S. <u>during</u> the Second World War.

18. I <u>was going to</u> call you, but I lost your phone number.

**PART 2**    Fill in the blanks with the simple past or the past continuous form of the verb in parentheses ( ).

**EXAMPLE:** He ___*was walking*___ to his car when he ___*lost*___ his glove.
    (walk)                            (lose)

1. What _____ at 4 p.m. yesterday afternoon? I tried
        (you/do)
   to call you, but you weren't home.

2. She _____ in Paris when the war _____ .
        (live)                              (start)

3. I _____ your necklace while I _____ for my
       (find)                              (look)
   watch.

4. She _____ a house three years ago.
        (buy)

5. He _____ his wife while he _____ in a restaurant.
       (meet)                          (work)

6. When my grandfather _____ to America, he _____
                        (come)                              (find)
   a job in a factory.

7. When he _____ at Ellis Island, his uncle _____
            (arrive)                                  (wait)
   for him.

8. While she _____ the computer, it _____.
   (use)                                    (crash)

9. He _____ dinner when the fire _____.
   (cook)                                  (start)

10. I _____ my car and _____ to the radio
    (drive)                     (listen)
    when I _____ that John F. Kennedy, Jr. died.
           (hear)

PART 3 Fill in the blanks with an appropriate time word. Choose *when,*
*whenever, while, until, before, after, by, ago, in, for,* or *during.*
In some cases, more than one answer is possible.

EXAMPLE: I will continue to work ___*until*___ I am 65 years old. Then I will retire.

1. _____ it snows, there are a lot of traffic accidents.

2. I was walking to my friend's house _____ it started to rain. I
   was glad I had my umbrella with me.

3. _____ I was driving to school, I was listening to the radio.

4. _____ I finished my homework last night, I watched the news
   on TV.

5. I got my visa _____ coming to the U.S.

6. He must stay in his country _____ he gets permission to come
   to the U.S.

7. _____ he dropped his glasses, they broke.

8. We have to finish this lesson _____ 10 o'clock.

9. He found a job two months _____.

10. He found a job three weeks _____ coming to the U.S.

11. He found a job _____ April.

12. It's 7:50. The movie will begin _____ ten minutes at 8:00.

13. _____ the movie began, everyone became quiet.

14. _____ she was watching the sad movie, she started to cry.

15. Einstein was 61 years old _____ he became a U.S. citizen.

16. Einstein lived in the U.S. _____ 22 years.

# EXPANSION ACTIVITIES

## CLASSROOM ACTIVITIES

1. Check (√) what was true for you before coming to the U.S. Find a partner and compare your list to your partner's list. Discuss any related information.

EXAMPLE:

_√_ I studied English.
Student A: I studied English for one year before coming to the U.S.
Student B: I didn't study English before coming to the U.S.

1. ____ I studied American history.
2. ____ I studied English.
3. ____ I finished college.
4. ____ I bought new clothes.
5. ____ I had a clear idea about life in the U.S.
6. ____ I was afraid about the future.
7. ____ I read about this city.
8. ____ I had a map of this city.

2. Form a small group. Turn to the person next to you and say a year or a specific time of the year. The person next to you tells what was happening in his or her life at that time.

EXAMPLES:

1996
I was living with my parents.
January, 1999
I was studying to be a nurse in my country.

## DISCUSSION

1. In a small group or with the entire class, discuss your experience of immigration. Was the process difficult? How did you feel during the process?

2. Einstein is often called a genius. Can you think of any other famous people who are geniuses?

3. In a small group or with the entire class, discuss the meaning of the fable in Exercise 14. What do you think this fable teaches us? Do you know anyone like the grasshopper or the ant in this fable?

## WRITING

1. Write a short fable like the one in Exercise 14.

2. Write a paragraph about the changes that took place after a major historical event in your country or elsewhere in the world.

EXAMPLES:

After the communists took over in Cuba . . .
After the Khmer Rouge took power in Cambodia . . .
After the coup failed in the former Soviet Union . . .
After the president of my country was assassinated . . .

3. Write about the life of a famous person who interests you.

4. Write about how you met your spouse or how your father and mother met.

## OUTSIDE ACTIVITIES

1. Most people remember what they were doing when they heard shocking news. Do you remember what you were doing when you heard the news that John Kennedy, Jr. died in a plane crash in July, 1999? Do you remember what you were doing when you heard that Princess Diana died in a car crash in August, 1997? Ask an American, "What were you doing when you heard the news?" You can ask an older American, "What were you doing when you heard the news that President Kennedy was killed in November, 1963?"

2. Is there a famous event in your native country that most people remember well? What was it? Ask people from your country what they were doing when this event happened. Report your findings to the class.

## Internet Activity

Look for the Ellis Island Web site. Find out what time the museum is open. See what names are on the wall of the museum. Is your family's name on the wall?

## GRAMMAR

Modals
Related Expressions

## CONTEXT

An Apartment Lease
Tenants' Rights
The New Neighbors
At a Garage Sale

## LESSON FOCUS

The modal auxiliaries are: *can, could, should, will, would, may, might, must.*

> She *can* swim well.
> I *must* return my library books.

Related expressions are: *be supposed to, be able to, have to, have got to, be allowed to, be permitted to, had better.*

> She *is able to* swim well.
> I *have to* return my library books.

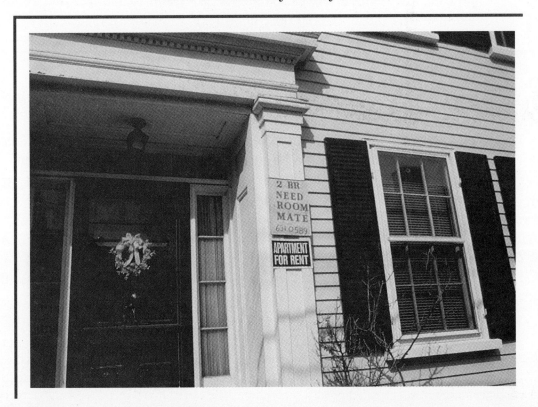

## 8.1   Overview of Modals and Related Expressions

| List of Modals | Facts About Modals |
|---|---|
| can<br>could<br>should<br>will<br>would<br>may<br>might<br>must | 1. The base form follows a modal. Never use an infinitive after a modal.<br>    You **must pay** your rent. (NOT: You must to pay your rent.)<br><br>2. Modals never have an *-s*, *-ed*, or *-ing* ending.<br>    He **can** go. (NOT: He cans go.)<br><br>3. To form the negative, put *not* after the modal.<br>    You **should not** leave now.<br><br>4. You can make a negative contraction with some modals.<br>    can't   couldn't   shouldn't   won't   wouldn't   mustn't<br>    Don't make a contraction for *may not* or *might not*.<br><br>5. Some verbs are like modals in meaning: *have to, be able to, be supposed to, be permitted to, be allowed to, had better*.<br>    He **must** sign the lease. = He **has to** sign the lease.<br><br>    I **must** pay my rent by the first of the month. = **I'm supposed to** pay my rent by the first of the month.<br><br>    He **can** pay the rent. = He **is able to** pay the rent. |

**Before You Read**
1. Do you live in an apartment? Do you have a lease? Did you understand the lease when you signed it?
2. Do renters in your hometown usually have to sign a lease?

Read the following article. Pay special attention to modals and related expressions.

# An Apartment Lease

When people rent an apartment, they often **have to** sign a lease. A lease is an agreement between the owner (landlord[1]) and the renter (tenant). A lease states the period of time of the rental, the amount of the rent, and rules the renter **must** follow. Some leases contain the following rules:

**Did you know...?**

In the U.S., renters pay about 26 percent of their income on rent.

- Renters **must** not have a waterbed.
- Renters **must** not have a pet.
- Renters **must** not change the locks without the owner's permission.
- Renters **must** pay a security deposit.

[1] A *landlord* is a man. A *landlady* is a woman.

smoke detector

The renter **does not have to** agree to all the terms of the lease. He can ask for changes before he signs. A pet owner, for example, can ask for permission to have a pet by offering to pay a higher security deposit.

Owners also have to follow rules. They **must** provide heat during the winter months. In most cities, they **must** put a smoke detector in each apartment and in the halls.

Many owners ask the renter to pay a security deposit, in case there are damages. When the renter moves out, the owner **is supposed to** return the deposit plus interest if the apartment is in good condition. If there is damage, the owner **can** use part or all of the money to repair the damage. However, he **may** not keep the renter's money for normal wear and tear (the normal use of the apartment).

When the lease is up, the owner **can** offer the renter a new lease or he can ask the renter to leave. The owner **is supposed to** give the renter notice (usually at least 30 days) if he wants the renter to leave.

An owner **can't** refuse to rent to a person because of sex, race, religion, nationality, or disability.

## 8.2 Statements and Questions with Modals

Compare affirmative statements and questions using a modal.

| *Wh-* Word | Modal (+ *n't*) | Subject | Modal | Verb (base form) | Complement | Short Answer |
|---|---|---|---|---|---|---|
| | | He | **can** | have | a cat in his apartment. | |
| | | He | **can't** | have | a dog. | |
| | **Can** | he | | have | a waterbed? | No, he **can't**. |
| What | **can** | he | | have | in his apartment? | |
| Why | **can't** | he | | have | a dog? | |
| | | Who | **can** | have | a dog? | |

---

**EXERCISE 1**  Fill in the blanks to complete these statements and questions.

**EXAMPLE:**  I can have a cat in my apartment, but I _____ *can't* _____ have a dog.

1. I can't have a dog. Why _____ a dog?

2. You should _____ the lease before you sign it.

3. Why _____ before I sign it?

4. We must pay a security deposit. How much _____ pay?

---

Modals; Related Expressions  **211**

5. My landlord says I must not _____ a waterbed in my apartment.

6. The landlord must _____ a smoke detector in each apartment.

7. If you damage something, the landlord can _____ some or all of your money to repair the damage.

8. How much money must _____ if I break a window?

9. _____ change the locks? No. You can't change the locks.

10. Why _____ change the locks?

11. The landlord can't _____ to rent to you because of your race or nationality.

12. _____ refuse to rent to me because of my religion? No, he can't.

## 8.3 Must, Have To, Have Got To, Be Supposed To

| Formal or Official | Informal | Explanation |
|---|---|---|
| The landlord **must** give you a smoke detector. | He **has to** give you a smoke detector. OR He**'s got to** give you a smoke detector. OR He**'s supposed to** give you a smoke detector. | Legal obligation |
| You **must** leave the building immediately. It's on fire! | You **have to** leave the building immediately. OR You**'ve got to** leave the building immediately. | Urgency |
| | My apartment is too small. We **have to** move. OR We**'ve got to** move. | Personal necessity |

## LANGUAGE NOTES

1. We use *must* in formal situations to describe rules and laws. It has an official tone. Avoid using *must* for personal necessities. It sounds too strong. *Have to* and *have got to* are more common.
   Student to teacher: I *have to* leave early today. My son is sick.

2. *Be supposed to* is much more common than *must* in reporting a rule. The creator or enforcer of the rule can say *must*. Someone who reports the rule usually says *be supposed to, have to,* or *have got to*.
   TEACHER TO STUDENT: You *must* write five compositions this semester.

STUDENT TO STUDENT: The teacher says we're *supposed to* write five compositions this semester. (OR: We *have to* write five compositions.)

PARENT TO TEENAGER: You *must* be home by 11 p.m.

TEENAGER TO FRIEND: I'm *supposed to* be home by 11 p.m. (OR: I've *got to* be home by 11 p.m.)

3. In fast, informal speech, *have to* is often pronounced "hafta." *Has to* is pronounced "hasta." *Got to* is often pronounced "gotta." Listen to your teacher pronounce the sentences in the preceding box.

4. We don't usually use *have got to* for questions and negatives.

5. *Must* has no past form. The past of both *must* and *have to* is *had to*.
   At the end of my lease last May, I *had to* move.
   I *had to* find a bigger apartment.

---

EXERCISE **2**   Fill in the blanks with *must* for rules and laws. Fill in the blanks with *have to* or *have got to* for personal necessities.

EXAMPLES:   The landlord _____*must*_____ give you heat in cold weather.

It's too hot in here. I _____*have to*_____ open a window.

1. To get a driver's license, you _____ take an eye exam.

2. Our apartment is too small for our family. We _____ move.

3. My stove doesn't work. I _____ talk to the landlord about it.

4. You _____ sign the lease with a pen. A pencil is not acceptable.

5. We _____ buy a new sofa. Our old one looks terrible.

6. I _____ cook dinner for my family tonight. It's my turn.

7. The landlord _____ return your security deposit if you leave your apartment in good condition.

8. The landlord _____ give you notice if he wants you to leave at the end of your lease.

9. I _____ ask the landlord about the laundry room.

10. I'm looking for a new apartment. I _____ buy the newspaper and look at the "for rent" section.

**EXERCISE 3**  Finish these sentences to talk about personal necessity.

**EXAMPLE:**  I always go to bed so late and then I'm tired the next morning. I've got to
*go to bed earlier.*

1. I won't have time to watch TV tonight. I've got to _____.

2. I can't talk to you now. I've got to _____.

3. I don't feel well. I have to _____.

4. I'm reading a novel, and I don't know the meaning of several words.
   I have to _____.

5. I'm gaining weight. I've got to _____.

6. We're going to have a test on modals next week. We've got to
   _____.

7. English is so important in the U.S. We've got to _____.

8. I eat too much junk food. I have to _____ or I'm
   going to get fat.

**EXERCISE 4**  Make a list of personal necessities you have.

**EXAMPLE:**  *I have to change the oil in my car every three months.*

1. _____

2. _____

3. _____

**EXERCISE 5**  Make a list of things you had to do last weekend.

**EXAMPLE:**  *I had to do my laundry.*

1. _____

2. _____

3. _____

Make these sentences less formal by changing from *must* to *be supposed to*.

EXAMPLE: You must wear a seat belt.
You're supposed to wear your seat belt.

1. You must carry your driver's license with you when you drive.

2. The teacher must give a final grade at the end of the semester.

3. Your landlord must give you notice if he wants you to leave.

4. You must stop at a red light.

5. We must put money in the parking meter during business hours.

6. The landlord must give me a smoke detector.

7. We must write five compositions in this course.

8. We must bring our books to class.

EXERCISE **7** Finish these statements. Use *be supposed to*.

EXAMPLE: I _'m supposed to pay my rent_____ on the first of the month.

1. Pets are not permitted in my apartment. I (not) _____ a pet.

2. The landlord _____ us heat in the winter months.

3. The tenants _____ before they move out.

4. The landlord _____ a smoke detector in each apartment.

5. I _____ my rent on the first of each month.

6. My stove isn't working. My landlord _____ it.

7. We're going to move out next week. Our apartment is clean and in good condition. The landlord _____ our security deposit.

Write three sentences to tell what you are supposed to do for this course. (You may work with a partner.)

EXAMPLE: *We're supposed to write three compositions this semester.*

1. _____

2. _____

3. _____

## 8.4 *Can, Could, May, Be Able To, Be Permitted To, Be Allowed To*

| Modal | Alternate expression | Explanation |
|---|---|---|
| I **can** pay up to $800 a month for an apartment. | **It is possible** for me to pay $800 a month. | Possibility |
| I **can't** understand the lease. | I **am not able to** understand the lease. | Ability |
| I **can't** have a pet in my apartment. | I **am not permitted to** have a pet. <br><br> I **am not allowed to** have a pet. | Permission |
| The landlord **may not** keep my deposit for no reason. | The landlord **is not permitted to** keep my deposit. <br><br> The landlord **is not allowed to** keep my deposit. | Permission |
| I **couldn't** speak English five years ago, but I can now. | I **wasn't able to** speak English five years ago, but I am able to now. | Past ability |
| I **could** have a dog in my last apartment, but I **can't** have one in my present apartment. | I **was permitted to** have a dog in my last apartment, but I **am not permitted to** have one in my present apartment. | Past permission |

## LANGUAGE NOTES

1. The negative of *can* is *cannot* (one word). The contraction is *can't*.
2. *Can* is not usually stressed in affirmative statements. Sometimes it is hard to hear the final *t*, so we must pay attention to the vowel sound to hear the difference between *can* and *can't*. Listen to your teacher pronounce these sentences:

I can gó. /kIn/
I cán't go. /kænt/
In a short answer, we pronounce *can* as /kæn/.
Can you help me later?
Yes, I can. /kæn/

3. We use *can* in the following common expression:
   I *can't afford* a bigger apartment. I don't have enough money.

4. The past of *can* is *could*.
   I *can* control the heat in my present apartment.
   I *couldn't* control the heat in my last apartment.

---

**EXERCISE 9**  Fill in the blanks with an appropriate permission word to talk about what is or isn't permitted at this school.

**EXAMPLES:**  We _____aren't allowed to_____ bring food into the classroom.

We _____can_____ leave the room without asking the teacher for permission.

1. We _____ eat in the classroom.

2. Students _____ talk during a test.

3. Students _____ use their dictionaries when they write compositions.

4. Students _____ write a test with a pencil.

5. Students _____ repeat a course a second time.

6. Students _____ sit in any seat they want.

7. Students _____ use their textbooks during a test.

8. Students _____ make a copy of their textbooks.

---

**EXERCISE 10**  Complete each statement.

**EXAMPLE:**  The landlord may not _____refuse to rent_____ to a person because of his or her nationality.

1. The tenants may not _____ the locks without the landlord's permission.

2. Each tenant in my building has a parking space. I may not _____ _____ in another tenant's space.

3. Students may not _____ during a test.

---

Modals; Related Expressions    **217**

4.  I took my camera to the art museum last week, but I couldn't use it.

    There was a sign that said, "You may not _____ the artwork."

5.  Teacher to students: "You don't need my permission to leave the room.

    You may _____ the room if you need to."

6.  Some teachers do not allow cell phones in class. In Mr. Klein's class,

    you may not _____ during class.

7.  My teacher says that after we finish a test, we may _____

    _____ . We don't have to stay in class.

8.  Some teachers do not allow food in the classroom. My teacher says

    we may not _____ in the classroom.

---

**EXERCISE 11** Write statements to tell what is or is not permitted in this class, in the library, at this school, or during a test. If you have any questions about what is permitted, write a question for the teacher. (You may work with a partner.)

**EXAMPLES:**   *We aren't allowed to talk in the library.*

                *May we use our textbooks during a test?*

                _____

                _____

                _____

---

**EXERCISE 12** Write three sentences telling about what you couldn't do in a classroom or school in your native country that you can do in an American school or classroom.

**EXAMPLE:**   *In my country, I couldn't call a teacher by his first name, but I*

               *can do it here.*

          1.   _____

          2.   _____

          3.   _____

**EXERCISE 13** Write three sentences telling about something that was prohibited in your native country that you can do in the U.S.

**EXAMPLE:** *I couldn't criticize the political leaders in my country, but I can do it now.*

1. _____

2. _____

3. _____

**Before You Read**

1. What are some complaints you have about your apartment? Do you ever tell the landlord about your complaints?
2. Is your apartment warm enough in the winter and cool enough in the summer?

Read the following conversation. Pay special attention to *should* and *had better*.

# Tenants' Rights

brochure

A. My apartment is always too cold in the winter. I've got to move.

B. You don't have to move. The landlord is supposed to give enough heat.

A. But he doesn't.

B. You **should** talk to him about this problem.

A. I did already. The first time I talked to him, he just told me I **should** put on a sweater. The second time I said, "You'**d better** give me heat or I'm going to move."

B. You **shouldn't** get so angry. That's not the way to solve the problem. You know, there are laws about heat. You **should** get information from the city so you can know your rights.

A. How can I get information?

B. Tomorrow morning, you **should** call the mayor's office and ask for a brochure about tenants' rights. When you know what the law is exactly, you **should** show the brochure to your landlord.

A. And what if he doesn't want to do anything about it?

B. Then you **should** report the problem to the mayor's office.

A. I'm afraid to do that.

B. Don't be afraid. You have rights. Maybe you **should** talk to other tenants and see if you can do this together.

| Examples | Explanation |
|---|---|
| You **should** talk to the landlord about the problem.<br><br>You **should** get information about tenants' rights.<br><br>You **shouldn't** get so angry. | For advice, use *should*.<br><br>   *Should* = It's a good thing.<br>   *Shouldn't* = It's a bad thing. |
| You **had better** give me heat, or I'm going to move.<br><br>You **had better not** miss the final exam, or you might fail the course. | For a warning, use *had better (not)*.<br><br>Something bad can happen if you don't follow this advice. |

## LANGUAGE NOTES

1. The contraction for *had* (in *had better*) is *'d*.
   
      I'd    you'd    he'd    she'd    we'd    they'd

2. Americans sometimes don't pronounce the *'d*. You will hear Americans say, "You better be careful."

3. Remember, *must* is very strong and is not for advice. It is for rules and laws.
   
      COMPARE:
      Your landlord *must* give you a smoke detector.
      You *should* check the battery in the smoke detector occasionally.

**EXERCISE 14** Fill in the blanks.

**EXAMPLE:** The students don't understand the lesson. The teacher should ___*explain*___

   *it again.*___

1. I can see you don't understand modals. You should _____ before the next test.

2. My mother is probably lonely. I should _____ more often.

3. You don't have enough gas in your tank. You should _____ very soon.

4. I always go to bed so late, and I feel terrible the next morning. I

   should _____ earlier.

5.  I work at a desk all day. Now I'm gaining weight. I should _____ _____ .

6.  It's going to get colder this afternoon. When you go out, you should _____ with you.

7.  You're taking too many classes and you don't have enough time to study. Next semester you shouldn't _____ .

8.  Children shouldn't lie. They should _____ to their parents.

---

**EXERCISE 15** Give advice using *should*.

**EXAMPLE:**  My landlord is going to raise the rent by 20 percent.
You should move.

1.  My next-door neighbors play their stereo loud all the time. I can't sleep at night.

2.  My landlady doesn't give us enough heat in the winter.

3.  I can't understand my lease.

4.  I broke a window in my apartment.

5.  My landlord doesn't want to return my security deposit.

6.  I have a job interview early tomorrow morning.

7.  Some students talk in the library, and other students can't study.

8.  My son doesn't want to do his homework. He just wants to be on the Internet all day.

---

**EXERCISE 16** Fill in the blanks to complete the statement.

**EXAMPLES:**  You'd better _take an umbrella_ , or you're going to get wet.

You'd better fill up your gas tank right away, or _you're going to run out of gas._

1.  Your stove is dirty. You'd better _____, or your landlord will keep your deposit.

2.  He'd better _____, or he'll lose his job.

3.  They'd better _____, or they'll fail this course.

4.  He'd better put enough postage on that letter, or _____

---

5. The class starts in 5 minutes. We'd better hurry, or _____

_____

6. My passport is ready to expire. I _____,
or I won't be able to travel this summer.

7. The teacher said, "No talking during a test." We _____

_____, or the teacher will get angry.

8. I forgot my driver's license. Before I get into my car, I _____

_____, or I can get a ticket.

## 8.6 Negatives of Modals and Related Expressions

| Examples | Explanation |
|---|---|
| You **must not** change the locks without the landlord's permission.<br><br>You **must not** take the landlord's smoke detector with you when you move. | Use *must not* for prohibition. These things are against the law or rule. *Must not* has an official tone. |
| I **can't** have a dog in my apartment.<br><br>I **may not** have a waterbed in my apartment. | Use *cannot* or *may not* to show no permission. The meaning is about the same as *must not*. (*May not* is more formal than *cannot*.) |
| The landlord **is not supposed to** keep your security deposit.<br><br>You **are not supposed to** talk to another student during the test.<br><br>You **are not supposed to** park at a bus stop. | Use *be not supposed to* for prohibition. These things are against the law or rule. When reporting a rule, people use *be not supposed to* more than *must not*. Remember, *must not* has an official tone. |
| My landlady offered me a new lease. I **don't have to** move when my lease is up.<br><br>The janitor takes out the garbage. I **don't have to** take it out. | These things are not necessary, not required. A person can do something if he wants, but he has no obligation to do this thing. |
| You **shouldn't** get angry.<br><br>If you turn on the air-conditioning, you **shouldn't** leave the windows open.<br><br>You **shouldn't** watch so much TV. | *Shouldn't* is for advice, not for rules. |
| You**'d better not** play your music so loud, or your neighbors will complain to the landlord. | *Had better not* is for a warning. |

# LANGUAGE NOTES

1. Remember, in affirmative statements, *have to, must,* and *be supposed to* have a very similar meaning. (Remember, *must* sounds more official.)

2. In negative statements, *must not, not have to,* and *shouldn't* have very different meanings.

    COMPARE:

    I *don't have to pay* my rent with cash. I can use a check.

    I *must not pay* my rent late.

    You *don't have to use* the elevator. You can use the stairs, if you like.

    There's a fire in the building. You *must not use* the elevator.

---

**EXERCISE 17** Practice using *must not* for prohibition. (Use *you* in the impersonal sense.)

EXAMPLE:   Name something you must not do.
You must not steal.

1. Name something you must not do on the bus.

2. Name something you mustn't do during a test.

3. Name something you mustn't do in the library.

4. Name something you must not do in the classroom.

5. Name something you mustn't do on an airplane.

---

**EXERCISE 18** Tell if you have to or don't have to do the following. For affirmative statements, you can also use *have got to*.

EXAMPLES:   work on Saturdays
I have to work on Saturdays. OR I've got to work on Saturdays.

wear a suit to work
I don't have to wear a suit to work.

1. speak English every day

2. use a dictionary to read the newspaper

3. pay rent on the first of the month

4. type my homework

5. work on Saturdays

6. come to school every day

---

7. pay my rent in cash

8. use public transportation

9. talk to the teacher after class

10. cook every day

---

**EXERCISE 19** Answer these questions about your native country.

1. In your native country, does a citizen have to vote?

2. Do men have to serve in the military?

3. Do schoolchildren have to wear a uniform?

4. Do divorced men have to support their children?

5. Do people have to get permission to travel?

6. Do students have to pass an exam to get their high school or university diploma?

7. Do students have to pay for their own books?

8. Do citizens have to pay taxes?

9. Do people have to make an appointment to see a doctor?

10. Do young people have to show an ID to enter nightclubs?

---

**EXERCISE 20** Fill in the blanks with *don't have to* (to show that something is not necessary) or *must not* or *be not supposed to* (to show that something is prohibited).

**EXAMPLES:** You ___*don't have to*___ bring your dictionary to class.

You ___*aren't supposed to*___ bring food into the computer lab.

1. You _____ talk to another student during a test.

2. You _____ drive through a red light.

3. You _____ speak English perfectly to become an American citizen. It's enough to speak simple English.

4. Resident aliens _____ become American citizens if they don't want to.

5. You _____ steal.

6. People over 17 years of age _____ attend school in the U.S. They can leave school if they want.

7. U.S. citizens _____ vote if they don't want to.

8. A U.S. citizen _____ support an enemy of the United States.

9. You _____ marry an American citizen to become a citizen of the U.S.

10. My lease says that I _____ have a dog in my apartment.

---

**EXERCISE 21** Students (S) are asking the teacher (T) questions about the final exam. Fill in the blanks with the negative form of *have to, should, must, had better, can, may, be supposed to*. (In some cases, more than one answer is possible.)

S. Do I have to sit in a specific seat for the test?

T. No, you ___*don't have to*___. You can choose any seat you want.
   *(example)*

S. Is it OK if I talk to another student during a test?

T. No. Absolutely not. You _____ talk to another student
   *(1)*
   during a test.

S. Is it OK if I use my book?

T. Sorry. You _____ use your book.
   *(2)*

S. What if I don't understand something on the test? Can I ask another student?

T. You _____ talk to another student, or I'll think you're
   *(3)*
   getting an answer. Ask me if you have a question.

S. What happens if I am late for the test? Will you let me in?

T. Of course I'll let you in. But you _____ come late.
   *(4)*
   You'll need a lot of time for the test.

S. Do I have to bring my own paper for the final test?

T. If you want to, you can. But you _____ bring paper.
   *(5)*
   I'll give you paper if you need it.

S. Must I write the test with a pen?

T. You can use whatever you want. You _____ use a
   *(6)*
   pen.

S. How long will the test take? The full period?

T. Probably not. You can use the full period, but you probably won't need so much time. Let me give you some advice: if you see an item that is difficult for you, go on to the next item. You

_____ spend too much time on a difficult item, or
(7)

you won't finish the test.

S. Can I bring coffee into the classroom?

T. The school has a rule about eating or drinking in the classroom.

You _____ bring food into the classroom.
(8)

S. If I finish the test early, must I stay in the room?

T. No, you _____ stay. You can leave.
(9)

---

**Before You Read**
1. Are people friendly with their neighbors in your community?
2. Do you know any of your neighbors now?

Read the following conversation. Pay special attention to *must*.

Two women meet for the first time in the hallway of their building and have this conversation.

---

# The New Neighbors

L. Hi. You **must be** the new neighbor. I saw the moving truck out front this morning. Let me introduce myself. My name is Lisa. I live downstairs of you.

P. Nice to meet you, Lisa. My name is Paula. We just moved in.

---

crib

L. I saw the movers carrying a crib upstairs. You **must have** a baby.

P. We do. We have a ten-month-old son. He's sleeping now. Do you have any kids?

L. Yes, I have a 16-year-old-daughter and an 18-year-old son.

P. It **must be** hard to raise teenagers.

L. Believe me, it is! I **must spend** half my time worrying about where they are and what they're doing. My daughter talks on the phone all day. She **must spend** half of her waking hours on the phone with her friends. They're always whispering to each other. They **must have** some big secrets.

P. I know what you mean. My brother has a teenage daughter.

L. Listen, I don't want to take up any more of your time. You **must be** very busy. I just wanted to bring you these cookies.

P. Thanks. That's very nice of you. They're still warm. They **must be** right out of the oven.

L. They are. Maybe we can talk some other time when you're all unpacked.

---

## 8.7 *Must* for Conclusions

| Examples | Explanation |
|---|---|
| The new neighbors have a crib. They **must have** a baby. Paula just moved in. She **must be** very busy. The teenage girls whisper all the time. They **must have** secrets. | *Must*, in these examples, shows a conclusion based on information we have or observations we make. *Must*, in these examples, talks about the present only, not the future. |
| I didn't see Paula's husband. He **must not** be home. Her daughter whispers on the phone. She **must not** want her parents to hear her conversation. | For a negative deduction, use *must not*. Do not use a contraction. |

**EXERCISE 22** A week later, Paula goes to Lisa's apartment and notices certain things. Use *must* + base form to show Paula's conclusions about Lisa's life.

EXAMPLE:    There is a cat box in the kitchen.
Lisa must have a cat.

1. There are pictures of Lisa and her two children all over the house. There is no picture of a man.

2. There is a nursing certificate on the wall with Lisa's name on it.

3. There are many different kinds of coffee on a kitchen shelf.

4. There are a lot of classical music CDs.

5. In Lisa's bedroom, there's a sewing machine.

6. In the kitchen, there are a lot of cookbooks.

7. There's a piano in the living room.

8. In the bookshelf, there are a lot of books about modern art.

9. On the kitchen calendar, there's an activity filled in for almost every day of the week.

10. There are pictures of cats everywhere.

Lisa's family

| Family Calendar | | | |
|---|---|---|---|
| **This Week** | MOM | Joey | Ann |
| Sunday | Church social dinner at Molly's | | |
| Monday | Carpool to school | Dentist 3:30 | |
| Tuesday | Art Class 11:00 | | Start science project |
| Wednesday | Take cat to Vet | Report Due | |
| Thursday | Carpool to school | | School play rehersal |
| Friday | PTA Meeting | | Library with Lisa |
| Saturday | | baseball game School Dance | piano lesson |

**EXERCISE 23**

Many people get vanity license plates that tell something about their profession, hobbies, or families. Often words are abbreviated: M = am, U = you, 4 = For, 8 = the "ate" sound. Words are often without vowels. If you see the following license plates, what conclusion can you make about the owner? (You may work with a partner and get help from the teacher.)

EXAMPLES:    EYEDOC    *The owner must be an eye doctor.*

1. I TCH ENGLSH _____

2. I LV CARS _____

3. I M GRANDMA _____

4. MUSC LVR _____

5. I LV DGS _____

6. TENNIS GR8 _____

7. I SK8 _____

8. CRPNTR _____

9. BSY MOM _____

10. SHY GUY _____

11. DAD OF TWO _____

12. RMNTIC GAL _____

13. NO TIME 4 U _____

14. CITY GAL _____

15. LDY DOC _____

16. LUV GLF _____

17. MXCAN GUY _____

18. I M GD COOK _____

19. ALWAYS L8 _____

20. WE DANCE _____

## 8.8  *Will* and *May/Might*

| Examples | Explanation |
|----------|-------------|
| My lease **will** expire on April 30. | Certainty about the future |
| My landlord **might** raise my rent at that time. I **may** move. | Possibility or uncertainty about the future |
| The teacher isn't here today. She **may** be sick. OR She **might** be sick. | Possibility or uncertainty about the present |

## LANGUAGE NOTES

1. *May* and *might* are modals. They both have about the same meaning: possibility or uncertainty, similar to the meaning of *maybe*. *Maybe* is an adverb. It usually comes at the beginning of the sentence.
   COMPARE:
   
   *Maybe* I will move.                I *may* move.
   *Maybe* he doesn't understand.      He *might* not understand.
   *Maybe* she is sick.                She *may* be sick.

2. We don't use a contraction for *may not* and *might not*.

**EXERCISE 24** The following sentences contain *maybe*. Take away *maybe* and use *may* or *might* + base form.

**EXAMPLE:**   Maybe your neighbors will complain if your music is loud.
Your neighbors might complain if your music is loud.

1. Maybe my sister will come to live with me.

2. Maybe she will find a job in this city.

3. Maybe my landlord will raise my rent.

4. Maybe I will get a dog.

5. Maybe my landlord won't allow me to have a dog.

6. Maybe I will move next year.

7. Maybe I will buy a house soon.

8. Maybe I won't stay in this city.

9. Maybe I won't come to class tomorrow.

10. Maybe the teacher will review modals if we need more help.

**EXERCISE 25** Fill in the blanks with a possibility.

**EXAMPLES:**   If you don't pay your rent on time, _you might have to pay a late fee._

If I make a lot of noise in my apartment, _the neighbors may complain._

1. When my lease is up, _____

2. If I don't clean my apartment before I move out, _____

_____

3. If a person doesn't graduate from high school, _____

_____

4. If I don't study for the next test, _____

5. If we don't register for classes early, _____

_____

6. If I don't pass this course, _____

**EXERCISE 26** Fill in the blanks with possibilities.

**EXAMPLE:**    One student isn't here today. She may _be out of town._

1.   My neighbor's name is Robert T. Harris. His middle name might

_____ or it might _____ .

2.   A. The school is getting a new teacher. Her name is Terry Karson.
     Do you know anything about her?

     B. Why do you say "her"? The new teacher may _____ .
     Terry is sometimes a man's name.

3.   A. I need a stamp. Do you have one?

     B. Let me look. I might _____ .

4.   A. Do you know where the nearest post office is?

     B. No, I don't. Ask the teacher. She might _____ .

5.   A. I don't have change for the vending machines. Do you have change
     for a dollar?

     B. Let me look in my pocket. I may _____ .

6.   A. Where is Linda Sanchez from?

     B. I don't know. That's a Spanish name. She might _____

     or she might _____ .

7.   A. Where's the dog? I can't find him.

     B. Did you look under the bed? He may _____ .

     Or he may _____ .

8.   A. Do we have any more soda?

     B. Look in the refrigerator.

     A. I can't find any.

     B. We may not _____ .

---

**Before You Read**  1.   People often have a garage sale or an apartment sale before they
     move. At this kind of sale, people sell things that they don't want or
     need anymore. Did you ever buy anything at this kind of sale?

2.   At a garage sale, it is usually not necessary to pay the asking price.
     You can bargain[2] with the seller. Can you bargain on prices in your
     native country? In a store? Where?

This is a conversation at a garage sale between a seller (S) and a buyer
(B). Read the conversation. Pay special attention to modals and related
expressions.

[2] When a buyer *bargains* with the seller, the buyer makes an offer lower than the asking price and hopes
that he or she and the seller will agree on a lower price.

# At a Garage Sale

S. I see you're looking at my microwave oven. **May** I help you with it?

B. Yes. I'm interested in buying one. Does it work well?

S. It's only two years old, and it's in perfect working condition. **Would you like** to try it out?

B. Sure. **Could** you plug it in somewhere?

S. I have an outlet right here. **Why don't we** boil a cup of water so you can see how well it works.

outlet

*A few minutes later . . .*

B. It seems to work well. **Would** you tell me why you're selling it, then?

S. We're moving next week. Our new apartment already has one.

B. How much do you want for it?[3]

S. $80.

B. **Will** you take $60?

S. **Can** you wait a minute? I'll ask my wife.

*A few minutes later . . .*

S. My wife says she'll let you have it for $65.

B. OK. **May** I write you a check?

S. I'm sorry. I**'d rather** have cash.

B. **Would** you hold it for me for an hour? I can go to the supermarket and cash a check.

S. **Could** you leave me a small deposit? Ten dollars, maybe?

B. Yes, I can.

S. Fine. I'll hold it for you, then.

---

## 8.9   Using Modals for Politeness

| To ask permission | Explanation |
|---|---|
| **May** <br> **Can** } I write you a check? <br> **Could** | *May* and *could* are considered more polite than *can* by some speakers of English. |

*(continued)*

---

[3] We ask "How much is it?" when the price is fixed. We ask "How much do you want for it?" when the price is negotiable. You can bargain for it.

| To request that another person do something | Explanation |
|---|---|
| Can <br> Could <br> Will <br> Would } you plug it in? | For a request, *could* and *would* are softer than *can* and *will*. |

| To express a want or desire | Explanation |
|---|---|
| **Would** you **like** to try out the microwave oven? <br><br> Yes, I **would like** to see if it works. <br><br> **I'd like** a cup of coffee. | *Would like* has the same meaning as *want*. *Would like* is softer than *want*. The contraction for *would* after a pronoun is **'d**. |

| To express preference | Explanation |
|---|---|
| **Would** you **rather** pay with cash or by credit card? <br><br> **I'd rather** pay by credit card (than with cash). | We use *or* in questions with *would rather*. We use *than* in statements. |

## LANGUAGE NOTES

1. Modals are often used to make direct statements more polite.
   COMPARE:

   Plug it in. (VERY DIRECT)
   *Would* you plug it in, please? (MORE POLITE)

   Give me a deposit. (VERY DIRECT)
   *Could* you give me a deposit, please? (MORE POLITE)

   I want to buy the microwave. (DIRECT)
   *I'd like* to buy the microwave. (MORE POLITE)

2. We can make a suggestion by using a negative question form.
   COMPARE:

   Go to the supermarket and cash a check. (DIRECT)
   *Why don't you* go to the supermarket and cash a check? (MORE POLITE)

   Let's boil a cup of water. (DIRECT)
   *Why don't we* boil a cup of water? (MORE POLITE)

**EXERCISE 27** Change each request to make it more polite. Practice *may, can, could + I?*

EXAMPLES:    I want to use your phone.
            May I use your phone?

            I want to borrow a quarter.
            Could I borrow a quarter?

1. I want to help you.          3. I want to leave the room.
2. I want to close the door.    4. I want to write you a check.

**EXERCISE 28** Change these commands to make them more polite. Practice *can, could, will, would + you?*

EXAMPLES:    Call the doctor for me.
            Would you call the doctor for me?

            Give me a cup of coffee.
            Could you give me a cup of coffee, please?

1. Repeat the sentence.    3. Spell your name.
2. Give me your paper.     4. Tell me your phone number.

**EXERCISE 29** Make these sentences more polite by using *would like.*

EXAMPLES:    Do you want some help?
            Would you like some help?

1.  I want to ask you a question.

2.  The teacher wants to speak with you.

3.  Do you want to try out the oven?

4.  Yes. I want to see if it works.

**EXERCISE 30** Make each suggestion more polite by putting it in the form of a negative question.

EXAMPLES:    Plug it in.
            Why don't you plug it in?

            Let's eat now.
            Why don't we eat now?

1. Take a sweater.          3. Turn left here.
2. Let's turn off the light. 4. Let's leave early.

**EXERCISE 31** Make a statement of preference using *would rather.*

EXAMPLE: work indoors/outdoors
I'd rather work indoors than outdoors.

1. live in the U.S./in my native country

2. live in the city/in a suburb

3. get up early/sleep late[4]

4. take a relaxing vacation/an active vacation

5. live in a house/a condo

6. read a story/write a composition

**EXERCISE 32** Ask a question with the words given. Another student will answer.

EXAMPLE: eat Chinese food/Italian food
A. Would you rather eat Chinese food or Italian food?
B. I'd rather eat Italian food.

1. read fact/fiction

2. watch funny movies/serious movies

3. listen to classical music/popular music

4. visit Europe/Africa

5. own a large luxury car/a small sports car

6. watch a soccer game/take part in a soccer game

7. write a letter/receive a letter

8. cook/eat in a restaurant

**EXERCISE 33** This is a conversation between a seller (S) and a buyer (B) at a garage sale. Make this conversation more polite by using modals and other polite expressions in place of the underlined words.

*May I help you?*
S. ~~What do you want?~~

B. I'm interested in that lamp. Show it to me. Does it work?

S. I'll go and get a light bulb. Wait a minute.

[4] *Sleep late* means to wake up late in the morning

*A few minutes later . . .*

B. Plug it in.

S. You see? It works fine.

B. How much do you want for it?

S. This is one of a pair. I have another one just like it. They're $10 each. I prefer to sell them together.

B. Give them both to me for $15.

S. I'll have to ask my husband. (*A few seconds later*) My husband says he'll sell them to you for $17.

B. Fine. I'll take them. Will you take a check?

S. I prefer to have cash.

B. I only have five dollars on me.

S. OK. I'll take a check. Show me some identification.

B. Here's my driver's license.

S. That's fine. Write the check to James Kucinski.

B. Spell your name for me.

S. K-U-C-I-N-S-K-I.

# SUMMARY OF LESSON 8

| Modal | Example | Explanation |
|---|---|---|
| can | I **can** stay in this apartment until March. | Permission |
| | I **can** type 75 words per minute. | Ability |
| | You **can't** park here. It's a bus stop. | Prohibition |
| | **Can** I borrow your pen? | Asking permission |
| | **Can** you turn off the light, please? | Request |
| should | You **should** be friendly with your neighbors. | A good idea |
| | You **shouldn't** leave the air conditioner on. It wastes electricity. | A bad idea |
| may | **May** I borrow your pen? | Asking permission |
| | You **may** leave the room. | Permission |
| | You **may not** talk during a test. | Prohibition |
| | It **may** rain tomorrow. | Future possibility |
| | The landlord **may** have an extra key. | Present possibility |

| Modal | Example | Explanation |
|---|---|---|
| might | It **might** rain tomorrow.<br><br>The landlord **might** have an extra key. | Future possibility<br><br>Present possibility |
| must | A driver **must** have a license.<br><br>You **must not** steal.<br><br>My neighbor has a cat box. She **must** have a cat. | Rule or law<br><br>Prohibition<br><br>Conclusion |
| would | **Would** you help me move? | Request |
| would like | I **would like** to use your pen. | Want |
| would rather | I **would rather** live in the city than in the suburbs. | Preference |
| could | In my country, I **couldn't** say bad things about our country's leaders.<br><br>Before I came to the U.S., I **couldn't** speak English.<br><br>**Could** you help me move?<br><br>**Could** I borrow your car? | Past permission<br><br><br>Past ability/inability<br><br>Request<br><br>Asking permission |
| have to | She **has to** leave.<br><br>He **had to** leave work early yesterday. | Personal necessity |
| have got to | She **has got to** see a doctor. | Personal necessity |
| not have to | You **don't have to** come back after the final exam, but you can if you want to. | No necessity |
| had better | You **had better** study, or you're going to fail the test. | Warning |
| be supposed to | I **am supposed to** pay my rent by the fifth of the month.<br><br>We**'re not supposed to** have dog in our apartment. | Reporting a rule |
| be able to | The teacher **is able to** use modals correctly. | Ability |
| be permitted OR allowed to | We**'re not allowed to** park here overnight.<br><br>We**'re not permitted to** park here overnight. | Permission |

1. After a modal, we use the base form.

   I must ~~to~~ study.

   I can help~~ing~~ you now.

2. A modal has no ending.

   He can~~s~~ cook.

3. We don't put two modals together. We change the second modal to another form.

   *have to*
   She will ~~must~~ take the test.

4. Don't forget *to* after *be permitted, be allowed, be supposed, be able*.

   *to*
   We're not permitted ^ talk during a test.

5. Don't forget *be* before *permitted to, allowed to, supposed to, able to*.

   *am*
   I ^ not supposed to pay my rent late.

6. Use the correct word order in a question.

   *should I*
   What ~~I should~~ do about my problem?

7. Don't use *can* for past. Use *could* + a base form.

   *couldn't go*
   I ~~can't went~~ to the party last week.

8. Don't forget *would* before *rather*.

   *'d*
   I ^ rather live in Canada than in the U.S.

9. Don't forget *had* before *better*.

   *'d*
   You ^ better take a sweater. It's going to get cold.

10. Don't forget *have* before *got to*.

    *'ve*
    It's late. I ^ got to go.

11. Don't use *maybe* before a verb.

    *may*
    It ~~maybe will~~ rain later.

**PART 1**     Find the grammar mistakes with the underlined words, and correct them. Not every sentence has a mistake. If the sentence is correct, write **C**.

**EXAMPLES:**     You must ~~to~~ stop at a red light.

You have to stop at a red light.     **C**

1. We're not permitted use our books during the test.

2. In my country, I couldn't traveled without permission from the government.

3. When she can leave?

4. What must I write on this application?

5. She has to taking her daughter to the doctor now.

6. What I should do about my problem?

7. You not supposed to talk during the test.

8. We're not allowed to take food into the computer lab.

9. He can't have a dog in his apartment.

10. Could I use your pen, please?

11. I rather walk than drive.

12. You'd better hurry. It's late.

13. I got to talk to my boss about a raise.

14. We maybe will buy a house.

15. She might buy a new car next year.

16. I may have to go home early tonight.

17. He can speak English now, but he can't spoke it five years ago.

**PART 2**     This is a conversation between two friends. Choose the correct expression in parentheses ( ) to complete the conversation.

A.   I'm moving on Saturday. ((Could)/ May) you help me?
            (example)

B. I (*should / would*) like to help you, but I have a bad back. I went to my
(1)
doctor last week, and she told me that I (*shouldn't / don't have to*) lift
(2)
anything heavy for a while. (*Can / Would*) I help you any other way besides
(3)
moving?

A. Yes. I don't have enough boxes. (*Should / Would*) you help me find some?
(4)

B. Sure. I (*have to / must*) go shopping this afternoon. I'll pick up some boxes
(5)
while I'm at the supermarket.

A. Boxes can be heavy. You (*would / had*) better not lift them yourself.
(6)

B. Don't worry. I'll have someone put them in my car for me.

A. Thanks. I don't have a free minute. I (*couldn't / can't*) go to class all last
(7)
week. There's so much to do.

B. I know what you mean. You (*might / must*) be tired.
(8)

A. I am. I have another favor to ask. (*Can / Would*) I borrow your van on
(9)
Saturday?

B. I (*should / have to*) work on Saturday. How about Sunday? I (*must not /*
(10)                                                          (11)
*don't have to*) work on Sunday.

A. That's impossible. I (*'ve got to / should*) move out on Saturday. The new
(12)
tenants are moving in Sunday morning.

B. Let me ask my brother. He has a van too. He (*must / might*) be able to let
(13)
you use his van. He (*has to / should*) work Saturday too, but only for half
(14)
a day.

A. Thanks. I'd appreciate it if you could ask him.

B. Why are you moving? You have a great apartment.

A. We decided to move to the suburbs. It's quieter there. And I want to have
a dog. I (*shouldn't / 'm not supposed to*) have a dog in my present apartment.
(15)
But my new landlord says I (*might / may*) have a dog.
(16)

B. I (*had / would*) rather have a cat. They're easier to take care of.
(17)

**CLASSROOM ACTIVITIES**

1. A student will read one of the following problems out loud to the class, pretending that this is his or her problem. Other students will ask for more information and give advice about this problem.

**EXAMPLE:**

My mother-in-law comes to visit all the time. When she's here, she always criticizes everything we do. I told my wife that I don't want her here, but she says, "It's my mother, and I want her here." What should I do?

A. How long do you think she will stay?
B. She might stay for about two weeks or longer.
C. How does she criticize you? What does she say?
B. She says I should help my wife more.
D. Well, I agree with her. You should help with housework.
B. My children aren't allowed to watch TV after 8 o'clock. But my mother-in-law lets them watch TV as long as they want.
E. You'd better have a talk with her and tell her your rules.

Problem 1. My mother is 80 years old, and she lives with us. It's very hard on my family to take care of her. We'd like to put her in a nursing home, where she can get better care. Mother refuses to go. What can we do?

Problem 2. I have a nice one-bedroom apartment with a beautiful view of a park and a lake. I live with my wife and one child. My friends from out of town often come to visit and want to stay at my apartment. In the last year, ten people came to visit us. I like to have visitors, but sometimes they stay from two to four weeks. It's hard on my family with such a small apartment. What should I tell my friends when they want to visit?

Problem 3. My best friend is married. Last week I saw her husband in a restaurant with another woman. They looked very romantic together. Do you think I should tell my friend?

Write your own problem to present to the class. It can be real or imaginary. (Suggestions: a problem with a neighbor, your landlord, a teacher or class, a service you are dissatisfied with)

_____

_____

_____

2.  Circle a game you like from the list following. Find a partner who also likes this game. Write a list of some of the rules of this game. Tell what you can, cannot, should, have to, and must not do. (If you and your partner are from the same country, you can write about a game from your country.)

> chess     tennis     football    poker     other _____
>
> checkers  baseball   soccer    volleyball

**EXAMPLE:**

> checkers
> You have to move the pieces on a diagonal. You can only move in one direction until you get a king. Then you can move in two directions.

_____

_____

_____

3.  Write a vanity license plate that says something about you. Write it on the chalkboard. Other people have to guess what it says about you.

4.  Work with a partner from your own country, if possible. Talk about some laws in your country that are different from laws in the United States. Present this information to the class.

**EXAMPLE:**

> Citizens must vote in my country. In the U.S., they don't have to vote.
> People are supposed to carry identification papers at all times. In the U.S., people don't have to carry identification papers.
> In my country, citizens must not own a gun.

## DISCUSSION

1.  Compare getting a driver's license in the U.S. with getting a driver's license in your native country. Are the requirements the same?

2.  How did you find your apartment?

## WRITING

1.  Write a short composition comparing rules in an apartment in this city with rules in an apartment in your hometown or native country.

2.  Write about the differences between rules at this college and rules at a college in your native country. Are students allowed to do things here that they can't do in your native country?

3.  Find out what a student has to do to register for the first time at this college. You may want to visit the registrar's office to interview a worker there. Write a short composition explaining to a new student the steps for admission and registration.

## OUTSIDE ACTIVITIES

1.  Find out what you must do to get one of the following. Report your information to the class.

    a.  a passport (Call or write to the U.S. Department of State.)
    b.  a credit card (Get a credit card application from a business or bank.)
    c.  a library card (Visit your public library.)
    d.  a marriage license (Call the marriage license department of this county.)

2. Call or write to the Mayor's office or department of housing in your city. Ask if this department can send you a list of rights and responsibilities of renters and landlords.

3. Look at the Sunday newspaper for notices about garage sales or apartment sales. What kind of items are going to be sold? If you have time, go to a sale. Report about your experience to the class.

4. Get a newspaper. Look for the advice column. Read the problems and the advice. Circle the modals. Do you agree with the advice?

## Internet Activities

1. Try to find information online about tenants' rights in the city where you live.

2. Find a phone directory online. Look up the names and addresses of moving companies in your city.

3. Find apartments for rent online.

# Appendices

## Spelling and Pronunciation of Verbs

### Spelling of the -*S* Form of Verbs

| Rule | Base Form | -*S* Form |
|------|-----------|-----------|
| Add *s* to most verbs to make the -*s* form. | hope<br>eat | hopes<br>eats |
| When the base form ends in *s*, *z*, *sh*, *ch*, or *x*, add *es* and pronounce an extra syllable, /əz/. | miss<br>buzz<br>wash<br>catch<br>fix | misses<br>buzzes<br>washes<br>catches<br>fixes |
| When the base form ends in a consonant + *y*, change the *y* to *i* and add *es*. | carry<br>worry | carries<br>worries |
| When the base form ends in a vowel + *y*, do not change the *y*. | pay<br>obey | pays<br>obeys |
| Add *es* to *go* and *do*. | go<br>do | goes<br>does |

### Pronunciation of the -*S* Form

The -*s* form has three pronunciations.

A.  We pronounce /s/ if the verb ends in these voiceless sounds: /**p t k f**/.

    hope—hopes       pick—picks

    eat—eats         laugh—laughs

B.  We pronounce /**z**/ if the verb ends in most voiced sounds.

    live—lives      read—reads      sing—sings

    grab—grabs     run—runs       borrow—borrows

C. When the base form ends in *s, z, sh, ch, x, se, ge,* or *ce,* we pronounce an extra syllable, /əz/.

| | | |
|---|---|---|
| miss—misses | watch—watches | change—changes |
| buzz—buzzes | fix—fixes | dance—dances |
| wash—washes | use—uses | |

D. These verbs have a change in the vowel sound.

do /**du**/—does /**dʌz**/

say /**sei**/—says /**sɛz**/

**Spelling of the *-ing* Form of Verbs**

| Rule | Base Form | *-ing* Form |
|---|---|---|
| Add *ing* to most verbs. | eat<br>go<br>study | eating<br>going<br>studying |
| For a one-syllable verb that ends in a consonant + vowel + consonant (CVC), double the final consonant and add *ing*. | p l a n<br> \| \| \|<br>C V C<br>s t o p<br> \| \| \|<br>C V C<br>s i t<br>\| \| \|<br>C V C | planning<br><br><br>stopping<br><br><br>sitting |
| Do not double final *w, x,* or *y*. | show<br>mix<br>stay | showing<br>mixing<br>staying |
| For a two-syllable word that ends in CVC, double the final consonant only if the last syllable is stressed. | refér<br>admít<br>begín | referring<br>admitting<br>beginning |
| When the last syllable of a two-syllable word is not stressed, do not double the final consonant. | lísten<br>ópen<br>óffer | listening<br>opening<br>offering |
| If the word ends in a consonant + *e*, drop the *e* before adding *ing*. | live<br>take<br>write | living<br>taking<br>writing |

## Spelling of the Past Tense of Regular Verbs

| Rule | Base Form | -ed Form |
|------|-----------|----------|
| Add *ed* to the base form to make the past tense of most regular verbs. | start<br>kick | started<br>kicked |
| When the base form ends in *e*, add *d* only. | die<br>live | died<br>lived |
| When the base form ends in a consonant + *y*, change the *y* to *i* and add *ed*. | carry<br>worry | carried<br>worried |
| When the base form ends in a vowel + *y*, do not change the *y*. | destroy<br>stay | destroyed<br>stayed |
| For a one-syllable word that ends in a consonant + vowel + consonant (CVC), double the final consonant and add *ed*. | s t o p<br> &#124; &#124; &#124;<br>C V C<br>p l u g<br> &#124; &#124; &#124;<br>C V C | stopped<br><br>plugged |
| Do not double final *w* or *x*. | sew<br>fix | sewed<br>fixed |
| For a two-syllable word that ends in CVC, double the final consonant only if the last syllable is stressed. | occúr<br>permít | occurred<br>permitted |
| When the last syllable of a two-syllable word is not stressed, do not double the final consonant. | ópen<br>háppen | opened<br>happened |

### Pronunciation of Past Forms That End in *-ed*

The past tense with *-ed* has three pronunciations.

A. We pronounce a /**t**/ if the base form ends in these voiceless sounds: /**p, k, f, s, š, č**/.

| | | |
|---|---|---|
| jump—jumped | cough—coughed | wash—washed |
| cook—cooked | kiss—kissed | watch—watched |

B. We pronounce a /**d**/ if the base form ends in most voiced sounds.

| | | |
|---|---|---|
| rub—rubbed | charge—charged | bang—banged |
| drag—dragged | glue—glued | call—called |
| love—loved | massage—massaged | fear—feared |
| bathe—bathed | name—named | free—freed |
| use—used | learn—learned | |

C. We pronounce an extra syllable /**əd**/ if the base form ends in a /**t**/ or /**d**/ sound.

| | | |
|---|---|---|
| wait—waited | want—wanted | need—needed |
| hate—hated | add—added | decide—decided |

# APPENDIX **B**

## Spelling of Short Comparative and Superlative Adjectives and Adverbs

A. For most short adjectives and adverbs, we add -*er* to make the comparative form and -*est* to make the superlative form.
old—older—oldest
tall—taller—tallest
fast—faster—fastest

B. If the word ends in -*e*, just add *r* or *st*.
nice—nicer—nicest
fine—finer—finest

C. For adjectives that end in -*y*, change *y* to *i* before adding –*er* or –*est*.
happy—happier—happiest
healthy—healthier—healthiest
sunny—sunnier—sunniest
NOTE: Do not add –*er* or –*est* to an -*ly* adverb.
quickly—more quickly—most quickly

D. For one-syllable words that end in consonant-vowel-consonant, we double the final consonant before adding –*er* or –*est*.
big—bigger—biggest
sad—sadder—saddest
hot—hotter—hottest
EXCEPTION: Do not double final *w*.
new—newer—newest

# APPENDIX **C**

## Spelling Rules for Adverbs Ending in -*ly*

1. Most adverbs of manner are formed by putting -*ly* at the end of an adjective.

| *Adjective* | *Adverb* |
| --- | --- |
| careful | carefully |
| quiet | quietly |
| illegal | illegally |

2. For adjectives that end in -*y*, we change *y* to *i*, then add -*ly*.
easy—easily
happy—happily
lucky—luckily

3. For adjectives that end in *-e*, we keep the *e* and add *-ly*.
>nice—nicely
>free—freely
>SMALL CAPS EXCEPTION:
>true—truly

4. For adjectives that end in a consonant + *-ly*, we drop the *e* and add *-ly*.
>simple—simply
>comfortable—comfortably
>double—doubly

5. For adjectives that end in *-ic*, add *-ally*.
>basic—basically
>enthusiastic—enthusiastically
>EXCEPTION:
>public—publicly

# APPENDIX D

## Metric Conversion Chart

### LENGTH

| When You Know | Symbol | Multiply by | To Find | Symbol |
| --- | --- | --- | --- | --- |
| inches | in | 2.54 | centimeters | cm |
| feet | ft | 30.5 | centimeters | cm |
| feet | ft | 0.3 | meters | m |
| yards | yd | 0.91 | meters | m |
| miles | mi | 1.6 | kilometers | km |
| centimeters | cm | 0.39 | inches | in |
| centimeters | cm | 0.32 | feet | ft |
| meter | m | 3.28 | feet | ft |
| meters | m | 1.09 | yards | yd |
| kilometers | km | 0.62 | miles | mi |

NOTE: 1 foot = 12 inches, 1 yard = 3 feet or 36 inches

# AREA

| When You Know | Symbol | Multiply by | To Find | Symbol |
|---|---|---|---|---|
| square inches | in² | 6.5 | square centimeters | cm² |
| square feet | ft² | 0.09 | square meters | m² |
| square yards | yd² | 0.8 | square meters | m² |
| square miles | mi² | 2.6 | square kilometers | km² |

| When You Know | Symbol | Multiply by | To Find | Symbol |
|---|---|---|---|---|
| square centimeters | cm² | 0.16 | square inches | in² |
| square meters | m² | 10.76 | square feet | ft² |
| square meters | m² | 1.2 | square yards | yd² |
| square kilometers | km² | 0.39 | square miles | mi² |

# WEIGHT (Mass)

| When You Know | Symbol | Multiply by | To Find | Symbol |
|---|---|---|---|---|
| ounces | oz | 28.35 | grams | g |
| pounds | lb | 0.45 | kilograms | kg |

| When You Know | Symbol | Multiply by | To Find | Symbol |
|---|---|---|---|---|
| grams | g | 0.04 | ounces | oz |
| kilograms | kg | 2.2 | pounds | lb |

NOTE: 16 ounces = 1 pound

# VOLUME

| When You Know | Symbol | Multiply by | To Find | Symbol |
|---|---|---|---|---|
| fluid ounces | fl oz | 30.0 | milliliters | mL |
| pints | pt | 0.47 | liters | L |
| quarts | qt | 0.95 | liters | L |
| gallons | gal | 3.8 | liters | L |

| When You Know | Symbol | Multiply by | To Find | Symbol |
|---|---|---|---|---|
| milliliters | mL | 0.03 | fluid ounces | fl oz |
| liters | L | 2.11 | pints | pt |
| liters | L | 1.05 | quarts | qt |
| liters | L | 0.26 | gallons | gal |

## TEMPERATURE

| When You Know | Symbol | Do This | To Find | Symbol |
|---|---|---|---|---|
| degrees Fahrenheit | °F | Subtract 32, then multiply by 5/9 | degrees Celsius | °C |

| When You Know | Symbol | Do This | To Find | Symbol |
|---|---|---|---|---|
| degrees Celsius | °C | Multiply by 9/5, then add 32 | degrees Fahrenheit | °F |

Sample temperatures:

| Fahrenheit | Celsius | Fahrenheit | Celsius |
|---|---|---|---|
| 0 | −18 | 60 | 16 |
| 10 | −12 | 70 | 21 |
| 20 | −7 | 80 | 27 |
| 30 | −1 | 90 | 32 |
| 40 | 4 | 100 | 38 |
| 50 | 10 | | |

# APPENDIX E

## The Verb *GET*

*Get* has many meanings. Here is a list of the most common ones:

- get something = receive

  I got a letter from my father.

- get + (to) place = arrive

  I got home at six. What time do you get to school?

- get + object + infinitive = persuade

  She got him to wash the dishes.

- get + past participle = become

| | | |
|---|---|---|
| get acquainted | get worried | get hurt |
| get engaged | get lost | get bored |
| get married | get accustomed to | get confused |
| get divorced | get used to | get scared |
| get tired | get dressed | |

They got married in 1989.

- get + adjective = become

| | |
|---|---|
| get hungry | get sleepy |
| get rich | get fat |
| get nervous | get dark |
| get well | get angry |
| get upset | get old |

It gets dark at 6:30.

- get an illness = catch

While I was traveling, I got malaria.

- get a joke or an idea = understand

Everybody except Tom laughed at the joke. He didn't get it.

The boss explained the project to us, but I didn't get it.

- get ahead = advance

He works very hard because he wants to get ahead in his job.

- get along (well) (with someone) = have a good relationship

She doesn't get along with her mother-in-law.

Do you and your roommate get along well?

- get around to something = find the time to do something

I wanted to write my brother a letter yesterday, but I didn't get around to it.

- get away = escape

The police chased the thief, but he got away.

- get away with something = escape punishment

He cheated on his taxes and got away with it.

- get back = return

He got back from his vacation last Saturday.

- get back at someone = get revenge

My brother wants to get back at me for stealing his girlfriend.

- get back to someone = communicate with someone at a later time

I can't talk to you today. Can I get back to you tomorrow?

- get by = have just enough but nothing more

    On her salary, she's just getting by. She can't afford a car or a vacation.

- get in trouble = be caught and punished for doing something wrong

    They got in trouble for cheating on the test.

- get in(to) = enter a car

    She got in the car and drove away quickly.

- get out (of) = leave a car

    When the taxi arrived at the theater, everyone got out.

- get on = seat yourself on a bicycle, motorcycle, horse

    She got on the motorcycle and left.

- get on = enter a train, bus, airplane

    She got on the bus and took a seat in the back.

- get off = leave a bicycle, motorcycle, horse, train, bus, airplane

    They will get off the train at the next stop.

- get out of something = escape responsibility

    My boss wants me to help him on Saturday, but I'm going to try to get out of it.

- get over something = recover from an illness or disappointment

    She has the flu this week. I hope she gets over it soon.

- get rid of someone or something = free oneself of someone or something undesirable

    My apartment has roaches, and I can't get rid of them.

- get through (to someone) = communicate, often by telephone

    She tried to explain the harm of eating fast food to her son, but she couldn't get through to him.

    I tried to call my mother many times, but her line was busy. I couldn't get through.

- get through with something = finish

    I can meet you after I get through with my homework.

- get together = meet with another person

    I'd like to see you again. When can we get together?

- get up = arise from bed

    He woke up at 6 o'clock, but he didn't get up until 6:30.

## *MAKE* and *DO*

Some expressions use *make*. Others use *do*.

**Make**

make a date/an appointment
make a plan
make a decision
make a telephone call
make a reservation
make a mistake
make an effort
make an improvement
make a promise

make money
make noise
make the bed

**Do**

do (the) homework
do an exercise
do the dishes
do the cleaning, laundry, ironing, washing, etc.
do the shopping

do one's best
do a favor
do the right/wrong thing
do a job
do business
What do you do for a living? (asks about a job)
How do you do? (said when you meet someone for the first time)

## APPENDIX **G**

# Nouns That Can Be Both Count or Noncount

In the following cases, the same word can be a count or a noncount noun. The meaning is different, however.

| Noncount | Count |
| --- | --- |
| I spent a lot of *time* on my project. | I go shopping two *times* a month. |
| I have a lot of *experience* with computers. | I had a lot of interesting *experiences* on my trip to Europe. |

In the following cases, there is a small difference in meaning. We see a noncount noun as a whole unit. We see a count noun as something that can be divided into parts:

| Noncount | Count |
| --- | --- |
| There is a lot of *crime* in a big city. | A lot of *crimes* are never solved. |
| There is a lot of *opportunity* to make money in the U.S. | There are a lot of job *opportunities* in my field. |
| She bought a lot of *fruit*. | Oranges and lemons are *fruits* that have a lot of Vitamin C. |
| I don't have much *food* in my refrigerator. | Milk and butter are *foods* that contain cholesterol. |
| I have a lot of *trouble* with my car. | He has many *troubles* in his life. |

# Verbs and Adjectives Followed by a Preposition

accuse someone of
(be) accustomed to
adjust to
(be) afraid of
agree with
(be) amazed at/by
(be) angry about
(be) angry at/with
apologize for
approve of
argue about
argue with
(be) ashamed of
(be) aware of
believe in
blame someone for
(be) bored with/by
(be) capable of
care about/for
compare to/with
complain about
(be) concerned about
concentrate on
consist of
count on
deal with
decide on
depend on/upon
(be) different from
disapprove of
(be) divorced from
dream about/of
(be) engaged to
(be) excited about

(be) familiar with
(be) famous for
feel like
(be) fond of
forget about
forgive someone for
(be) glad about
(be) good at
(be) grateful to someone for
(be) guilty of
(be) happy about
hear about
hear of
hope for
(be) incapable of
insist on/upon
(be) interested in
(be) involved in
(be) jealous of
(be) known for
(be) lazy about
listen to
look at
look for
look forward to
(be) mad about
(be) mad at
(be) made from/of
(be) married to
object to
(be) opposed to
participate in
plan on
pray to

pray for
(be) prepared for
prevent someone from
prohibit from
protect from
(be) proud of
recover from
(be) related to
rely on/upon
(be) responsible for
(be) sad about
(be) satisfied with
(be) scared of
(be) sick of
(be) sorry about/for
speak about
speak to/with
succeed in
(be) sure of/about
(be) surprised at
take care of
talk about
talk to/with
thank someone for
(be) thankful to someone for
think about/of
(be) tired of
(be) upset about
(be) upset with
(be) used to
wait for
warn (someone) about
(be) worried about
worry about

---

# Direct and Indirect Objects

1. The order of direct and indirect objects depends on the verb you use.

$$\text{IO} \qquad \text{DO}$$

He told his friend the answer.

$$\text{DO} \qquad \qquad \text{IO}$$

He explained the answer to his friend.

---

2. The order of the objects sometimes depends on whether you use a noun or a pronoun object.

```
S   V     IO        DO
He gave the woman the keys.

S   V    DO    IO
He gave them to her.
```

3. In some cases, the connecting preposition is *to;* in some cases, *for.* In some cases, there is no connecting preposition.

She'll serve lunch *to* her guests.
She reserved a seat *for* you.
I asked him a question.

Each of the following groups of words follows a specific pattern of word order and preposition choice.

**Group I**   **Pronouns affect word order.** The preposition is *to.*

Patterns:  He gave a present to his wife. (DO to IO)
He gave his wife a present. (IO/DO)
He gave it to his wife. (DO to IO)
He gave her a present. (IO/DO)
He gave it to her. (DO to IO)

Verbs:

| bring | lend | pass | sell | show | teach |
|-------|------|------|------|------|-------|
| give | offer | pay | send | sing | tell |
| hand | owe | read | serve | take | write |

**Group II**   **Pronouns affect word order.** The preposition is *for.*

Patterns:  He bought a car for his daughter. (DO for IO)
He bought his daughter a car. (IO/DO)
He bought it for his daughter. (DO for IO)
He bought her a car. (IO/DO)
He bought it for her. (DO for IO)

Verbs:

| bake | buy | draw | get | make |
|------|-----|------|-----|------|
| build | do | find | knit | reserve |

**Group III**   **Pronouns don't affect word order.** The preposition is *to.*

Patterns:  He explained the problem to his friend. (DO to IO)
He explained it to her. (DO to IO)

Verbs:

| admit | introduce | recommend | say |
|-------|-----------|-----------|-----|
| announce | mention | repeat | speak |
| describe | prove | report | suggest |
| explain | | | |

**Group IV** **Pronouns don't affect word order.** The preposition is *for*.

Patterns: He cashed a check for his friend. (DO for IO)
He cashed it for her. (DO for IO)

Verbs:
| | | | | |
|---|---|---|---|---|
| answer | change | design | open | prescribe |
| cash | close | fix | prepare | pronounce |

**Group V** **Pronouns don't affect word order.** No preposition is used.

Patterns: She asked the teacher a question. (IO/DO)
She asked him a question. (IO/DO)
It took me five minutes to answer the question. (IO/DO)

Verbs: ask    charge    cost    wish    take (with time)

# APPENDIX J

## Capitalization Rules

- The first word in a sentence: **My** friends are helpful.

- The word "I": My sister and **I** took a trip together.

- Names of people: **Michael Jackson**; **George Washington**

- Titles preceding names of people: **Doctor** (**Dr.**) **Smith**; **President Lincoln**; **Queen Elizabeth**; **Mr. Rogers**; **Mrs. Carter**

- Geographic names: the **United States**; **Lake Superior**; **California**; the **Rocky Mountains**; the **Mississippi River**
    NOTE: The word "the" in a geographic name is not capitalized.

- Street names: **Pennsylvania Avenue** (**Ave.**); **Wall Street** (**St.**); **Abbey Road** (**Rd.**)

- Names of organizations, companies, colleges, buildings, stores, hotels: the **Republican Party**; **Heinle and Heinle Publishers**; **Dartmouth College**; the **University of Wisconsin**; the **White House**; **Bloomingdale's**; the **Hilton Hotel**

- Nationalities and ethnic groups: **Mexicans**; **Canadians**; **Spaniards**; **Americans**; **Jews**; **Kurds**; **Eskimos**

- Languages: **English**; **Spanish**; **Polish**; **Vietnamese**; **Russian**

- Months: **January**; **February**

- Days: **Sunday**; **Monday**

- Holidays: **Christmas**; **Independence Day**

- Important words in a title: **Grammar in Context**; **The Old Man and the Sea**; **Romeo and Juliet**; **The Sound of Music**
    NOTE: Capitalize "the" as the first word of a title.

## Glossary of Grammatical Terms

- **Adjective** An adjective gives a description of a noun.

    It's a *tall* tree.　　He's an *old* man.　　My neighbors are *nice*.

- **Adverb** An adverb describes the action of a sentence or an adjective or another adverb.

    She speaks English *fluently*.　　I drive *carefully*.

    She speaks English *extremely* well.　　She is *very* intelligent.

- **Adverb of Frequency** An adverb of frequency tells how often the action happens.

    I *never* drink coffee.　　They *usually* take the bus.

- **Affirmative** means *yes*.

- **Apostrophe** '

- **Article** The definite article is *the*. The indefinite articles are *a* and *an*.

    I have *a* cat.　　I ate *an* apple.　　*The* President was in New York last weekend.

- **Auxiliary Verb** Some verbs have two parts: an auxiliary verb and a main verb.

    He <u>*can't*</u> study.　　We <u>*will*</u> return.

- **Base Form** The base form of the verb has no tense. It has no ending (*-s* or *-ed*): *be, go, eat, take, write*

    I didn't *go* out.　　He doesn't *know* the answer.　　You shouldn't *talk* loud.

- **Capital Letter** A B C D E F G . . .

- **Clause** A clause is a group of words that has a subject and a verb. Some sentences have only one clause.

    *She speaks Spanish.*

Some sentences have a **main clause** and a **dependent clause**.

| **MAIN CLAUSE** | **DEPENDENT CLAUSE (reason clause)** |
|---|---|
| She found a good job | because she has computer skills. |
| **MAIN CLAUSE** | **DEPENDENT CLAUSE (time clause)** |
| She'll turn off the light | before she goes to bed. |
| **MAIN CLAUSE** | **DEPENDENT CLAUSE (*if* clause)** |
| I'll take you to the doctor | if you don't have your car on Saturday. |

- **Colon** :

- **Comma** ,

- **Comparative Form** A comparative form of an adjective or adverb is used to compare two things.

    My house is *bigger* than your house.

    Her husband drives *faster* than she does.

- **Complement** The complement of the sentence is the information after the verb. It completes the verb phrase.

    He works *hard*.     I slept *for five hours*.     They are *late*.

- **Consonant** The following letters are consonants: *b, c, d, f, g, h, j, k, l, m, n, p, q, r, s, t, v, w, x, y, z.*

    NOTE: *y* is sometimes considered a vowel.

- **Contraction** A contraction is made up of two words put together with an apostrophe.

    *He's* my brother.          *You're* late.          They *won't* talk to me.
    (*He's = he is*)          (*You're = you are*)          (*won't = will not*)

- **Count Noun** Count nouns are nouns that we can count. They have a singular and a plural form.

    1 pen / 3 pens     1 table / 4 tables

- **Dependent Clause** See **Clause.**

- **Direct Object** A direct object is a noun (phrase) or pronoun that receives the action of the verb.

    We saw *the movie*.     You have *a nice car*.     I love *you*.

- **Exclamation Mark !**

- **Hyphen -**

- **Imperative** An imperative sentence gives a command or instructions. An imperative sentence omits the word *you*.

    *Come* here.     *Don't be* late.     Please *sit* down.

- **Indefinite Pronoun** An indefinite pronoun (*one, some, any*) takes the place of an indefinite noun.

    I have a cell phone. Do you have *one*?

    I didn't drink any coffee, but you drank *some*. Did he drink *any*?

- **Infinitive** An infinitive is *to* + base form.

    I want *to leave*.     You need *to be* here on time.

- **Linking Verb** A linking verb is a verb that links the subject to the noun or adjective after it. Linking verbs include *be, seem, feel, smell, sound, look, appear, taste.*

    She *is* a doctor.     She *seems* very intelligent.     She *looks* tired.

- **Modal** The modal verbs are *can, could, shall, should, will, would, may, might, must.*

    They *should* leave.     I *must* go.

- **Negative** means *no*.

- **Nonaction Verb** A nonaction verb has no action. We do not use a continuous tense (*be* + verb *-ing*) with a nonaction verb. The nonaction verbs are: *believe,* *cost, care, have, hear, know, like, love, matter, mean, need, own, prefer, remember, see, seem, think, understand, want*

- **Noncount Noun** A noncount noun is a noun that we don't count. It has no plural form.

  She drank some *water*.   He prepared some *rice*.   Do you need any *money*?

- **Noun** A noun is a person (*brother*), a place (*kitchen*) or a thing (*table*). Nouns can be either count (*1 table, 2 tables*) or noncount (*money, water*).

  My *brother* lives in California. My *sisters* live in New York. I get *mail* from them.

- **Noun Modifier** A noun modifier makes a noun more specific.

  *fire* department   *Independence* Day   *can* opener

- **Noun Phrase** A noun phrase is a group of words that form the subject or object of the sentence.

  *A very nice woman* helped me at registration.

  I bought *a big box of candy*.

- **Object** The object of the sentence follows a verb or a preposition.

  He bought *a car*.   I saw *a movie*.   She travels with *me*.

- **Object Pronoun** Use object pronouns (*me, you, him, her, it, us, them*) after the verb or preposition.

  He likes *her*.   I saw the movie. Did you see *it*?

- **Parentheses** ( )

- **Paragraph** A paragraph is a group of sentences about one topic.

- **Participle, Present** The present participle is verb + *-ing*.

  She is *sleeping*.   They were *laughing*.

- **Period** .

- **Phrase** A group of words that go together.

  *Last month* my sister came to visit.

  There is a strange car *in front of my house*.

- **Plural** Plural means more than one. A plural noun usually ends with *-s*.

  She has beautiful *eyes*.

- **Possessive Form** Possessive forms show ownership or relationship.

  *Mary's* coat is in the closet.   *My* brother lives in Miami.

- **Preposition** A preposition is a short connecting word: *about, above, across, after, around, as, at, away, back, before, behind, below, by, down, for, from, in, into, like, of, off, on, out, over, to, under, up, with.*

- **Pronoun** A pronoun takes the place of a noun.

    I have a new car. I bought *it* last week.

    John likes Mary, but *she* doesn't like *him*.

- **Punctuation** Period . Comma , Colon : Semicolon ; Question Mark ? Exclamation Mark !

- **Question Mark ?**

- **Quotation Marks " "**

- **Regular Verb** A regular verb forms its past tense with *-ed*.

    He *worked* yesterday.      I *laughed* at the joke.

- **Sense-Perception Verb** A sense-perception verb has no action. It describes a sense.

    She *feels* fine.      The coffee *smells* fresh.      The milk *tastes* sour.

- **Sentence** A sentence is a group of words that contains a subject[1] and a verb (at least) and gives a complete thought.

    Sentence: She came home.

    Not a sentence: When she came home

- **Simple Form of Verb** The simple form of the verb has no tense; it never has an *-s*, *-ed*, or *-ing* ending.

    Did you *see* the movie?

    I couldn't *find* your phone number.

- **Singular** Singular means one.

    She ate *a sandwich*.      I have one *television*.

- **Subject** The subject of the sentence tells who or what the sentence is about.

    *My sister* got married last April. *The wedding* was beautiful.

- **Subject Pronoun** Use subject pronouns (*I, you, he, she, it, we, you, they*) before a verb.

    *They* speak Japanese.      *We* speak Spanish.

- **Superlative Form** A superlative form of an adjective or adverb shows the number one item in a group of three or more.

    January is the *coldest* month of the year.

    My brother speaks English the *best* in my family.

- **Syllable** A syllable is a part of a word that has only one vowel sound. (Some words have only one syllable.)

    change (one syllable)      after (af·ter = 2 syllables)

    look (one syllable)      responsible (re·spon·si·ble = 4 syllables)

---

[1] In an imperative sentence, the subject *you* is omitted: *Sit down. Come here.*

- **Tag Question** A tag question is a short question at the end of a sentence. It is used in conversation.

    You speak Spanish, *don't you?*

    He's not happy, *is he?*

- **Tense** A verb has tense. Tense shows when the action of the sentence happened.

    SIMPLE PRESENT: She usually *works* hard.

    FUTURE: She *will work* tomorrow.

    PRESENT CONTINUOUS: She *is working* now.

    SIMPLE PAST: She *worked* yesterday.

- **Verb** A verb is the action of the sentence.

    He *runs* fast.      I *speak* English.

    Some verbs have no action. They are linking verbs. They connect the subject to the rest of the sentence.

    He *is* tall.      She *looks* beautiful.      You *seem* tired.

- **Vowel** The following letters are vowels: *a, e, i, o, u. Y* is sometimes considered a vowel (for example, in the word *mystery*).

# APPENDIX L

## Special Uses of Articles

| No Article | Article |
|---|---|
| Personal names:<br>    John Kennedy<br>    Michael Jackson | The whole family:<br>    the Kennedys<br>    the Jacksons |
| Title and name:<br>    Queen Elizabeth<br>    Pope John Paul | Title without name:<br>    the Queen<br>    the Pope |
| Cities, states, countries, continents:<br>    Cleveland<br>    Ohio<br>    Mexico<br>    South America | Places that are considered a union:<br>    the United States<br>    the former Soviet Union<br>    the United Kingdom<br>Place names: the _____ of _____<br>    the Republic of China<br>    the District of Columbia |
| Mountains<br>    Mount Everest<br>    Mount McKinley | Mountain ranges:<br>    the Himalayas<br>    the Rocky Mountains |
| Islands:<br>    Coney Island<br>    Staten Island | Collectives of islands:<br>    the Hawaiian Islands<br>    the Virgin Islands<br>    the Philippines |

| No Article | Article |
|---|---|
| Lakes:<br>Lake Superior<br>Lake Michigan | Collectives of lakes:<br>the Great Lakes<br>the Finger Lakes |
| Beaches:<br>Palm Beach<br>Pebble Beach | Rivers, oceans, seas, canals:<br>the Mississippi River<br>the Atlantic Ocean<br>the Dead Sea<br>the Panama Canal |
| Streets and avenues:<br>Madison Avenue<br>Wall Street | Well-known buildings:<br>the Sears Tower<br>the World Trade Center |
| Parks:<br>Central Park<br>Hyde Park | Zoos:<br>the San Diego Zoo<br>the Milwaukee Zoo |
| Seasons:<br>summer    fall<br>spring    winter<br>Summer is my favorite season.<br>NOTE: After a preposition, *the* may be used.<br>In (the) winter, my car runs badly. | Deserts:<br>the Mojave Desert<br>the Sahara Desert |
| Directions:<br>north    south<br>east    west | Sections of a piece of land:<br>the Southwest (of the U.S.)<br>the West Side (of New York) |
| School subjects:<br>history<br>math | Unique geographical points:<br>the North Pole<br>the Vatican |
| Name + *college* or *university:*<br>Northwestern University<br>Bradford College | The University (College) of _____<br>the University of Michigan<br>the College of DuPage County |
| Magazines:<br>*Time*<br>*Sports Illustrated* | Newspapers:<br>the *Tribune*<br>the *Wall Street Journal* |
| Months and days:<br>September<br>Monday | Ships:<br>the *Titanic*<br>the *Queen Elizabeth* |
| Holidays and Dates<br>(Month + Day)<br>Thanksgiving<br>Mother's Day<br>July 4 | The day of (month)<br>the Fourth of July<br>the fifth of May |
| Diseases:<br>cancer<br>polio<br>AIDS<br>malaria | Ailments:<br>a cold<br>a headache<br>a toothache<br>the flu |

| No Article | Article |
|---|---|
| Games and sports:<br>    poker<br>    soccer | Musical instruments, after *play:*<br>    the drums<br>    the piano<br>NOTE: Sometimes *the* is omitted.<br>    She plays (the) drums. |
| Languages:<br>    French<br>    English | The _____ language:<br>    the French language<br>    the English language |
| Last month, year, week, etc. = the one before this one:<br>    I forgot to pay my rent last month.<br>    The teacher gave us a test last week. | The last month, the last year, the last week, etc. = the last in a series:<br>    December is the last month of the year.<br>    Summer vacation begins the last week in May. |
| In office = in an elected position:<br>    The president is in office for four years. | In the office = in a specific room:<br>    The teacher is in the office. |
| In back/front:<br>    She's in back of the car (1). | In the back/the front:<br>    He's in the back of the bus (2). |

# APPENDIX M

## Alphabetical List of Irregular Verb Forms

| Base Form | Past Form | Past Participle | Base Form | Past Form | Past Participle |
|---|---|---|---|---|---|
| be | was/were | been | choose | chose | chosen |
| bear | bore | born/borne | cling | clung | clung |
| beat | beat | beaten | come | came | come |
| become | became | become | cost | cost | cost |
| begin | began | begun | creep | crept | crept |
| bend | bent | bent | cut | cut | cut |
| bet | bet | bet | deal | dealt | dealt |
| bind | bound | bound | dig | dug | dug |
| bite | bit | bitten | do | did | done |
| bleed | bled | bled | draw | drew | drawn |
| blow | blew | blown | drink | drank | drunk |
| break | broke | broken | drive | drove | driven |
| breed | bred | bred | eat | ate | eaten |
| bring | brought | brought | fall | fell | fallen |
| broadcast | broadcast | broadcast | feed | fed | fed |
| build | built | built | feel | felt | felt |
| burst | burst | burst | fight | fought | fought |
| buy | bought | bought | find | found | found |
| cast | cast | cast | fit | fit | fit |
| catch | caught | caught | flee | fled | fled |

| Base Form | Past Form | Past Participle | Base Form | Past Form | Past Participle |
|---|---|---|---|---|---|
| fly | flew | flown | shut | shut | shut |
| forbid | forbade | forbidden | sing | sang | sung |
| forget | forgot | forgotten | sink | sank | sunk |
| forgive | forgave | forgiven | sit | sat | sat |
| freeze | froze | frozen | sleep | slept | slept |
| get | got | gotten | slide | slid | slid |
| give | gave | given | slit | slit | slit |
| go | went | gone | speak | spoke | spoken |
| grind | ground | ground | speed | sped | sped |
| grow | grew | grown | spend | spent | spent |
| hang | hung | hung[2] | spin | spun | spun |
| have | had | had | spit | spit | spit |
| hear | heard | heard | split | split | split |
| hide | hid | hidden | spread | spread | spread |
| hit | hit | hit | spring | sprang | sprung |
| hold | held | held | stand | stood | stood |
| hurt | hurt | hurt | steal | stole | stolen |
| keep | kept | kept | stick | stuck | stuck |
| know | knew | known | sting | stung | stung |
| lay | laid | laid | stink | stank | stunk |
| lead | led | led | strike | struck | struck/stricken |
| leave | left | left | strive | strove | striven |
| lend | loaned/lent | loaned/lent | swear | swore | sworn |
| let | let | let | sweep | swept | swept |
| lie | lay | lain | swim | swam | swum |
| light | lit/lighted | lit/lighted | swing | swung | swung |
| lose | lost | lost | take | took | taken |
| make | made | made | teach | taught | taught |
| mean | meant | meant | tear | tore | torn |
| meet | met | met | tell | told | told |
| mistake | mistook | mistaken | think | thought | thought |
| pay | paid | paid | throw | threw | thrown |
| prove | proved | proven/proved | understand | understood | understood |
| put | put | put | upset | upset | upset |
| quit | quit | quit | wake | woke | woken |
| read | read | read | wear | wore | worn |
| ride | rode | ridden | weave | wove | woven |
| ring | rang | rung | weep | wept | wept |
| rise | rose | risen | win | won | won |
| run | ran | run | wind | wound | wound |
| say | said | said | withdraw | withdrew | withdrawn |
| see | saw | seen | wring | wrung | wrung |
| seek | sought | sought | write | wrote | written |
| sell | sold | sold | | | |
| send | sent | sent | | | |
| set | set | set | | | |
| shake | shook | shaken | | | |
| shed | shed | shed | | | |
| shine | shone/shined | shone | | | |
| shoot | shot | shot | | | |
| show | showed | shown/showed | | | |
| shrink | shrank | shrunk | | | |

The past and past participle of some verbs can end in *-ed* or *-t*. Americans generally prefer the *-ed* form:

| | |
|---|---|
| burn | burned or burnt |
| dream | dreamed or dreamt |
| kneel | kneeled or knelt |
| learn | learned or learnt |
| spill | spilled or spilt |
| spoil | spoiled or spoilt |

[2] *Hanged* is used as the past form to refer to punishment by death. *Hung* is used in other situations: She *hung* the picture on the wall.

# The United States of America

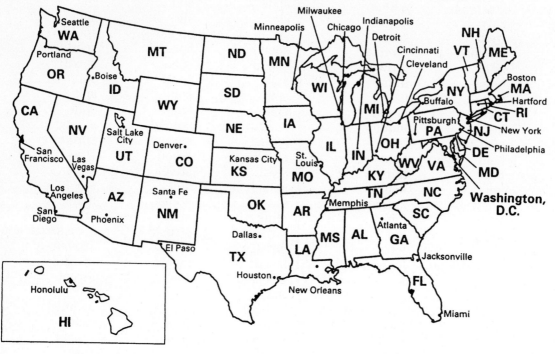

| AL | Alabama | IN | Indiana | NE | Nebraska | SC | South Carolina |
|----|---------|----|---------|----|----------|----|----------------|
| AK | Alaska | IA | Iowa | NV | Nevada | SD | South Dakota |
| AZ | Arizona | KS | Kansas | NH | New Hampshire | TN | Tennessee |
| AR | Arkansas | KY | Kentucky | NJ | New Jersey | TX | Texas |
| CA | California | LA | Louisiana | NM | New Mexico | UT | Utah |
| CO | Colorado | ME | Maine | NY | New York | VT | Vermont |
| CT | Connecticut | MD | Maryland | NC | North Carolina | VA | Virginia |
| DE | Delaware | MA | Massachusetts | ND | North Dakota | WA | Washington |
| FL | Florida | MI | Michigan | OH | Ohio | WV | West Virginia |
| GA | Georgia | MN | Minnesota | OK | Oklahoma | WI | Wisconsin |
| HI | Hawaii | MS | Mississippi | OR | Oregon | WY | Wyoming |
| ID | Idaho | MO | Missouri | PA | Pennsylvania | DC* | District of Columbia |
| IL | Illinois | MT | Montana | RI | Rhode Island | | |

*The District of Columbia is not a state. Washington D.C. is the capital of the United States. Note: Washington D.C. and Washington state are not the same.

# North America

Alaska

CANADA

U. S. A.

Hawaii

MEXICO

Puerto Rico

# Index